PRENTICE HALL STUDIES
IN INTERNATIONAL RELATIONS
ENDURING QUESTIONS IN CHANGING TIMES

CHARLES W. KEGLEY, JR., *SERIES EDITOR*

In the era of globalization in the twenty-first century, people cannot afford to ignore the impact of international relations on their future. From the value of one's investments to the quality of the air one breathes, international relations matter. The instantaneous spread of communications throughout the world is making for the internationalization of all phenomena, while the distinction between the domestic and the foreign, the public and the private, and the national and the international is vanishing. Globalization is an accelerating trend that is transforming how virtually every field of study in the social sciences is being investigated and taught.

Contemporary scholarship has made bold advances in understanding the many facets of international relations. It has also laid a firm foundation for interpreting the major forces and factors that are shaping the global future.

To introduce the latest research findings and theoretical commentary, a new publication series has been launched. *Prentice Hall Studies in International Relations: Enduring Questions in Changing Times* presents books that focus on the issues, controversies, and trends that are defining the central topics dominating discussion about international relations.

ETHICS AND THE FUTURE OF CONFLICT
LESSONS FROM THE 1990S

EDITORS

ANTHONY F. LANG, JR.
Albright College

ALBERT C. PIERCE
Center for the Study of Professional Military Ethics
The United States Naval Academy

JOEL H. ROSENTHAL
Carnegie Council on Ethics and International Affairs

PEARSON

Prentice
Hall

UPPER SADDLE RIVER, NEW JERSEY 07458

172.42
E 84

Library of Congress Cataloging-in-Publication Data

Ethics and the future of conflict: lessons from the 1990s/editors, Anthony F. Lang, Jr., Albert
C. Pierce, Joel H. Rosenthal.
    p. cm.—(Prentice Hall studies in international relations)
Includes bibliographical references and index.
    ISBN 0-13-183993-4
    1. Just war doctrine. 2. World politics—1989– . 3. United States—Military policy.
4. Military history—20th century. 5. United States—History, Military—20th century.
6. United States—Foreign relations—1989–1993. 7. United States—Foreign relations—
1993–2001. I. Lang, Anthony F. II. Pierce, Albert C. III. Rosenthal, Joel H.
IV. Series.
    U22.E8288 2004
    172'.42—dc22

                                                                                2003015911

Editorial Director: Charlyce Jones Owen
Acquisitions Editor: Glenn Johnston
Assistant Editor: John Ragozzine
Editorial Assistant: Suzanne Remore
Director of Marketing: Beth Mejia
Marketing Assistant: Jennifer Bryant
Prepress and Manufacturing Buyer: Sherry Lewis
Interior Design: John P. Mazzola
Cover Design: Kiwi Design
Composition/Full-Service Project Management: Kari Callaghan Mazzola and John P.
    Mazzola
Printer/Binder: Courier Companies, Inc.
Cover Printer: Coral Graphics

This book was set in 10/12 Electra.

Pearson Education LTD.   Pearson Education North Asia Ltd
Pearson Education Singapore, Pte. Ltd Pearson Educación de Mexico, S.A. de C.V.
Pearson Education, Canada, Ltd   Pearson Education Malaysia, Pte. Ltd
Pearson Education–Japan   Pearson Education, Upper Saddle River, NJ
Pearson Education Australia PTY, Limited

10 9 8 7 6 5 4 3 2 1
ISBN 0-13-183993-4

CONTENTS

v

PREFACE

It is tempting to think of 1991–2001 as the "post–Cold War" decade. As such, it is a transitional period, a relatively benign time when the great powers paused before a new mortal challenge appeared. Such an interpretation is terribly mistaken.

While the Persian Gulf War and the interventions in Somalia, Haiti, and the Balkans will inevitably register as relatively minor episodes in the broad sweep of American history, tectonic changes occurred in the 1990s that will be felt for years to come. All of the fault lines that look so dangerous today preceded the earthquake of September 11, 2001. The agenda for the future has been hidden in plain sight for quite some time.

In geopolitical terms, the question of ethics and force is now largely about the values and goals of the United States. As the predominant military force in the world—far exceeding the capabilities of even the most advanced industrialized nations—the United States has demonstrated its willingness and capability to deliver lethal force to enforce a stable and predictable world order. The key concept for the next decade is the same as the last: asymmetry.

Asymmetry—a situation in which the combined military and economic power of one state creates a radical imbalance in power—is the result of American political will as well as the fruit of American technology. Americans have made it a priority to conduct research and development in military systems ranging from precision-guided munitions to satellite intelligence-gathering and missile defense. In political terms, Americans have also signaled willingness, beyond any other nation or group of nations, to spend the resources necessary to purchase and deploy these sophisticated systems. While this willingness might be reaching new heights after September 11, again, the pattern is nothing new.

One place where the pattern of the past may take a new turn is in the tendency of American planners to minimize risk to U.S. forces, to engage in force protection

or riskless war. Michael Ignatieff has written about "virtual war"—war in technological superiority allows all risk to be exported to the enemy. The current war against
terrorism will put stress on this notion. Hard choices will need to be made regarding risk and reward. What is it worth—in terms of U.S. casualties—to apprehend elusive terrorists? What should be done when long-range bombing is not sufficient?
For the moment, Americans are clinging to the benefits of virtual war with understandable tenacity.

Another place where a familiar pattern will be tested is in the strict interpretation of noncombatant status and immunity. Military operations in the 1990s—largely humanitarian in nature—featured strong emphasis on maintaining the firewall
between combatants and noncombatants. Human rights advocates and ethics critics
often pointed to policies such as long-range bombing, dual-use targeting, and even
the use of relatively indiscriminate economic sanctions as testing the limits of noncombatant immunity. But few doubted the intent of planners to limit collateral damage as much as possible. The struggle in the future will be over defining standards for
"as much as possible." What is considered an acceptable amount of collateral damage in a war of self-defense might be different, and more permissive, than a war with
humanitarian goals.

For all of the new stressors on our familiar pattern, the ultimate purposes for resorting to force are likely to continue unchanged. In addition to self-defense and the
pursuit of human rights goals, force will be used to punish and deter. Peacekeeping
and peace enforcement are also likely to continue, as states will no longer be allowed
to "fail." Failed states are obvious refuges for terrorists. In fighting what President
George W. Bush has called the "axis of evil," there is pressure to put a face on that
evil so that it can be eliminated. Whether that face is Osama bin Laden, Saddam Hussein, or some other foe, we can anticipate ongoing efforts at targeting specific leaders as well as the states in which they are found.

New forms of warfare are already beginning to surface, although none are without precedent. We have seen the beginning of a new phase in the development of
weapons of mass destruction (WMD). The anthrax attack of fall 2001 may be a precursor of future threats. The first response has been the creation of the Office of
Homeland Defense. Whether further reform of the U.S. defense establishment is
necessary to meet this threat remains to be seen. It is not hard to imagine a re-
assessment of the National Security Act of 1947—the act that created the current
structure in anticipation of the Cold War that followed. In addition to the real threat
of chemical and biological attacks, cyberwarfare lurks as yet another threat to American security.

As American policymakers think about their options for defense, they will face
the question of how much offense do we need to provide a good defense? Should the
United States and its allies seek regime changes in places such as Iraq, Iran, and
North Korea? Is preemption the wave of the future? Fighting nonstate terror networks raises the question of how much responsibility can be assigned to the states
where terrorism and threats to Western interests reside. Strategists are facing a world
with no clearly defined defense perimeter.

American hegemony raises as many questions for the ethicist as it does for the strategist. As the United States fights its wars of the next decade, it will surely follow both the law of armed conflict, and to the extent possible, evolving human rights law and the principles of the just war tradition. But clear-cut answers as to the most ethical policy choices are not likely to be available. The war against the al Qaeda terrorist network has raised controversial questions regarding nonstate actors and their status under international law. We can anticipate more such cases where the law is unclear and precedents will be set.

The best assurance of an ethical foreign policy is an assurance that new policies will be openly debated—that interested citizens will test these policies against the principles and standards that American policymakers themselves profess. Taking a realist perspective, this book is premised on the idea that ethics is not always about achieving consensus on moral ideals. Sometimes the best we can do is to articulate and negotiate differences.

Realists understand that the journey to "a just world" is a journey that can never be completed. But in reflecting on where we have been and where we are going, we can surely strive to do our part well. At the top of our agenda for the future should be a commitment to relate reason to experience, to test principles against tough cases, and to hold our policies up to scrutiny. In the end, this process is what ultimately will make our foreign policies as ethical as they can be.

The editors would like to thank the numerous individuals who helped organize the meetings that produced these chapters, and those who helped in the editing process. At the Carnegie Council, Eva Becker, Vice President for Finance and Administration, provided assistance throughout the project. Matt Mattern and Lotta Hagman helped in planning and organizing the meetings. Janice Gabucan and Vivek Nayar helped in the editing stages. The editors would also like to thank all the Prentice Hall staff who helped in producing the book, especially John Ragozzine, Kari Callaghan Mazzola, and Heather Shelstad. Cathal J. Nolan of Boston University provided insightful comments on the draft. And Charles Kegley deserves a special note of thanks for shepherding this book through the entire process, from idea to finished product.

Joel H. Rosenthal

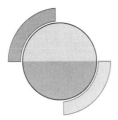

ABOUT THE CONTRIBUTORS

MARTIN COOK is a Professor in the Department of Philosophy at the United States Air Force Academy.

CONRAD C. CRANE is Research Professor of Military Strategy at the United States Army War College.

MARTHA CRENSHAW is a professor in the Department of Government at Wesleyan University.

CHARLES J. DUNLAP, JR., United States Air Force, is a Staff Judge Advocate in the Army Education and Training Command at Randolph Air Force Base, Texas.

FRANCES V. HARBOUR is a professor in the Department of Public and International Affairs at George Mason University.

JAMES TURNER JOHNSON is a professor in the Department of Religion at Rutgers University.

CHARLES W. KEGLEY, JR. is Pearce Professor of International Relations at the University of South Carolina.

ANTHONY F. LANG, JR. is a professor in the Department of Political Science at Albright College.

JOHN P. LANGAN, S. J., is the Rose Kennedy Professor of Christian Ethics at the Kennedy Institute of Ethics, Georgetown University

STEVEN LEE is a professor in the Department of Philosophy at Hobart and William Smith Colleges.

ALBERT C. PIERCE is Director of the Center for the Study of Professional Military Ethics at the United States Naval Academy.

GREGORY A. RAYMOND is Director of the Honors College at Boise State University.

JOEL H. ROSENTHAL is President of the Carnegie Council on Ethics and International Affairs.

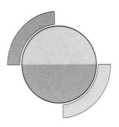

ETHICS AND THE FUTURE OF CONFLICT

INTRODUCTION

ANTHONY F. LANG, JR.

Albright College

The military tactics, strategy, and capabilities of the United States changed rapidly during the 1990s. The end of the Cold War, the Persian Gulf War, the Revolution in Military Affairs, geopolitical strategies based on humanitarian purposes—these and other developments forced U.S. political and military leaders to develop new ideas and doctrines. The terrorist attack of September 11, 2001, the ensuing military campaign in Afghanistan, and the war against Iraq have exponentially increased the pace of those changes. Fighting terrorists and responding to the threat of chemical and biological attacks raises serious questions about previous military assumptions.

Tactics and strategy have changed. But have the political and moral ends that justify military force changed? What moral purposes should guide decisions to employ force? What ethical rules should govern the use of force once a military action has begun? These are old questions, but the events of the past ten years demand new answers. Moral frameworks may remain the same, but they are surely being tested in new ways.

This book reflects the judgments of a working group of professionals in the areas of ethics, military affairs, and political and diplomatic studies. Sponsored by the Carnegie Council on Ethics and International Affairs and the National War College, the working group commissioned papers in order to produce ethically competent analyses well grounded in political, diplomatic, and military realities. These papers were debated and discussed in the context of eight meetings over the course of four years. Authors were given the opportunity to defend their arguments and revise their

This introduction has benefited from extensive feedback from Joel H. Rosenthal, Albert C. Pierce, and Scott Silliman. All errors are the responsibility of the author alone.

1

papers based on comments made during the meetings. As a result, the papers benefited from the synergy generated by the expertise of the working group members, in-
suring that philosophical, military, and diplomatic considerations were taken into
account. The editors have selected the best papers from the project, ones that speak
to the challenges currently facing the United States and the international community. The purpose of this volume is to better understand and evaluate the role that military force has played and will continue to play in the world of global politics.

   This introduction will lay out three different ways in which ethics and the use
of force have been addressed in recent years: the just war tradition, international law,
and international relations theory. These approaches to the study of ethics and the
use of force are found throughout this volume, although no single author adopts one
wholeheartedly. Rather, each author draws on these different frameworks in their
analyses. These approaches provide three frames of reference for those who wish to
analyze and assess the difficult moral choices facing those engaged in the use of military force.

THE JUST WAR TRADITION

The editors have employed a loose version of the just war framework as the basic organizing principle for the book. This does not mean, however, that all authors employed this frame in their individual papers. Rather, the editors believe that moral
evaluation makes sense when looking at the purpose behind the use of force (*jus ad
bellum*) and the strategies and tactics employed in the context of armed conflict (*jus
in bello*). In the course of editing and revising the papers, it has become clear that this
framework may fail to capture the overlap between these two categories of moral
evaluation. Topics such as the law of armed conflict and terrorism do not lend themselves well to clear distinctions between what is allowable in warfare and what justifies warfare in the first place. Despite these concerns, the just war framework provides
a useful starting point to consider the ethics of the use of force.

   The just war tradition,[1] with its roots in ancient philosophy and Judeo-Christian
theology and philosophy, is less a coherent, single theory and more a body of reflections on the justice of using military force. While its roots have been traced to Aristotle, Cicero, Augustine, and Aquinas, a number of contemporary theorists such as
James T. Johnson and Michael Walzer have applied this ancient and medieval legacy to more current dilemmas.[2] Catholic theologians and bishops have long been
leaders in this field and they continue today to engage just war theory to evaluate
weapons of mass destruction, along with evaluations of the military response to the
attacks of September 11, 2001. Protestant thinkers have also been prominent in this
tradition, most notably the mid-twentieth-century contributions of Reinhold Niebuhr
and Paul Ramsey.[3]

   The just war tradition provides two sets of criteria to guide both the decision to resort to war (*jus ad bellum*) and the conduct of war (*jus in bello*). The *jus ad bellum* criteria include: right authority, just cause, right intention, aim of peace, proportionality,

last resort, and reasonable hope of success. The *jus in bello* criteria include discrimination (or noncombatant immunity) and proportionality. Proportionality in both cases has to do with the ratio of harm done to good accomplished: In *ad bellum* it has to do with the assessment of good to be achieved as well as resulting harm in deciding to use force against another sovereign, and in *in bello* it has to with the balancing of good that is accomplished against collateral harm done in attacking a particular military objective.

The just war tradition remains the dominant set of ethical concepts in the West, certainly in the United States, for guiding decision making about war and peace. The pacifist tradition is equally ancient, but represents a minority within both the scholarly and activist communities. A few attempts have been made to apply Immanuel Kant's classic essay, *Perpetual Peace*, to international conflicts, but these have not yet been influential.[4]

A more recent development in just war thinking has been the argument put forward by some scholars to change its focus from a criteria checklist for *limiting* the use of force, back to what they say is a more historically rooted *obligation* to use force for appropriate reasons. Found most often in works that draw on its religious foundations, such works frame just war as an obligation upon states and leaders to seek justice and create the conditions of peaceful order. These approaches, while keeping firm the restraints that should condition any use of force, do not begin with a presumption against the use of military force. Rather, they begin with the sense that the most powerful have an obligation to use force to protect rights and establish peace.[5]

As noted, not all the contributors to this volume employed the just war tradition. All, however, know of the tradition and are conversant with it. It has shaped the discussions that produced this volume and will continue to shape discourse on the use of force.

INTERNATIONAL LAW

Prior to the twentieth century, international law did not consider the use of force, even large-scale war, to be illegal. The father of modern international law, the seventeenth-century Dutch jurist Hugo Grotius, sought to codify a diverse range of sources, including just war theory, in an attempt to limit, but not to eliminate, the use of military force in European affairs.[6] In the nineteenth century, international law developed slowly toward a prohibition on the use of force, but never outlawed it completely. It was not until the peace-through-arbitration movements of the late nineteenth and early twentieth century that international lawyers sought to explicitly ban the use of force. The convening of international jurists led to the 1899 and 1907 Hague Conventions, the first treaties that sought to formally codify a series of rules governing when and how force could be used.

Following World War I, political activists and scholars found support amongst government leaders for outlawing war; the General Treaty for Renunciation of War as an Instrument of National Policy, also known as the Kellogg-Briand Pact, was signed and ratified in 1928.[7] Although this treaty, along with the creation of the League of Nations, sought to make war illegal, the outbreak of World War II suggests that these norms were less widely accepted than their supporters hoped they would be.

The charter of the United Nations, drafted during the last stages of World War II, further attempted to make war illegal. Article 2(4) of the charter states:

> All Members shall refrain in their international relations from the threat or use of force against the territorial integrity or political independence of any state, or in any other manner inconsistent with the Purposes of the United Nations.

The framers of the charter, however, hoping to avoid the fate of the League of Nations, added Article 51:

> Nothing in the present charter shall impair the inherent right of individual or collective self-defense if an armed attack occurs against a member of the United Nations, until the Security Council has taken measures necessary to maintain international peace and security. Measures taken by Members in the exercise of this right of self-defense shall be immediately reported to the Security Council and shall not in any way affect the authority and responsibility of the Security Council under the present charter to take at any time such action as it deems necessary in order to maintain or restore international peace and security.

Of course, the charter also recognizes that the Security Council can authorize the use of force by member states when it acts pursuant to Chapter VII in dealing with a threat to the peace, breach of the peace, or act of aggression. These passages from the UN Charter remain the most important treaty law provisions concerning the decision to use military force.[8] The presumption in international law, then, is that waging war is generally considered illegal, unless a state is acting in self-defense or with the sanction of the UN Security Council.

Treaty law, however, is not the only source of international law. Just as important are the provisions that arise from customary international law—a general and consistent practice of states based upon a sense of legal obligation (*opinio juris*). Locating and defining this customary law is not always easy. In light of the fact that states have certainly not stopped using military force over the past fifty years (i.e., since the passage of the UN Charter), one might think that customary international law would be more permissive than treaty law in dealing with the use of force. However, some have argued that customary and treaty law both tend toward the prohibition of the use of military force, arguing that exceptions have been justified through appeals to self-defense, an appeal that would not be necessary if the use of force were accepted as a legitimate means of pursuing policy.[9]

One of the most important developments in recent years that may challenge these prohibitions is the use of military force to enforce human rights provisions for humanitarian purposes. American interventions in Somalia, Bosnia-Herzegovina, and Kosovo have been justified as actions undertaken to support broader human rights and humanitarian concerns rather than for purposes of self-defense. Nor are these changes confined to American actions; the Kosovo intervention was undertaken by NATO, albeit led by the United States. Some have contended that while these actions remain illegal according to international law, they represent an inchoate shift in the legitimate legal justifications for using force—from limiting the ability to use force, to defending relatively newer concepts like human rights.[10]

Despite this development, however, international law can be seen primarily as providing a series of restraints on the use of military force. Excluding domestic legal provisions that govern the use of military force, the UN Charter stipulates that any use of force must be taken either in self-defense under Article 51 or as approved by the Security Council. The charter does allow for authorizations to use force by the General Assembly, but only in cases where the Security Council is incapable of addressing an issue. These institutional structures create further restraints on the use of force by compelling states to justify their decisions publicly, in a global context.

INTERNATIONAL RELATIONS THEORY

International relations theory offers a third way to analyze the use of military force. While social scientists have traditionally been hesitant to explore normative issues, recent developments in international relations demonstrate a recognition that without an understanding of normative issues, political analysis will lack an essential dimension.

Theories such as neorealism and neoliberalism have discouraged scholars from addressing either the descriptive or prescriptive ethical analyses of decisions to use military force. For neorealists, decisions to use military force arise from the structure of the international system, a structure defined as anarchic. The motivation for all actors in the system is survival, leading to the conclusion that any international policy, especially one that leads to the use of force, can be explained as a necessary response to threats.[11] For neoliberals, the assumption of complete anarchy is somewhat exaggerated. They argue that institutions intervene to structure decisions on uses of force. While neoliberals also support the assumption that agents (primarily states) are self-interested actors, they see ways in which force can be constrained by institutional structures.[12]

Recent work in political science has sought to expand these models by suggesting ways in which norms can be considered important factors in decisions to use military force. This new approach, sometimes called constructivism, locates normative factors in the contexts and decisions of national security.[13] These works examine how norms combine with national and international structures to produce outcomes that would not be predictable if those norms did not exist. As one recent work suggests:

> . . . moral principles are fundamentally important to understanding norms governing the use of force, although they are seldom applied in their unadulterated form. This is because norms are products of political processes and therefore cannot be divorced

from considerations of power and interest, which often distort—but do not obliterate—moral principles. Nevertheless, norms are neither merely epiphenomenal reflections of power and interest nor aspirational statements of ideal behavior. Rather they can in their own right not only constrain states in how they pursue their interests but more fundamentally shape state interests themselves. Norms are both products of power and sources of power in the international system. . . . [E]thics are "embedded" in international relations in two senses: First, abstract moral principles are embedded in specific international norms governing the use of force; and second, these norms constitute part of the structure of the international system itself and thereby become embedded in state interests.[14]

This more recent literature on the relationships among norms, moral principles, and international politics seeks to describe the moral principles that stand at the base of certain assumptions that frame our sense of feasible policy options. This literature explains how those principles are shaped by political processes.

A final dimension of political analyses of military force has been a more explicit focus on history and case studies, using historical material to reflect on experience that might be relevant for the future. Historians and political scientists have not always been in agreement on the ways in which historical material ought to be used in drawing lessons about current politics. Often seen as distortions of historical narratives, case studies by political scientists and scholars of international affairs can be overly general and used out of context. Used judiciously, however, historical analyses of decisions to use force can highlight the normative issues with great effectiveness. Perhaps because history often focuses on individual decisions, narrative descriptions of difficult decisions can provide an important source of material on the descriptive normative aspects of military force. Indeed, almost all of the constructivist work in political science has been historically grounded, drawing on narrative descriptions.[15]

CONCLUSION

These three approaches to the study of military force allow both analysis and evaluation. They are only broad frameworks that provide markers for the chapters that follow. Indeed, the real work takes place in the chapters—the difficult task of applying general theories and norms to concrete historical cases.

One final point concerns the largely American focus of the papers. The United States has been the most prone to use military force outside its borders in the past twenty years, a function of both American foreign policy goals and the ability to accomplish those goals. Although this volume focuses primarily on U.S. military force, the editors do not assume that an American perspective on these questions is the only relevant one. Rather, the choice to focus on the United States arises from a recognition of the overwhelming power of the U.S. military and the propensity of policymakers in the United States to use that power. The current war on terrorism has certainly made this focus central.

This book should be seen as a part of an ongoing dialogue on the ethics of the use of force and not as a last word. The decision to use deadly force to coerce others is one of the most difficult and challenging a policymaker will ever make. The chapters in this book explore the complexities behind those decisions. If this book prompts policymakers, citizens, and military leaders to see the moral dilemmas behind those decisions, it will have accomplished its task.

NOTES

1. Just war is less a "theory" and more a tradition, since it does not supply a single coherent framework for explaining and interpreting uses of force. Rather, it is a body of knowledge that requires interpretation within a standard set of guidelines. See Terry Nardin and David Mapel, *Traditions of International Ethics* (Cambridge: Cambridge University Press, 1989) for an example of how the concept of a tradition can produce certain modes of moral evaluation. See also, Albert C. Pierce in Chapter 1 of this volume for a further elaboration of this point.
2. See James Turner Johnson, *Just War Tradition and the Restraint of War: A Moral and Historical Inquiry* (Princeton: Princeton University Press, 1981); James Turner Johnson, *Morality and Contemporary Warfare* (New Haven: Yale University Press, 2001); James Turner Johnson and George Weigel, *Just War and the Gulf War* (Lanham: University Press of America, 1991); and Michael Walzer, *Just and Unjust Wars: A Moral Argument with Historical Examples*, 3rd ed. (New York: Basic Books, 1999).
3. Paul Ramsey. *The Just War: Force and Political Responsibility* (New York: Rowman and Littlefield, 1968/2002).
4. See Brian Orend, *War and International Justice: A Kantian Perspective* (Ontario: Wilfred Laurier University Press, 2000) for one of the few examples of this approach.
5. One of the most important proponents of this position is George Weigel; see *Tranquillitas Ordinis: The Present Failure and Future Promise of American Catholic Thought on War and Peace* (Oxford: Oxford University Press, 1987).
6. See texts by Grotius, Samuel Pufendorf, Samuel Rachel, Christian von Wolff, and Emmerich de Vattel in "'The Emergence of International Law,'" in *International Relations in Political Thought: Texts from the Ancient Greeks to the First World War*, ed. Chris Brown, Terry Nardin, and Nicholas Rengger (Cambridge: Cambridge University Press, 2002), pp. 311–378.
7. Although many claim the treaty was an attempt by French diplomats to limit German power; see E. H. Carr, *The Twenty Years' Crisis* (New York: Harper Press, 1939/1962) for an argument along these lines.
8. There exists a vast body of literature concerning what is allowed in the conduct of war, or *jus in bello* criteria, much of which has been codified in the Protocols to the Geneva Conventions, issued in 1979. These treaties, however, rarely address the question of what justifies launching a war.
9. See Yoram Dinstein, *War, Aggression, and Self-Defence*, 3rd ed. (Cambridge: Cambridge University Press, 2002), pp. 90–91. For other important works in this area, see Anthony Clark Arend and Robert J. Beck, *International Law and the Use of Force: Beyond the UN Charter Paradigm* (New York: Routledge, 1993) and Ingrid Detter, *The Law of War*, 2nd ed. (Cambridge: Cambridge University Press, 2000).
10. For an argument that the use of force in these contexts is generally illegal, see Simon Chesterman, *Just War or Just Peace: Humanitarian Intervention and International Law* (Oxford: Oxford University Press, 2000).
11. See Kenneth Waltz, *Theory of International Politics* (Boston: Addison-Wellesley, 1979) and John Mearshimer, *The Tragedy of Great Power Politics* (New York: W. W. Norton and Company, 2002) for two of the clearest statements of this theoretical approach.
12. See Robert Keohane, *After Hegemony: Cooperation and Discord in World Politics* (Princeton: Princeton University Press, 1984) for a statement of the neoliberal approach.
13. Peter Katzenstein, ed., *The Culture of National Security: Norms and Identity in World Politics* (New York: Columbia University Press, 1996) remains the best collection of articles on this approach, including some critical commentary on attempts to include norms in analyses of national security.

14. Ward Thomas, *The Ethics of Destruction: Norms and Force in International Relations* (Ithaca: Cornell University Press, 2002), pp. 3–4.
15. See Colin Elman and Miriam Fendius Elman, eds., *Bridges and Boundaries: Historians, Political Scientists, and the Study of International Relations* (Cambridge, MA: MIT Press, 2001) for a selection of papers on the overlap between the methods of political scientists and historians in the area of international affairs.

WAR, STRATEGY, AND ETHICS

ALBERT C. PIERCE

United States Naval Academy

The larger project from which this book arose aimed to produce competent ethical analyses well grounded in diplomatic, political, and military realities. That intellectual process drove the directors and participants to the nexus of strategy and ethics. Each of these two fields has its own well-developed body of literature, which are usually shelved in different parts of the library. This chapter begins with the question, what is and what ought to be the relationship between these two fields, these two literatures, which also amount to two distinct logics and two separate languages?

One answer, that of the pacifist, is that ethics and strategy (as the latter is usually construed and applied regarding the use of military force) are fundamentally in conflict, i.e., that violence is always wrong and that strategies for the use of violence, including military force, all run counter to the basic ethic of pacifism. For the pacifist, ethics trumps strategy, with the obvious exception of nonviolent strategies.

Another answer, that of classical and contemporary realism, has a similar bottom line, though arrived at by a quite different route. The realist argues that war is a function of state interests, especially vital national interests; that as such, it is too important to be impeded by considerations of ethics; and thus that ethics must be set aside in favor of strategy. Here strategy trumps ethics.

For both the pacifist and the realist, strategy and ethics are not just two bodies of literature. Rather they are two sets of ideas applied by two different sets of people for two quite different purposes, resulting in a fundamental opposition. The two languages do not translate well into each other, and the two logics point in different directions.

A third answer is the basic thesis of this chapter—that, while there often is tension between the demands of strategy and the demands of ethics, there is no *necessary* or *fundamental* conflict between the two, and further that they can, and often do, point in the same direction, i.e., *toward limits on war and more broadly on the resort to and the use of military force.* I do not argue that strategy and ethics are identical, or that they are always mutually reinforcing, only that they are not diametrically opposed in any fundamental sense.

This chapter unfolds in three parts: (1) an elaboration of how strategy points toward such limits, (2) a companion elaboration of how ethics does the same, and (3) some concluding observations.

STRATEGY

Carl von Clausewitz, the eighteenth-century Prussian soldier and scholar, still has the most comprehensive view of war, the clearest and soundest strategic logic, and is the theorist most widely taught and applied among the U.S. armed forces. Clausewitz's classic book *On War* begins with the theory of war, which, he tells us, "is an act of force and there is no logical limit to the application of that force."[1] At least at the beginning of the book, war is an all-out thing: "To introduce the principle of moderation into the theory of war itself would always lead to logical absurdity."[2] This extreme or absolute nature of war results in large part from the hostile feelings that war inevitably invokes and evokes, on the battlefield and at home. "If war is an act of force, the emotions cannot fail to be involved"[3] — and the emotions war generates are among the most powerful in human experience.

The dominant emotions on the battlefield are triggered by danger and fear: "Without an accurate conception of danger we cannot understand war."[4] In a long paragraph important enough to be quoted here in full, Clausewitz, to contrast the soldier's experience of war with the scholar's examination of it, vividly describes a novice soldier's introduction to the terrifying realities of the battlefield:

> . . . As we approach, the rumble of guns grows louder and alternates with the whir of cannonballs, which begin to attract his attention. Shots begin to strike close around us. We hurry up the slope where the commanding general is stationed with his large staff. Here cannonballs and bursting shells are frequent, and life begins to seem more serious than the young man had imagined. Suddenly someone you know is wounded; then a shell falls among the staff. You notice that some of the officers act a little oddly; you yourself are not as steady and collected as you were: Even the bravest can become slightly distracted. Now we enter the battle raging before us, still almost like a spectacle, and join the nearest divisional commander. Shot is falling like hail, and the thunder of our own guns adds to the din. Forward to the brigadier, a soldier of acknowledged bravery, but he is careful to take cover behind a rise, a house or a clump of trees. A noise is heard that is a certain indication of increasing danger — the rattling of grapeshot on roofs and on the ground. Cannonballs tear past, whizzing in all directions, and musketballs begin to fall around us. A little further we reach the firing line, where the infantry endures the hammering for hours with incredible steadfastness. The air is filled with hissing bullets that sound like a sharp crack if they pass close to one's head. For a final shock, the sight of men being killed and mutilated moves our pounding hearts to awe and pity.[5]

Clausewitz then observes, "The novice cannot pass through these layers of increasing intensity of danger without sensing that here ideas are governed by other factors, that the light of reason is refracted in a manner quite different from that which is normal in academic speculation."[6] War in the classroom and war on the battlefield are two different phenomena: The first unfolds in safety, while the latter is fraught with danger, fear, and anger.

But the emotions that drive war are not confined to the battlefield. Indeed, some of the most powerful of them are well away from the sounds of the guns, and Clausewitz identifies them as one element of his famous trinity:

> As a total phenomenon its dominant tendencies always make war a remarkable trinity—composed of primordial violence, hatred, and enmity, which are to be regarded as a blind natural force; of the play of chance and probability within which the creative spirit is free to roam; and of its element of subordination, as an instrument of policy, which makes it subject to reason alone.[7]

Interestingly, the "primordial violence, hatred, and enmity," Clausewitz tells us, reside *not* in the soldier on the battlefield, but rather "this blind natural force . . . mainly concerns *the people*" of the nation at war [emphasis added]. "The passions that are to be kindled in war must already be inherent in the people."[8] Clausewitz had been on the receiving end of Napoleonic warfare and the *levée en masse*, so he understood the nation *mobilized* for war.

Danger, fear, and anger on the battlefield, combined with primordial violence, hatred, and enmity back home drive war toward the extreme. But, Clausewitz's trinity contains not only the emotions that drive war toward the extreme, but also the principal source of restraint on those powerful emotions—"its element of subordination, as an instrument of policy, which makes it subject to reason alone." Policy and reason bring us to Clausewitz's starting point for strategy—the *political objective*.

> No one starts a war—or rather, no one in his sense ought to do so—without first being clear in his mind what he intends to achieve by that war and how he intends to conduct it. The former is its political purpose [or objective]; the latter its operational [or military] objective. This is the governing principle which will set its course, prescribe the scale of means and effort which is required, and make its influence felt throughout down to the smallest operational detail.[9]

For Clausewitz the political objectives drive everything else: "The political [objective] is the goal, war is the means of reaching it, and means can never be considered in isolation from their purpose."[10] Everything else in war must be subordinated to, must serve, the political objectives.

Political objectives must be defined at the very beginning:

> The first, the supreme, the most far-reaching act of judgment the statesman and commander have to make is to establish . . . the kind of war on which they are embarking; neither mistaking it for, nor trying to turn it into, something that is alien to its nature. This is the first of all strategic questions, and the most comprehensive.[11]

Political leadership sets the political objectives, which in turn define "the [nature] kind of war" on which the nation is embarking, and *strategy* ensures that the war is conducted so as to serve and achieve those political objectives—and *only those political objectives*. "War, therefore, is an act of policy."[12]

Strategy, then, can usefully be thought of as the art and science of how policy—and policymakers—wrestle primordial violence, hatred, and enmity and the other powerful emotions of war to the ground—on the battlefield, at higher headquarters, in the corridors of power, and among the people. Strategy makes these emotions, and the violence they generate, purposeful. It channels them, constrains them, directs and limits them so as to make them productive, that is, to serve the interests of the state as defined by the political objectives.

All strategy is about ends and means, and for Clausewitz there is an iron relationship between the two: *Means must be kept proportionate to ends.* The means include not only the forces to be committed to the effort, but the casualties that will be incurred, and the other financial, political, and social costs of the war effort. "Since war is not an act of senseless passion, but is controlled by its political [objective], the value of this [objective] must determine the sacrifices to be made for it in *magnitude* and *duration*. Once the expenditure of effort exceeds the value of the political [objective], the [objective] must be renounced and peace must follow."[13]

Here Clausewitz's view on the relationship between ends and means runs directly counter to that expressed in the famous line from General Douglas MacArthur: "There is no substitute for victory." MacArthur seems to be saying that victory is so important that no price is too high to pay. In contrast, Clausewitz argues that victory is defined by achieving the political objectives, and that every political objective *has its own price*, determined by the value of the political objective, and that one should never pay a price for victory higher than the value of that particular political objective. If it can't be "purchased" at its proper price, then it shouldn't be "bought" at all.

At times, everything else seems to conspire against this iron linkage. Even when two nations begin a war with limited political objectives, and they commit forces, and are willing to keep costs, proportionate to the value of those political objectives, the internal dynamics of war, the struggle between contending forces and wills, the pursuit of victory and the desire to avoid defeat—all tend to push things out of control.

> Such an interaction could lead to a maximum of effort if such a maximum could be defined. But in that case all proportion between action and political demands would be lost: Means would cease to be proportionate to ends, and in most cases a policy of maximum exertion would fail on account of the domestic problems it would raise. In this way the belligerent is again driven to adopt a middle course. He would act on the principle of using no greater force, and setting himself no greater military aim, than would be sufficient for the achievement of his political purpose. To turn this principle into practice he must renounce the need for absolute success in each given case, and he must dismiss remoter possibilities from his calculations.[14]

This iron linkage, this strict application of strategy, this politically imposed restraint are how and why "warfare thus eludes the strict requirement that extremes of force be applied."[15]

It is *strategy* that must establish and enforce this iron relationship, and in doing so, it runs counter to some of our deepest, most basic, and most powerful emotions. Strategy is a demanding taskmaster. Each war can—and should be—limited so as to serve the particular set of political objectives that define it. It can—and should be—limited by government policy, which must restrain the primordial violence, hatred, and enmity that drive war out of control. There is a standard against which the conduct of war should be measured—the political objectives—and there is someone responsible for holding it to that standard—political leadership. This is the essence of strategy.

ETHICS

If for Clausewitz strategy is the effort to prevail over primordial violence, hatred, and enmity, then for the earliest author of just war principles, the fifth-century African bishop, Augustine of Hippo, and for his religious successors in the just war tradition, ethics is perhaps the effort to prevail over the effects of original sin.

Just war "tradition," is preferable to just war "theory" because "theory" is a term too easily misunderstood or misconstrued here. For example, one might think, "well, that's *just a theory*." Or, one might believe that *theories* are only about abstractions, not real-world practical matters. Or, one might believe that *theory* implies some sort of scientific validity, as in the theory of relativity, while just war cannot offer that kind of certainty. The just war *tradition* is, rather, a set of criteria to guide and evaluate the decisions and conduct of statesmen and soldiers in this deadly business of war. It bridges the ideal and the real.

Further, as James Turner Johnson has so authoritatively and eloquently explained, it is a *tradition*, with many sorts of roots and many kinds of contributors—philosophers, theologians, lawyers, statesmen, and soldiers, among them.[16] It has evolved over time, accommodating basic principles to vastly different geopolitical environments (from the Roman empire and city-states, to medieval kingdoms and fiefdoms, through the early and modern nation-state) and adapting to greatly different challenges (barbarian invasions, religious wars, twentieth-century total wars, nuclear weapons, genocide, ethnic cleansing,[17] and terrorism).

Though it certainly has been invoked to justify war, the just war tradition's basic aim and contribution has been to limit both the resort to war and the conduct of war. Customarily divided into the *jus ad bellum*, which limits the resort to war, and the *jus in bello*, which limits the conduct of war, the just war tradition, put another way, limits the *why*, *when*, and *how* of war.

Two of the *jus ad bellum* criteria restrict the morally acceptable reasons for going to war—the *why*. *Just cause* says, in effect, that not all political objectives clear the bar for what is a morally legitimate reason for resorting to war. While there have certainly been heated debates over what constitutes *just cause*, and while authoritative thinking on this issue has evolved over the millennia, self-defense and defense of a third party under attack have been the prevailing, most consistently endorsed "just causes" for war.

In the aftermath of the Holocaust, the civilized world added prevention of genocide to the list of just causes, formally declaring it in a United Nations General Assembly resolution,[18] but generally articulating it in the two-word slogan "Never again." In the 1990s, the debates raged over just which humanitarian crises (how much suffering, of what kind, by how many people, for how long) constituted legitimate just causes for outside military intervention.

But at no period in history has the just war tradition sanctioned *any and all* political objectives established by governments; the thrust of the tradition has been to constrain the list of acceptable reasons for going to war, or even for outside military intervention short of war.

A second *jus ad bellum* criterion—*right intention*—also serves to constrain governments on their decisions about war, on the *why* of war. This is a criterion of conscience, which says that the declared reason for going to war has to constitute a just cause, and that the declared reason is the real reason. This is a "no-hidden-agendas" criterion. Expressed in arithmetic terms, it says: declared reason = real reason = just cause.

Four additional *jus ad bellum* criteria serve to limit *when* it is morally acceptable to go to war—proper authority, proportionality, probability of success, and last resort. These are prudential, pragmatic criteria.

Proper authority says that only the duly constituted government of the nation is morally empowered to declare war. War is not the legitimate business of any group of citizens, no matter how just their cause or sincere their intentions. In the 1990s debates over humanitarian intervention, there was much discussion over, outside the self-defense and defense of third parties against aggression cases, whether some level, and what level, of multilateral authorization should be required for humanitarian interventions, both to protect sovereignty and to restrain the impulses of powerful nations. In the U.S. constitutional system, one could extend this principle down one step and argue that only the legislative branch constitutes proper authority, or at least that the president alone does not constitute such. But all formulations of proper authority limit who has legitimate moral authority to take a nation to war.

In the *jus ad bellum*, *proportionality* says that the harm that will be done in and by the war must not outweigh the overall good to be accomplished by the war. Of course, such judgments are made prospectively with only limited ability to predict how events will play out once the shooting starts. There are, of course, no guarantees, but proportionality drives the statesman to make reasonable, conscientious, and prudent calculations, and not to use rose-colored glasses in the attempt, and not to succumb to the temptations of overly optimistic assumptions and scenarios.[19]

Conventional wisdom seems to argue that the contemporary U.S. doctrine of "overwhelming force" violates proportionality. The two concepts seem similar, but are quite different. Overwhelming force has to do with how much force one side commits, compared with the other side in a conflict. Proportionality has to do with how much harm is done, compared with how much good is accomplished. Overwhelming force has to do with the ratio of *inputs* proportionality with the ratio of *outcomes*. While in some scenarios, overwhelming force could produce more harm than good, it does not inevitably do so. Thus overwhelming force does not necessarily violate proportionality.

Probability of success also serves to limit the resort to force, by placing a burden on the statesman to ascertain whether his war effort has a reasonable probability of achieving the just cause that triggers it. Here too, there are no guarantees and no mathematical formulae to calculate the results. As with proportionality, with probability of success, one is in the realm not of mathematics, but of reasoned and reasonable judgment. Here the just war tradition runs counter to some of our most treasured stories, factual and fictional, of valiant but futile struggles, stories that embody some of the values and virtues we celebrate. But the just war tradition does not approve, let alone encourage, futile wars, no matter how noble or just the cause and no matter how valiant and self-sacrificing the soldiers. Here too, there is an echo of the realm of military strategy: Probability of success sounds much like what military planners call "feasibility."

A fourth *jus ad bellum* criterion—*last resort*—also serves to limit when a nation may embark on war. Again, prudence and judgment are the order of the day, not hard-and-fast mathematics or absolute requirements abstracted from reality. Last resort drives the statesman either to try other, nonviolent means to resolve the conflict or issue at hand, or to ascertain that other means or instruments of statecraft cannot achieve the political objectives, or accomplish the just cause. Once again, one hears echoes of the world of political-military deliberation and debate, for example, the "let's-give-sanctions-a-chance" argument often invoked to delay or defer the resort to military force in times of crisis.

Taken together, these four *jus ad bellum* criteria place limits on when it is morally acceptable to wage war. They place serious burdens on political leaders to take difficult, often time-consuming, procedural and substantive steps before launching on a war, no matter how just the cause. Added to the two criteria of intention—just cause and right intention—they constitute an at-times formidable set of hurdles, each of which has equal merit and weight. Indeed, the tradition holds that all six must be met; even five out of six does not meet the demanding standard.

The second set of the just war criteria—the *jus in bello*—are clearly in the realm of limits. The tradition holds that the two sets of criteria are independent, that all four combinations are possible—a just war waged justly, an unjust war waged justly, an unjust war waged justly, and an unjust war waged unjustly. The just war tradition does not hold that the ends justify the means, i.e., that even if the war is just (according to the six *jus ad bellum* criteria), not all means are permissible in pursuit of that just war.

The *jus in bello* criteria limit both intention and consequences. The first criterion—discrimination—limits who may be attacked, and the second—proportionality—places limits on the acceptable bad consequences, intended and unintended.

Discrimination is in the realm of intention. The underlying principle here is noncombatant immunity, which states that noncombatants may never be the object of a deliberately intended direct attack. Some clarifications are in order here. First, the distinction is between combatants and noncombatants, not precisely between military personnel and civilians. Some military personnel, even while still wearing uniforms, may not be attacked—for example, those who have surrendered, or who are seriously wounded and out of the fight—because they are *non*combatants. On the other hand, some civilians *may* be attacked—for example, those driving ammunition trucks to the frontline to resupply enemy troops, or those working their shift in a tank factory turning out the engines of war—because they are combatants.

The combatant/noncombatant distinction places severe limits on how war may be conducted—by restricting who may be targeted or attacked. Noncombatants are those who "have done nothing, and are doing nothing, that entails the loss of their rights,"[20] including the right not to be attacked. They are, as Michael Walzer describes them, "not currently engaged in the business of war."[21]

Proportionality, in the *jus in bello* sense, says that the harm that is done *in any particular military operation*, may not exceed the good that is accomplished by *that particular military operation*. It is the same concept as in *jus ad bellum*, only here it is applied at a lower level, not that of the war overall. *Jus in bello* proportionality does not allow one to "cook the books," i.e., by measuring the harm done in a particular military operation (a raid, or an assault, or a bombing run) against the good to be accomplished by the overall war. Such calculations would make the concept meaningless in any just war. This is the realm of collateral damage. The *jus in bello* acknowledges that noncombatants will, almost inevitably, be killed in war *unintentionally*. It does require, however, that those unintended good effects not outweigh the good effects. Proportionality is in the realm of consequences.

Taken together, then, the *jus in bello* criteria cover both intentions and consequences, and in both cases limit how wars, even just wars, may be conducted. *Jus in bello* says that all violence in war must be *both* discriminate and proportional. Any violence that is not militarily necessary violates *jus in bello*, but not all violence that is deemed militarily necessary is morally permissible; to pass that test, it must meet the criteria of discrimination and proportionality.

The two sets of just war criteria—*jus ad bellum* and *jus in bello*—combine to place limits, at times stringent limits, on the resort to war and the conduct of war. Both sets involve an ethic of intent and an ethic of consequences, and both require formidable calculations in advance about an uncertain future whose specifics and even contours may defy precise prediction.

CONCLUDING OBSERVATIONS

This chapter hardly exhausts all that is worth saying about the relationship between strategy and ethics. Its purpose has been twofold: First, it refutes the common argument, i.e., that the two sets of concepts are fundamentally opposed to each other.

Second, it persuasively advances another, i.e., that the two can and sometimes do point in the same direction—toward placing limits on the resort to war and on the conduct of war. As the succeeding chapters in this book will at least implicitly demonstrate, there are certainly times when the two logics and languages are in tension with each other, and there are also times when the demands of the two can be reconciled in ways that do not do serious damage to either one.

Going to war, or even committing military forces in contingencies short of war, is among the most weighty decisions a nation, through its political leaders, makes. In the best of circumstances, this is a very difficult business, as military history illustrates in at times painful detail. If we are to do better, if we are to do as well as we could and should, at this inherently difficult business, we need statesmen and soldiers, scholars and citizens, who, if not fluent in the two languages of strategy and ethics, and if not masters of both logics, are at least conversant with and minimally competent in both.

NOTES

1. Edited and translated by Michael Howard and Peter Paret, *On War* (Princeton: Princeton University Press, 1976), p. 77.
2. Ibid., p. 76.
3. Ibid.
4. Ibid., p. 114.
5. Ibid., p. 113.
6. See the first two paragraphs of Book 1, Chapter 4, ibid., p. 113.
7. Ibid., p. 89.
8. Ibid.
9. Ibid., p. 579.
10. Ibid., p. 87.
11. Ibid., pp. 88–89.
12. Ibid.
13. Ibid., p. 92.
14. Ibid., p. 585.
15. Ibid., p. 80.
16. See James Turner Johnson, *The Just War Tradition and the Restraint of War* (Princeton: Princeton University Press, 1981).
17. "Ethnic cleansing" is the current term of art, used here only reluctantly because it fails to clarify just who or what is cleansed by ethnic cleansing.
18. The Convention on the Prevention and Punishment of the Crime of Genocide. See United Nations General Assembly Res. 260A(III), UN Doc. A/760, at 9 (1948).
19. Clausewitz's caution that the strategist "must dismiss remoter possibilities from his calculations" incorporates the same burden of rigorous calculations.
20. Michael Walzer, *Just & Unjust Wars*, 3rd ed. (New York: Basic Books, 2000), p. 146.
21. Ibid., p. 43.

THE POLITICS AND ETHICS OF RESCUE

JOHN P. LANGAN, S. J.
Georgetown University

Rescuing persons in distress from those who are pursuing them is the core idea of humanitarian intervention. Whether the call comes from Kosovo or Rwanda, from Bosnia or Liberia, the basic scenario is much the same: Members of an alien and despised group are driven forth from their homes to be the likely victims of famine and disease or are gathered together to be slaughtered. Some leaders are ready to stir up this dreadful process and to tell the stories from the remote or the recent past that will motivate their compatriots to take up arms against their neighbors and to attempt to even—in the bodies of unarmed men and women and children—the unresolved scores of previous generations of ethnic conflict and imperial oppression. Driven by fear and resentment, their followers turn to force, defy outside criticisms and humanitarian rebukes, and see in indiscriminate slaughter the surest and most reliable means of protecting their fatherland and their culture from the debasing effects of allowing the continued presence of ancient enemies and new cosmopolitan migrants.

This chapter explores some ethically significant aspects of the political and military responses that Western governments and more particularly the United States can make to the call for rescue. Such calls arise from the midst of ethnic conflict in societies often very different from our own but which nonetheless have the ability to appeal to a sense of compassion and justice thus creating an obligation to come to their rescue. Their ability to do this is not surprising, for they have easy access to Western notions of human rights and the rule of law. These commitments have been constantly affirmed over the past fifty years by the highest political authorities and by numerous religious and nongovernmental organizations, ensuring that appeals using the language of human rights are readily understood and evoke passionate responses from already existing networks of activists and experts. The Western electronic media are able and are often willing to present the more

18

dramatic atrocities in a form that arouses sympathy for the victims along with in-dignation and even loathing directed at the oppressors, though their ability to con-vey a clear understanding of causes and remedies for these appalling situations is considerably less. To borrow from the parable of the Good Samaritan, the media are able to bring the victims from the side of the road, where it is comparatively easy to pass them by while we proceed about our business, to the center of the screen and often enough to the center of the political process. This is especially the case when the victims have, as they often do, compatriots, whether emigrants or exiles, who have learned to present the case of their people to the Western societies in which they live and work.

This chapter explores three aspects of the public debate that these calls to res-cue provoke. First, the changed shape of public debate on these matters that resulted from the collapse of the Soviet Union and of the Cold War paradigm for the con-duct of public policy and public debate. Second, a set of three dilemmas that will afflict any new paradigm of humanitarian intervention for the sake of rescuing vic-tim populations: linking moral principle and national interest in these situations; attempting to combine consistency and local applicability, the universal norm and the particular challenges, in a workable policy; and, finding means and resources to implement a policy that will be adequate to the needs of the situation and ac-ceptable in its costs and risks. Third, the task of arriving at a new paradigm that will not collapse because of its neglect of the lessons of realism and the constraints of contemporary American political life.

PARADIGM SHIFTS

One of the most common visual aids used by politicians and others doing popu-lar presentations on foreign policy and national security issues during the years from 1948 to 1989 was the map. The central feature of the map was red ink, which was used to indicate the areas of the world under communist control. Often the map was presented in sequential fashion to show the coming of communist con-trol first to the Soviet Union (1917), then to the neighboring states in eastern and central Europe and the Balkans (1945) as well as to the zones of occupation in east-ern Germany and in the northern half of the Korean peninsula (1945), then to Czechoslovakia (1948), to China (1949), to Vietnam (1955 and 1975) along with Laos and Cambodia, then, most irritatingly, to Cuba (1959), to Angola, to Nicaragua, and, finally, to Afghanistan (1979). The only area of qualified dimin-ishment of the red empire was in southern Europe, where Tito's Yugoslavia was often represented with a red-white mixture of some sort, since it was clearly not under Moscow's control but was patterned to a large extent in its institutional structure along communist lines. The message conveyed graphically by the map was that communism was a growing and irreversible menace, that its reach and as-pirations were global, and that it had an inner unity and coherence as well as an impressive dynamism.

The map or the series of maps conveyed important information both directly and indirectly. Directly, what it said about communist parties coming to power in different countries was incontestable, at least in its general outlines. Indirectly, what it exemplified and implied about the way in which general public perception of the security threat to the United States and to "the free world" was channeled along the lines of a bipolar world was also not to be denied. For it pointed to an important set of presuppositions for most public debate that was usually not subjected to serious question in the multitude of more specific debates over defense budgets, foreign aid requests, weapons procurement decisions, and alliances with particular countries that were thought to be under the threat of communist subversion or domination. Even those who assumed the communist threat much exaggerated or mistakenly seen as present in various fundamentally nationalist movements had to admit the powerful influence of the Cold War paradigm exemplified by the map on the imagination of the general public and on the range of options that policymakers were willing to consider. Scholars, unless they were willing to be labeled as radical or naive, often felt that they might introduce minor modifications to the paradigm, might point out overlooked elements in various local situations, might speak of the weight of ancient dogmas and the illusion created around received myths, and might challenge some distortions in the way the paradigm was applied to these particular situations. But they were also likely to feel that rejecting the general applicability of the paradigm in discussion and research would probably be damaging to their credibility and to their career prospects.

If we look back at the Cold War paradigm, which is the last broadly shared reading of the situation and responsibilities of the United States within the world and which sustained two generations of broadly bipartisan foreign policy, from the vantage point of contemporary discussions of human rights and of the need to rescue victims in a world of violence and intolerance, we can see that the Cold War paradigm had both a great advantage and a great disadvantage. The great advantage was that it provided a crucial and easy way of connecting considerations of both moral values and national interest with the resources of the national security apparatus and so with the possibilities for action in a wide range of locations around the world. The great disadvantage was correlative to this, since the tendency to interpret local and regional conflicts along the lines of the Cold War paradigm was very powerful and frequently led people to overlook or misconstrue important features of these conflicts. This was most famously and obviously the case in Vietnam. Often enough, this meant that the terms of American involvement in a given area were shaped predominantly by "our side" in the local conflict, since our own understanding of the local situation was obviously less detailed, less nuanced, and less engaged than the views of those who were keen to involve American power on their side. This could work out well in the hands of skilled and perceptive local leaders who were anxious to reunite and energize their divided societies and to keep them from falling under communist control. But it could also mean that the United States wound up backing local leaders who were unacceptable to their own people and who ranged from the corrupt to the murderous. As time went on, efforts to present the kleptocratic rulers in the Philippines and Zaire and the Argentine colonels and their counterparts in other Latin American regimes and the white racists of Rhodesia and South Africa as defenders of "the free world" became less and less plausible, even though it was undeniably true that many of the opponents of these regimes were themselves Marxists and were fundamentally illiberal and undemocratic.

The institutionalization of human rights policy in the Carter administration occurred at a time when the Soviet Union was still continuing to support national liberation movements on all continents and when it was preparing its own disastrous intervention into Afghanistan. But the policy pushed the United States in the direction of attempting a more comprehensive evaluation of the internal performance of its allies and clients with regard to human rights and began the process of disentangling the defense and promotion of freedom and human rights from the still ongoing process of waging the Cold War. Development of the policy was a signal of widespread dissatisfaction that had built up over many aspects of the U.S. stance toward Third World countries, but at the same time it was intended to provide an ideological basis for continuing criticism of the Soviet Union. While the Cold War could no longer provide comprehensive legitimation for cooperation with authoritarian and dictatorial regimes, it had not ceased to be the central concern of policymakers and of the general public. Serious criticism of the human rights abuses of Tito's regime in Yugoslavia, for instance, was not on the agenda. If the shah of Iran had been threatened by communist subversion rather than by a populist Islamic revolution, the response of both Carter and his critics to the human rights abuses of the Savak would in all likelihood have been significantly different. A useful point of comparison here is the lack of concern that the United States showed in 1965 when Suharto seized power in Indonesia and destroyed large numbers of ethnic Chinese along with the cadres of the communist party.

But the broad scope of the annual reports by the State Department on human rights manifested a growing tendency to universalism in the moral judgments of a generation that had lived through the debacle of Vietnam and that had grown skeptical about the uses of Cold War rhetoric. The map of communist advance was seen to be less and less enlightening about the actual course of events once Nixon and Kissinger played "the China card," which involved treating the Sino–Soviet split not merely as an important fact about how things went on the other side of the wall but also as an opportunity for a more complex and less ideological style of diplomacy. This diplomacy might or might not concern itself with human rights, but it had to give greater weight to local factors and to maneuvers across and around the great ideological divide. This gave legitimacy to ways of thinking that could be driven either by calculations of national interest as classically conceived or by proclamations of universal norms as articulated by the lawyers and political activists who were attempting to construct institutions and norms for the protection of the victims of this bloodiest of centuries, without regard to their political orientation or ethnic background. What is common to both these ways of thinking despite their clear opposition to each other (commonly

discussed as realism vs. idealism or moralism or legalism) is that they treat the categories of the Cold War opposition as secondary. For the Cold War paradigm in its
prime (1948–1967) bound together the defense of U.S. national interest and the protection of such universal moral-political values as freedom and democracy in an international system that was both cooperative and adversarial and that embodied
itself and the pursuit of its goals in an institutional network, of which NATO was
the centerpiece.

In the internal political life of the United States, during the period of the Cold
War after 1967, that is, after the difficulty and the costs of carrying out that intervention in Vietnam became obvious to all, a pattern emerged in which most of
those who were customarily on the left side of political debates, with the important
exception of organized labor, were increasingly critical of both armed and covert
U.S. interventions and of the Cold War legitimations that U.S. governments routinely offered for these activities. The left developed reflex patterns for interpreting
these interventions as manifestations of U.S. imperialism and discounted both humanitarian and anticommunist rationales. More reliable support for these exercises came from the political right, even in areas of the country that had been
traditionally isolationist, since there was in these quarters more readiness to bear any
burden in the task of opposing communism and more willingness to accept the
self-descriptions and self-evaluations of Third World anticommunists.

The collapse of the Berlin Wall, the collapse of the satellite regimes, and then
the collapse of the Soviet Union itself meant the end of the Cold War and called
into question the meaning and continued worth of many Cold War activities. There
was no longer a comprehensive communist threat from which people needed to be
rescued, a threat that might justify ignoring lesser evils or allowing them to occur
because attempting to remedy them might undermine the position of the "free
world" in some way or might bring closer the possibility of nuclear annihilation. At
the same time, the opening of countries that had previously been under communist control meant that the West and other countries concerned about human rights
abuses had more extensive opportunities to contemplate the results of ethnic conflict and of dictatorial misrule, since the veil of secrecy that had previously obscured human rights violations had been torn away, at least for a time. Some of the
worst catastrophes occurred in regions in which stable government collapsed and
in which the rule of law had ceased to be effective. Of course, some of the greatest slaughters occurred in areas such as Central and West Africa, which had never
figured prominently on the Cold War map. But the course of events in the Horn
of Africa exhibited the transition from subsidized Cold War confrontations to the
collapse of the state in the brutalities of clan warfare in Somalia and the resulting
famine. The end of the Cold War clearly did not mean the coming of the peace-
able kingdom. In many areas of the world it made humanitarian intervention easier to carry out since it removed the likelihood of communist counterintervention
and the dangers of escalating conflict; at the same time, by removing the global foe,
it made intervention more difficult to justify to the general public.

NEW DILEMMAS

The children with swollen bellies in Somalia and Sudan, the skulls of the victims buried in mass graves in Srebrenica, the rivers swollen with bodies in Rwanda, the roads blocked with corpses in Liberia, the twisted figures of the victims of sniping in Sarajevo—all made stunning visuals that generated public sentiment for action and intervention. People were appalled that such things should happen at this late time in the twentieth century and felt indignant that their own governments and organizations with which they dealt would have traffic with regimes or movements that either committed or permitted such things. It was not merely ordinary people reading newspapers or watching television who were moved; journalists and policymakers themselves showed that they felt the chilling effects of perceiving evil working its destructive way even as they watched. One person who was deeply moved by what he saw on several visits to Bosnia was Richard Holbrooke, who played a large part in the achievement of the Dayton Accords. In January 1993, shortly before Clinton's first inauguration, Holbrooke sent a memorandum to Warren Christopher, who was to be secretary of state, and to Anthony Lake, who was to be national security advisor. He begins his memo by stressing the high political stakes that a policy for Bosnia would entail:

> Bosnia will be the key test of American policy in Europe. We must therefore succeed in whatever we attempt. The Administration cannot afford to begin with either an international disaster or a quagmire. Despite the difficulties and risks involved, I believe that inaction or a continuation of the Bush policies in Bosnia by the Clinton administration is the least desirable course. Continued inaction carries long-term risks that could be disruptive to U.S.–European relations, weaken NATO, increase tension in Greece and Turkey, and cause havoc with Moscow.

The language of this passage speaks the general contemporary political language of risk and challenge. It attempts to link the painful and destructive situation on the ground in Bosnia, which it takes as a given without further description or analysis but which its author knows at firsthand, to national interest as this is commonly specified in terms of relationships with allies and potential adversaries. The context is the transition between administrations, a time of both flexibility and vulnerability but also usually a time when policies can be reassessed and fundamental assumptions can be reconsidered. The primary motivation for what is being proposed, the protection of the Muslims of Bosnia, is moral and in principle universal, but the language itself is political and conflictual.

Holbrooke went on to propose four objectives for the new administration in its Bosnia policy. These were as follows:

> [F]irst, "to save as many lives as possible in Bosnia"; second, "to make containment of the war a top priority"; third, "to punish the Serbs for their behavior . . . and to brand certain individuals war criminals"; fourth, "to use this crisis as an opportunity

to strengthen the U.N. system." We should act, I added, "in concert with other nations," even creating "some sort of ad hoc military coalition," but avoid getting dragged into a ground war in the region.

These all count as morally commendable objectives, but they lack the close connection with national interest and national priorities that a comparable crisis in Europe would have produced in the days of continuing struggle with the Soviet Union. Internal strife in Yugoslavia would have been seen as inviting Soviet meddling and perhaps even intervention, as endangering a state whose security we had agreed to protect, as putting the southern members of NATO in a position where they would be liable to Soviet pressure, and as threatening the balance of forces in Europe. It would have engaged all the central players in the shaping of national security policy and would have provoked continued deliberations at the highest levels of the alliance. Ending bloodshed in an appalling ethnic conflict and containing a local armed conflict on the European continent, punishing those guilty of war crimes, and strengthening the UN are all tasks that, if successfully accomplished, would enhance U.S. prestige and national interest, but in ways that are marginal and that do not affect the core of American power and interests.

At this point Holbrooke has come up against the triple dilemma that confronts those who would move from recognizing the ethical imperative of rescue to forging a policy of rescue. The victims of the large-scale human rights violations that are inherent in ethnic cleansing and in civil wars and that are the manifest objective in genocide invariably belong to groups that are not dominant or powerful, though they should not be thought of as completely lacking in resources. In fact, their unacceptability to their neighbors may in many cases be based on their greater perceived success in certain areas of life or on superior access to outside resources or on closer connections with past oppressors. (It is this last factor that is especially important in the case of the Muslims in Bosnia). But they are at a disadvantage in terms of numbers or access to the instruments of violence. This means that there will be serious risks and costs in attempting to rescue them or in standing between them and those who would destroy them. Rescuing victims will be an uphill task with the likelihood in most cases of serious difficulties and scant rewards. The situation that makes rescue ethically compelling also usually makes it politically unappealing.

The three dilemmas that I mentioned earlier are to some extent interlocked, though they are distinct. The first dilemma arises from the fact that the appeal to moral principle in rescue situations focuses our attention on the victims, the persons who are in need of rescue and whose rights are in jeopardy. This means that the actions taken to aid them will be in the first instance other-regarding, that is, they will be aimed primarily at providing goods and preventing evils for others. The connection with what is to our advantage or interest will be contingent, complex, hypothetical, indirect, often long-term; it will require some argument, steps in which may well be open to dispute. These connections may in fact be powerful and reliable for society as a whole, even while they may not be motivating or rewarding for the individuals who have to carry the burdens and the risks of implementing the policy. The benefits of a more stable international system may be quite real and may provide powerful reasons for our government to act; but they may not necessarily work to the advantage of those who have to make sacrifices and take risks in order to attain them. They are also less likely to be clearly perceptible for many people than they were in the adversarial situation of the Cold War period, where stopping or surpassing the other side could readily be understood as a positive outcome worth striving and sacrificing for. The complex and often highly uncertain relationship between the aid brought to the victims and the enhancement of our national interest means that it is always an open possibility for critics of rescue proposals to present them as having a negative or merely speculative impact on the national interest. It requires farsighted and courageous national leadership to articulate the connections in a persuasive way and to elicit from a broad range of citizens and interest groups the trust that will be needed if truly difficult policy choices have to be made. Leadership of this sort will need to have a broad vision of how accomplishing the task of rescue really does advance America's situation in the world.

The dilemma arises in the political forum precisely because narrow views of what the national interest is about will rule out any broadly interventionist policy and because support for humanitarian intervention not firmly and clearly related to the national interest will be unstable. The United States, as even such practitioners of realpolitik as Henry Kissinger have had to admit, is a country that strongly desires its foreign policy to express its moral values; and there will be significant support for many types of victims in need of rescue, even though this will not always lead people to endorse a policy of intervention. For instance, there was widespread concern for the Chechens; but virtually no one argued for a policy that would have gone beyond pressure on the Russians to intervention on their territory. Considerations of sovereignty, international order, and wider networks of international relationships drove such a course of action out of the minds of most participants in the public debate even before they could formulate it as a logical possibility. But in most cases there is a shifting community of NGOs, compatriots and friends of the victim group, religious and humanitarian organizations, concerned journalists and academics who will be ready to throw themselves into advocacy work for the victims and who in many cases will be ready to provide money, food, medicine, and arms for the relief and protection of the victims. These people will have contacts and more or less close relationships with officials in Western governments and international organizations. The resulting network can be highly effective both in shaping public debate and in helping to alter conditions in the troubled area. Consider, for example, the activities of Croatian communities in the United States, Canada, and Australia and their sympathizers in Germany and Italy. Even when narrow and isolationist conceptions of the national interest are dominant, humanitarian considerations will not be banished from the public debate in the United States. They will customarily exhibit a mixture of the broad sympathy that appeals to a universalist ethic evoke and of the passionate intensity that animates those who are kith and kin of the victims.

But a brief comparison between the Croatian and the Bosnian cases will illustrate some of the limits of a purely moral demand for rescue. Briefly, the Croats
were more powerful and were asking less; with a limited amount of outside assistance, much of it not highly visible, the Croats were able to help themselves and
to drive the Serbs out of Croatian areas they had occupied. The Bosnians were in
greater need and hoped for a large-scale intervention that would provide Western
military protection against their Serb adversaries. Eventually this came, but only
after tremendous suffering and human rights violations and the partition of their
country.

Attempting to argue for rescue or intervention on purely or even primarily humanitarian grounds will always be vulnerable to shifts in both public and elite
opinion. These shifts can be produced by quite diverse causes: by compassion fatigue, as the crisis extends beyond the length of the public's attention span; by the
emergence of larger or more proximate crises, which deprive the remote or familiar crisis of the media exposure that it needs if the public is to be motivated; by the
bad behavior of the victims and heroes who need protection but who can sometimes
lapse into savagery after long persecution; by the countermeasures of the other side
in the field of propaganda and public persuasion; by the suspicion, often rooted in
a lazy high-mindedness or a proceduralist desire to be evenhanded, that there must
be parallel crimes and causes of suffering on both sides. Interest, as the philosophers
and social theorists of the eighteenth century saw with their desire for clarity and
simplicity, is a more reliable indicator of policy and behavior than humanitarian
sentiment. But it is also possible to link national interest to sympathy once a commitment to undertake the tasks of intervention and rescue has been made. National interest is then seen primarily as the ability to carry through successfully on
our commitments and as the perception of others in the international arena that
we are appropriately steadfast, competent, and powerful and that our protection is
eminently worth having. This, it should be acknowledged, is a voluntaristic and ex-
trinsic view of the national interest; and it did not provide much in the way of intelligent guidance in our long struggle in Vietnam.

Short of a decisive national commitment that incorporates the rescue into the
sphere of the national interest, it is very likely that responses to calls for rescue and
intervention will be slower than the progress of the tragedy on the ground and that
they will be reluctant and less than fully reliable. This is not surprising, since the
overcoming of bureaucratic inertia and of political skepticism takes more time than
the mobilization of sympathetic networks in the ordinary civilian population to
provide public support for the rescue of the victims and since it is only rarely that
the national political leadership will find that it has sufficient clarity about the issues in a local conflict and sufficient passion about what is being done to the victims to take a decisive initiative from the top in favor of rescue. The response is even
less likely to be speedy when it has to come from a multilateral organization such
as a military alliance or a part of the UN system.

The second dilemma arises from the need to devise rescue policies that will neither cost too much nor risk too much but that will at the same time be effective in

rescuing and protecting those who are in danger and, if possible, situations of conflict from deteriorating to the level of massacre and genocide. This dilemma is closely related to the previous one, since one of the central concerns in determining what costs or risks are excessive is the political acceptability of these costs and risks. This is not something that can be reliably predicted with any degree of precision and that seems to vary from generation to generation, depending on the level of casualties and the political outcomes of recent wars and uses of force by the government. The shadows of Vietnam still hang over the policymakers and military leaders of the United States, even if they evoke boring reminiscences rather than haunting memories for the young. If a rescue mission or humanitarian intervention is perceived to be only loosely related to core concerns in the national interest or if it is thought to be poorly conceived or poorly managed, the levels of acceptable cost and risk as these are informally determined by the American public will go down rapidly. The most dramatic illustration of this tendency was the intervention in Somalia. As this example shows, a great deal depends on how the intervention is presented by the media and on what expectations have been generated in the public by previous media treatments of the crisis.

It should also be noted that costs and risks will not always move in the same direction. One standard way to minimize risk, whether this be risk of failure or risk of casualties, in the exercise of force is to make a massive deployment of available forces so that local resistance by the aggressors becomes an extremely unattractive option. But this, of course, makes the operation correspondingly expensive in financial terms and increases the political costs if large numbers of troops have to be maintained on active deployment for long periods of time. Another way to minimize risk and to increase the prospects for success in the deployment of military forces is to move with surprise. But this in turn runs up against the standard requirement in just war theory that the use of force be a last resort after alternatives have been exhausted. At the same time the forces deployed must be adequate to the mission, and their instructions and rules of engagement must be sufficiently flexible and must allow for sufficient escalation in the use of force so that the humanitarian objectives can be attained with a reasonable certainty of success. Failure to establish control of a given region is only too likely to result in further harm to the victims or in some of them becoming hostages and thus victims for the future. The resolution of this dilemma requires a prudent adjusting of means to ends and a just distribution of risks and costs. Successful previous experience is obviously an enormous help in developing the skills and attitudes that are present in this process of prudent adjustment; but previous successes should not blind those who have operational responsibilities to the new difficulties and to the surprises that a new local situation is likely to present.

The third dilemma is also shaped by the distinctiveness of the new local situation; but the difficulty it presents is more theoretically challenging than the second, which is concerned with the immediate practical response to the needs of a particular situation and with arriving at a sustainable and effective policy for handling a particular crisis. But, like the second dilemma, it is conditioned by the limits on resources that act as a constraint on how much can be done to aid the victims of even the worst atrocities. The third dilemma is the problem of achieving practical consistency in the resolution of crises involving humanitarian intervention and aiming at the rescue of those innocent persons who are in peril in situations of group conflict. Stated from a somewhat different perspective, it is the problem of selecting in a world marked by limitations of money, personnel, media access, time and attention available to policymakers, and public support just which groups are to be rescued. This problem is especially salient because the most common ethical justification for intervention is a universalist ethic that invokes the human rights possessed by all persons, regardless of their status, racial and ethnic background, religious affiliation, sexual orientation, and political preferences. From such a universalist perspective, there seems to be no reason to prefer the cries for help of Bosnian Muslims to the similar cries of Tutsi refugees or Afghan rebels or Sudanese Christians or Chechen tribesmen or Albanians in Kosovo or Palestinian refugees or Chinese dissidents or Catholics in East Timor or Indians in Chiapas or Guatemala. For a strict universalist, all these cries seem to present the same demand for rescue and to have the same moral urgency, no matter what may be the differences in history, context, and likely consequences.

Often enough, there surfaces in the public debate the claim that similar cases are to be treated in a similar fashion and that if intervention is justified or required in one of these cases, it will be required in all of them. In itself this is a formal point, and it may be advanced by both the advocates and the opponents of intervention. In response to this point, it is necessary to separate the ethics and the politics of rescue. On the one hand, similar violations of rights and similar atrocities do require similar responses and remedies. This point, it seems to me, must be granted to the proponents of a consistent universalism. The central part of the practical response to a crisis situation, however, has to be specific practical measures that will bring an end to the grievous violations of human rights that justify rescue and intervention in the first place. What these measures are, how effective they are likely to be, and how serious their negative consequences will be are all matters that are context dependent. Calls for identical treatment of similar offenders effectively ignore the variations in contexts and likely outcomes and are a less than intelligent response to a troubled and difficult situation, even though they may be rhetorically attractive and even politically persuasive in working through some hard cases. Similarity is itself a very elastic category, and using it requires some selection of relevant categories in terms of which judgments of similarity are to be made. Situations calling for major decisions in foreign policy will normally be complex, and decision makers will have some freedom of judgment in assessing the relative importance of various factors. It is the primary task of human rights organizations and of the religious bodies that overlap with them to remind decision makers of the fundamental importance of human life and of basic human rights and to argue strenuously for protective measures, even when these bring with them very high costs and risks. While policymakers may claim that no more can reasonably be done to help various classes of victims and while they may argue that further measures would jeopardize other morally important values and while their judgments may actually be correct and worthy of respect, individuals and groups will also be right to feel a repugnance in conscience to decisions that abandon groups of victims to a fate administered by hostile powers. The facts may force us to admit our inability to rescue certain groups; they do not require us to admit that such an outcome is morally satisfactory. We are likely to do no better than to accept the often arbitrary limits to what we can do in rescues and humanitarian interventions. Certainly our actually available resources do not allow us to attempt to rescue all. Candor and a search for knowledge of ourselves as moral and political agents require us to acknowledge a certain contingency and even arbitrariness in our choices of which groups to rescue. For the foreseeable future, our choices will be shaped by journalistic sympathies, photo opportunities, ethnic alliances in our own political community, presidential and congressional campaigning needs. Democracy is a messy business and the United States is not in the position of a supreme and impartial magistrate setting right the wrongs of the world but is one society striving to meet its obligations to its own citizens and to those who look to it for help. For a purely universalist ethic, this is a seriously unsatisfactory situation; but we should also recognize that there are more specific justifications for intervention, the acknowledgment of which would give moral justification for the unevenness of the pattern of responses to evil that we have been worrying about. These more specific justifications include alliances and treaties, promises and public statements that encouraged subject and victim peoples to expect rescue, the moral necessity to undo the effects of previous complicity in the activities of unjust and oppressive regimes, and concerns about consequences in other societies.

The effort to achieve a consistent application of principles such as the imperative to protect human life and human rights and the duty of rescue to ethnic conflicts and instances of genocide is difficult. The contexts are too various, the forms of resistance are too numerous. But the concessions to obstructing forces in these humanitarian crises are not mere departures from a certain aesthetic ideal, departures that may actually lead to a richer and more complex aesthetic and a plan that draws out the more varied and more interesting possibilities of a mountainous terrain. Rather, they are acts of tragic acceptance in which people of good will and nations with strong humanitarian commitments acknowledge their inability to rescue without producing greater harms. This inability may well involve their own past moral failures (as when anti-Semitic attitudes and acts by non-Nazi nations and governments helped to make the Holocaust a conceivable project or when Jewish refugees were turned away from places where they expected to find security) or their own present lack of political will to bear the burdens that a serious project of rescue would bring with it. There is a special responsibility that falls on governments that provide encouraging signals to dissidents and separatist groups that their human rights will be protected even if their political goals cannot be achieved and that then effectively abandon those to whom they initially offered access and support. The acceptance of a tragic situation, particularly when the acceptance is done by one group and the tragedy is endured by another, does not automatically bring with it moral absolution.

CONCLUSIONS

After reviewing the collapse of the Cold War paradigm for thinking about intervention and rescue and after struggling with the dilemmas that are inherent in undertaking the task of rescue in contemporary circumstances, what outlines can we offer for a new paradigm for deliberation about what will probably be a series of crises in the transition from the twentieth to the twenty-first century?

Because of the complexity of these issues, only tentative conclusions are possible. This list springs from the issues addressed thus far in this chapter:

1. Should there be an acceptance of ethical universalism rather than Cold War adversarialism as the starting point for development of policy?
2. Should we acknowledge at the start that there are areas where actively interventionist policies are likely to be prohibitively dangerous (the territories of the former Soviet Union) or are likely to be assimilated into ongoing adversarial relationships (South Asia, Iraq) or are going to be interpreted as an effort to maintain a legacy of colonialism and imperialism (parts of Africa and Latin America)?
3. What would it mean to recognize that actively interventionist policies can have serious destabilizing effects by encouraging secessionist movements?
4. What would it mean to recognize the importance of preventive and proactive measures that will attempt to prevent conflict from developing to the point where violence becomes endemic and where massive slaughter becomes a possibility?
5. What would it mean to recognize that it is morally, economically, and politically preferable to spend resources on preventive measures rather than on interventions after catastrophes have occurred?
6. Can international and national institutions develop a pragmatic and contextualized view of the merits of multilateral and unilateral, regional or UN bases for conducting interventions rather than canonizing one instrument or approach?
7. What would be required to develop a broad bipartisan coalition endorsing the moral requirement of intervention in cases of genocide and of informal political norms sanctioning those politicians who attempt to gain partisan advantage from difficulties and costs of the policy?
8. What would be required to recognize that the national interest of the United States, which has a strong and continuing concern for the stability of the international status quo, at least in its broad outlines, should be broadly interpreted to include a minimum level of security and peace that is incompatible with genocide?
9. What would be required to recognize that rescues and humanitarian interventions are an important but extraordinary means of meeting a fundamental ethical obligation arising from human solidarity?
10. Can the international community develop measures to resolve ethnic and religious conflicts that may involve the creation of new structures that will move beyond traditional conceptions of sovereignty and boundaries?

11. Can the international community generate the political will to use force in a steady and reliable way in the early stages of humanitarian crises, given that the slide to catastrophe can be extraordinarily rapid in situations where hostility has been longstanding?

12. Can there be a recognition that consistency in the handling of a single case is practically more important than achieving consistency across cases, which are likely to be vastly different?

These questions represent just a small sample of possible future areas of consideration. They are not posed to any single profession or institution, but represent questions that we all must ask. In order to understand ethics and the use of force in the twenty-first century, we must begin to consider difficult questions such as these.

RESPONDING TO TERRORISM

ETHICAL IMPLICATIONS

MARTHA CRENSHAW

Wesleyan University

This chapter addresses the question of the applicability of the principles of just war to American decisions to use military force in response to international terrorism. Before the attacks of September 11 and the declaration of the "war on terrorism," the American government was ambivalent as to whether terrorism should be defined as crime or as warfare. The normative aspects of policy choices were addressed only infrequently. After September 11, the question of whether justice can be achieved in the use of force against terrorism has become an issue on the public agenda. Both ethical and political considerations must be used to judge responses to terrorism, since policymakers must contend with political pressures as well as moral principles. However, the two requirements need not be contradictory, and it is important to include ethical principles in evaluations of political judgment. This analysis first describes the policies and actions that constitute the American response to terrorism, and then discusses the criteria by which they should be evaluated.

AMERICAN POLICY OVERVIEW

IDENTIFICATION OF THE THREAT

The official conception of terrorism has not always been clear, although terrorism has posed a serious policy problem for the United States since the late 1960s. In 1972, the president created a Cabinet Committee to Combat Terrorism, which centered the response to international terrorism in the State Department. Since then terrorism has figured prominently on the national agenda and been the subject of periodic institutional reorganizations, well before the establishment of a Department of Homeland Security in 2002. The approach to terrorism before September 11 was frequently ambivalent. Terrorism was described both as crime and as warfare, and as both a domestic and an international problem. For example, President Nixon's public speeches typically equated terrorism with domestic unrest as much as foreign threats. He described Palestinian hijackings and a bombing at the University of Wisconsin as the same "cancerous disease." President Carter, faced with the Iran hostage crisis, defined terrorism as a threat to civilization and the rule of law and as a test of American values.

The Reagan administration perceived terrorism as a direct threat to the national interest, and defined it as both an attack on democracy and a form of surrogate warfare practiced by states. In fact, it was during the Reagan administration that the issue of "state sponsorship" of terrorism came to the fore. At the same time, President Reagan labeled terrorists as criminals and contended that civilization itself was at stake, along with the democratic principles of the rule of law and respect for individual life. State Department legal adviser Abraham Sofaer also approached terrorism as crime. He disagreed strongly that the law of war applied to terrorism while arguing simultaneously that national self-defense was at stake.[1] Secretary of State George Shultz referred to terrorists as "depraved opponents of civilization itself."[2] He recognized the political intent behind terrorist violence (which would distinguish it from "mere" crime), but he countered that the political goals of terrorism could never justify it. Shultz called terrorism a threat to democracy because it rejects the principle of settling disputes through legitimate political processes. Not facing up to terrorism would be giving in to "lawlessness." Yet he also referred to terrorism as a threat to U.S. strategic interests, because it was sponsored by totalitarian states (i.e., the Soviet Union) and occurred in areas of importance to Western interests. Thus terrorism was both a mode of warfare and an attempt to destroy the moral values of democracy.

The vice president's Task Force on Combating Terrorism issued its report in February 1986.[3] It explicitly recognized the dilemma of defining terrorism as crime vs. warfare but did not take sides, although the report defined terrorism as a threat to national security. The report also contradicted some of Shultz's assertions by suggesting that addressing the grievances behind terrorism was not a sign of moral confusion. The report was also cautious about the efficacy of military force as a response to terrorism.

President Bush had little to say about terrorism, despite having chaired the 1986 Task Force, probably because the Gulf War dominated his agenda. The Clinton administration, however, introduced a new conception, one that reflected both a different worldview and the changes of the post–Cold War world. Deliberately avoiding descriptions of terrorism as a threat to civilization, the administration stressed the pursuit of justice and law enforcement. Terrorism was categorized as one of a collection of modern "border-crossing" or "transnational" threats, including proliferation, organized crime, drugs, disease, and environmental disasters. All these problems were interpreted as global threats that resulted inevitably from modern life—open societies, open borders, technological advance, and access to information. The State Department in its 1994 edition of *Patterns of Global Terrorism* explained that a general rule of U.S. counterterrorism policy was to "treat terrorists as criminals and apply the rule of law." In 1997 Kenneth McCune, then the acting Coordinator for Countert-errorism, testified to Congress that one of the three principles of overall counterter-rorism policy was treating terrorists as criminals, considering their actions as crimes, and making every effort to apprehend and prosecute them according to the rule of law. The other two elements of policy were listed as refusing concessions to terrorist demands and pressuring countries that supported terrorism through economic, diplo-matic, and political sanctions. No mention was made of the use of military force, al-though McCune's testimony was explicitly about "Sudan and Terrorism," and Sudan was the target of retaliation only a year later.[4]

The Clinton administration also emphasized the risks of terrorism using weapons of mass destruction, a result of new technological advances as much as new political motivations. The possibilities of "bioterrorism" and "cyberterrorism" attracted par-ticular attention. A noteworthy shift in institutional focus was the growing role of the Department of Defense in defending against or coping with terrorist attacks using "WMD" on American territory, the pursuit of "homeland defense." The difficulty of distinguishing between domestic and foreign threats was becoming increasingly ob-vious, especially after the 1993 bombing of the World Trade Center and the 1995 Ok-lahoma City bombing. The president also established the position of a National Coordinator for Terrorism on the National Security Council.

The 1998 bombings of the American embassies in Kenya and Tanzania pro-duced another change in threat conception. A National Security Council staff member was quoted as saying "For the first time, the White House is treating ter-rorism as a national-security problem, and not as a law-enforcement problem. Amer-ica has joined the battle."[5] In justifying the attacks on Sudan and Afghanistan in August, the president and high-ranking representatives of the administration warned of a long struggle against terrorism, with no clear victory in sight. President Clin-ton referred to terrorists as the enemies of peace, democracy, tolerance, and secu-rity. In his speech to the United Nations opening session in September, he referred to terrorism "not as a clash of cultures or political action by other means, or a di-vine calling, but a clash between the forces of the past and the forces of the future, between those who tear down and those who build up, between hope and fear, chaos and community."[6] Secretary of State Albright introduced a World War II analogy yet also resisted defining terrorism as warfare by announcing that "the na-tion whose finest planted the flag at Iwo Jima and plunged into hell at Omaha Beach will not be intimidated by the murderers who have chosen to make our na-tion their enemy."[7]

POLICY RESPONSES

Between 1968 and 2001, the use of military force was an exception, and it was lim-ited to armed rescues of hostages and brief retaliatory strikes. Over that period, the United States developed an extensive range of responses to terrorism, which will only be outlined here in order to focus on the role of military operations as a choice among alternatives.[8]

Force was used in hostage rescue attempts by special operations forces, including the failed Iran hostage rescue in 1980 and the thwarted *Achille Lauro* mission in 1985. This use was a way of solving the humanitarian dilemma posed by the policy of no concessions to terrorist demands, which was a centerpiece of official policy since the Nixon administration. The credibility of the no-concessions policy was badly damaged by the Iran-Contra scandal, and lapses in practice were relatively common, but official commitment to the principle was consistently reiterated. However, high-profile hostage seizures declined significantly in the 1990s, so the policy has not recently been put to the test.

Force was also employed in the service of law enforcement, to arrest suspects abroad and return them to the United States for trial, as in the arrest of Fawaz Yunis in 1987. This policy was strengthened after the FBI gained powers of extraterritorial jurisdiction through legislation enacted in 1986. The forcing down of the Egyptian airliner carrying the hijackers of the *Achille Lauro* in 1985 could also be considered as an attempt to apprehend the perpetrators. The alternative to forcible seizure was persuading other governments to arrest and extradite or expel suspects, which remains a central component of a law enforcement strategy. The rewards program administered by the State Department was and is a means of persuading individuals to provide information leading to the arrest of suspects. Sanctions, such as those implemented against Libya for refusing to turn over suspects in the bombing of Pan Am 103, and which resulted in their trial in an international court, are also an alternative to forceful apprehension. Preventive and defensive measures, which are alternatives to the use of force because they impede the commission of acts of terrorism in the first place, include improving security at airports, embassies, military bases, and other targets favored by terrorists. In order both to defend against terrorism and to implement sanctions, the United States consistently promotes international cooperation. The government also provides assistance and training to foreign governments largely on a bilateral basis, which introduces the question of American responsibility for the possibly unethical behavior of the recipients of such aid.

Retaliatory or preemptive military strikes (via aerial bombings or cruise missile attacks) were carried out against Libya in 1986, against Iraq in 1993, and against targets in Sudan and Afghanistan in 1998. The first two attacks were directed specifically against the governments of states accused of organizing terrorism against Americans, in the first instance the bombing of a discotheque frequented by American soldiers in Berlin, and in the second a plot to assassinate former President Bush during a visit to Kuwait. The 1998 strikes targeted al Qaeda training camps in Afghanistan and a pharmaceuticals factory in Khartoum presumed to be manufacturing precursor chemicals for weapons that would come into al Qaeda's hands. The governments of Afghanistan and Sudan were not explicitly threatened.

The "war on terrorism" thus represented a dramatic escalation. The deployment of ground troops in a major intervention on hostile territory in order to overthrow a regime harboring terrorists and to destroy a nonstate terrorist organization was unprecedented. The response to terrorism now includes military campaigns, whether directly or by proxy, against any terrorism "of global reach" as well as efforts to overthrow regimes considered part of the "axis of evil," one attribute of which is support for terrorism or at least the potential for supporting terrorism. Thus mobilization for war against Iraq was partially justified in the name of counterterrorism.

Another recent expansion of the resort to force involves covert CIA operations, which can be considered as examples of the use of force even though they need not involve military units or personnel. The CIA was prohibited from assassinations until after the 1998 embassy bombings, when the Clinton administration authorized attempts to apprehend bin Laden that could include killing him should he try to leave Afghanistan.[9] After September 11, the Bush administration has moved further in this direction, for example, by employing Predator drones to assassinate al Qaeda operatives in Yemen.

Since the beginning of the "war on terrorism," law enforcement has become the primary alternative to the use of military force. While many of the sanctions previously implemented against states accused of sponsoring terrorism remain in place, the imminence of the threat and the independence of al Qaeda from state support make this option less relevant.

NORMATIVE CRITERIA

Evaluation of policy toward terrorism must strike a balance between morality and political prudence or practicality. Decision makers apply ethical principles in complex and hazardous circumstances, with weighty consequences. In the end, their decisions about terrorism are political, and they will have to choose among competing values. Furthermore, scholars disagree about the interpretation of moral principles as well as their applicability. Nevertheless, a discussion of normative guidelines for policy can at least be initiated by examining the issues involved in applying principles of just war, focusing on *jus ad bellum* criteria.[10]

RIGHT AUTHORITY AND STATE SOVEREIGNTY

Applying the criterion of right authority to counterterrorism policy refers of course to the right of a government to respond to terrorism, but it can also be interpreted generally as the protection of territorial integrity and sovereignty, a right protected by the UN Charter and the mainstay of order in the international system. First, the response to terrorism must be undertaken by a lawful government, not vigilantes or other private actors. On the other hand, the response to terrorism is likely to involve formal violations of the sovereignty of other states. Uninvited military strikes against persons or property within the jurisdiction of another state, whether or not the state directly controls those persons or property, as well as direct attacks on a state, whether limited strikes or large-scale military interventions, are violations. So, too, are armed rescues of hostages on the territory of other states without their permission.

However, potentially mitigating factors can be balanced against respect for sovereignty. There may be cogent and explicable reasons for violations, which should be specified in advance of action.

In the first instance, the government of the offended state may be complicit. If a government participates in terrorist activities, it is not living up to its obligations even though it exercises control over a defined territory and is recognized internationally as the legitimate government of that state. Similarly, if a state passively assists acts of terrorism by knowingly allowing terrorist groups to use its territory as a base for operations, it is culpable. A state cannot avoid exposing itself to counterattack simply by refusing to accept responsibility. Clandestine support for terrorism is a form of deliberate deception, designed precisely to elude detection and blame. Even when the evidence is indisputable, states invariably deny that they have resorted to terrorism. The view that passive and active complicity justifies infringements on territorial integrity is not, however, universally accepted. Michael Schmitt, for example, contends that "Harboring terrorists is simply insufficient for attribution of an armed attack to the harboring State."[11]

What if a state is unable to control its territory or lacks the capacity to deny it to terrorists? In this case, using force against the terrorist organization is more justifiable than attacking the host state. However, it should be noted that any use of force, however precisely targeted, is technically a violation of territorial integrity and sovereign authority if the host country has not consented. In practical terms, the government will be weakened as a result, and its diminished control might actually permit more terrorism in the long run. Punitive or preemptive military action directed against nonstates causes necessary but secondary effects on state sovereignty. The critical issue is the extent to which the government maintains control over the use of violence within its sovereign jurisdiction. A government that is unwilling or unable to prevent nonstate terrorists from using its territory undermines its claim to sovereignty.[12] Furthermore, if punishment is justified, states that are the victims of nonstates may have no other way of defending themselves other than to use force against states that harbor terrorists and facilitate terrorism.

Consider the ambiguous record of armed rescues of hostages in terms of state sovereignty. It shows that both decisions to act and reactions to those actions were primarily political. The first modern instance that provoked controversy was the Israeli raid on Entebbe in 1976, in order to free the passengers of a hijacked airliner. Even though the Ugandan government of Idi Amin was complicit, and the lives of the hostages were manifestly in danger, Israel was subjected to severe criticism in the United Nations because of the violation of sovereignty. The government of Somalia did not oppose the German rescue of airline passengers at Mogadishu in 1978. The American attempt to rescue the diplomatic hostages in Iran resembled the Entebbe raid in intent if not in execution. The Iranian government was even more openly complicit in the harm being inflicted on American representatives.

Respect for sovereignty has also complicated the use of force to apprehend suspected terrorists abroad. In 1985, the Joint Special Operations Command (JSOC) forced an Egyptian airplane to land at an American base in Sicily, surrounded the plane with American troops in an effort to seize the Palestinian hijackers of the cruise ship *Achille Lauro*, and followed the plane on to Rome.[13] In this case, Egypt may indeed have been complicit, since the government not only allowed the hijackers to leave Egyptian territory but facilitated their departure when it was known that an

American passenger on the ship had been killed. However, the violation of Italian sovereignty was hard to justify. The reaction of Antonio Cassese, an Italian judge, is instructive: "The United States sailed into a sea of political and diplomatic troubles. Not only did it fail to achieve its purpose . . . it also antagonized and deeply offended two allies, one a member of NATO."[14] He argued that the United States managed to destroy the international consensus against terrorism that had resulted from the initial seizure of the cruise ship.

The United States subsequently grew more cautious and circumspect. For example, in 1987 Fawaz Yunis was first lured into international waters and then arrested by agents of the FBI. He was transported back to the United States in military vessels, tried in a civilian court, and convicted. No further apprehensions outside the United States have raised questions of sovereignty, especially since September 11, due to the cooperation of the governments where suspects were located. However, after 1998 the Clinton administration was willing to seize Bin Laden on Afghanistan's territory without the Taliban's consent, had it been possible.

The record indicates that past U.S. restraint in retaliating directly against states was due more to considerations of national security than respect for the abstract principle of sovereignty. For example, the Carter administration considered retaliatory military action against Iran in the early days of the hostage crisis, but rejected it because of the risk of escalation in U.S.–Soviet relations after the Soviet invasion of Afghanistan. National Security Adviser Zbigniew Brzezinski initially favored a retaliatory strike in combination with the rescue mission, and he continued to believe that the United States should retaliate militarily if the rescue mission failed.[15]

The United States viewed the bombing of Libya in 1986 as an act of war against a state that had mounted attacks on American interests (including the bombing of the La Belle discotheque in Germany as well as military challenges in the Mediterranean). Syria, however, had also supported anti-American terrorism but was not targeted. Libya, by contrast, had few allies and held little strategic importance for the United States. Still the attack was widely criticized, even by NATO allies who refused the United States overflight permission rights.

In 1993, the Clinton administration launched a cruise missile strike on Baghdad in retaliation for Iraqi involvement in an attempt to assassinate former President Bush during a visit to Kuwait. Iraq had just been defeated in the Gulf War, and the 1993 bombing was a pinprick in comparison to the Gulf air war. Retaliation was easy because of Iraq's weakness and isolation. On the other hand, the United States considered but rejected retaliation against Iran in response to evidence of Iran's involvement in the Khobar Towers bombing in 1996. The reasons for restraint had less to do with sovereignty than with the timing of the information that permitted the United States to ascertain Iran's responsibility. By the time that the United States had evidence it considered sufficient, moderates had gained some influence in Iran. Furthermore, many European states favored a more constructive policy toward Iran, rather than containment as the United States preferred, and their opposition limited U.S. options.

In 1998, the governments of both Sudan and Afghanistan were isolated and largely friendless. By 2001, Afghanistan was even more ostracized due to the Taliban's continued support for Bin Laden and sanctions imposed by the Security Council. The Taliban regime was only recognized as a legitimate authority by three other governments (Pakistan, Saudi Arabia, and United Arab Emirates).

JUST CAUSE AND RIGHT INTENTION

The reasons for the resort to military force are critical to normative evaluation, including the judgment as to whether or not states are justified in violating the sovereignty of others. Under international law, self-defense, enshrined in Article 51 of the UN Charter, is the most widely recognized justification for the use of force and the one most often proposed by states that have used force against terrorism. The question is the expansiveness of the conception of self-defense. American justifications for the use of force have typically combined self-defense with preemption and deterrence.

Paul Gilbert proposed that "defensive just war theory" is limited by the self-defense requirement to restoring one's security, removing a threat, or forestalling harm.[16] However, in his view, an alternative theory of punitive justice also accepts the use of force as punishment or retribution for a wrong that has been done. Michael Schmitt, on the other hand, argues that the only acceptable purpose of the use of force is defeat of the enemy or direct prevention of an impending attack. A state is not allowed to act to punish or in order to sustain a policy of general deterrence. As William O'Brien explained, the use of force must be limited to what is necessary to achieve the just cause, "sticking to the pursuit of the just cause and nothing more, repressing emotions of hatred and vengeance. . . ."[17] Thus the goal of military action can only be defense against terrorism. This criterion is highly restrictive. Retaliating against suspected terrorists for general purposes of demonstrating resolve or upholding reputation and credibility would not be justifiable in terms of the right intention requirement. Nor would it be permissible to retaliate simply because a frustrated domestic public demanded action. Effects such as retribution may be a consequence but they cannot be the primary purpose. Yet Schmitt also notes that "deterrent self-defense has become, or is at least in the process of becoming, accepted."[18]

On the other hand, both James Turner Johnson and Jean Bethke Elshtain argue that states *can* punish those who have inflicted an injury.[19] States have an obligation to prevent further harm to their citizens and to punish those responsible for the harm that has already occurred. Punishment is not identical to revenge, however. In Elshtain's view, just punishment is restrained, whereas revenge observes no limits. Moral outrage is never just cause for a forceful response to terrorism.[20]

Thus the use of military force to preempt anticipated attacks—to disrupt the organizational infrastructure of the terrorists or deprive them of resources in the short term—is usually justified as a means of forestalling harm. The purpose of the 1998 bombing in Afghanistan, Secretary Albright said, was to disrupt the Osama bin Laden organization's ability to conduct additional terrorist activities.[21] She argued that the bombing was justified both as a response to the embassy bombings and as a way of forestalling future harm to American interests. The bombing of Libya in 1986 was explained as both retribution for the La Belle disco bombing and deterrence of future Libyan attacks. The 1986 Task Force report (released before the April bombing) explained that "our principles of justice will not permit random retaliation against groups or countries. However, when perpetrators of terrorism can be identified and located, our policy is to act against terrorism. . . . A successful deterrent strategy may require judicious employment of military force to resolve an incident."[22] President Reagan's speech after the attack called the evidence of Libyan responsibility for the disco bombing direct, precise, and irrefutable. He also said, "Self-defense is not only our right, it is our duty. It is the purpose behind the mission undertaken tonight—a mission fully consistent with Article 51 of the UN Charter."[23] He also justified it as a preemptive action that would alter Libya's behavior.

Critics of the U.S. bombing of Libya referred explicitly to this normative framework. They claimed that the use of force was not to pursue justice but to relieve frustration and demonstrate power. For example, Mary Kaldor asserted, "The inadequacy of the American explanation may be due to the fact that the Libyan airstrike was not about terrorism at all. It was about the global role of the United States. It was about the exercise of military power, and the reassertion of a dominant American position. . . . The attack on Libya was the culmination of a series of developments in U.S. foreign policy and military strategy which are intended to increase the visibility and utility of the American arsenal."[24] In fact, she continues, "In this worldview, the reality of the Libyan role in terrorism is irrelevant." The same criticism has been made of American policy toward Iraq.

The bombing of the pharmaceuticals plant in Khartoum in 1998 was controversial precisely because the link between the plant and terrorism was hard to demonstrate. Secretary of State Albright claimed, "I think that if we had not taken this action, we would not have been exercising our right of self-defense, and we would be more in danger, I think, of other actions coming down the road. So we had no choice. We know that this is, as I said, a long-term-issue battle for us."[25] However, the evidence linking the plant to chemical weapons and to bin Laden was said to be weak.[26] Michael Barletta, for example, argued that although it was possible that some precursor chemicals might at some time have been present at the plant, the facility probably played no role in the actual development of chemical weapons.[27]

On the other hand, Paul Pillar, an official of the Central Intelligence Agency, defended the work of the intelligence agencies. He claimed that there was good reason to be suspicious of the Al-Shifa plant and its relationship to the Sudanese government. However, he also pointed out that the intelligence agencies did not indicate that there was an active chemical weapons program or that destroying the plant would affect the likelihood of bin Ladin attacking the United States with chemical weapons. The issue was not one of poor intelligence but whether the use of military force was a prudent choice.[28]

Pillar also argued that the use of force was actually retaliatory rather than pre-emptive. The evidence in itself did not justify preemption. In his view, the United States should not have lowered the standard of evidence for preemption because of the desire to retaliate.

The 1998 bombings of Sudan and Afghanistan were criticized on similar grounds, even from within the administration. The president's motives for ordering the attacks were questioned. Critics in the press referred to the *wag the dog* syndrome, an allu-sion to the diversionary use of military force.[29] The administration vigorously de-fended its motives, insisting that the sole motivation was protecting the American people from terrorism and that no other consideration was involved.[30]

This discussion points to problems in stretching the concept of self-defense to jus-tify force as preemption or "anticipatory self-defense."[31] Self-defense may be con-fused with retribution or revenge. For security reasons, governments may not be able to fully disclose evidence that substantiates the claim that there is an imminent threat. Sometimes they lack tactical warning and must proceed on the assumption that acts of terrorism are part of an ongoing campaign, not isolated incidents that will not be repeated. The harm inflicted by the September 11 attacks was so great that preemp-tion was easier to justify. The greater the anticipated harm, the lower the standard of proof that another attack is likely.

NECESSITY OR LAST RESORT

The use of force must be the last, not the first, resort. Peaceful means must have been exhausted. It is not clear whether this requirement means that other alterna-tives must be tried first, or that they must only be explored or contemplated. A thor-ough comparison of alternative courses of actions is a practical requirement of rational decision making as well as a normative criterion for the use of force. How-ever, in a crisis situation, policymakers may not have time to try other options or even to collect and assess information about them. Does lack of full consideration of options due to the pressure of time remove moral justification from the use of force? Applying this criterion also requires comprehensive knowledge of the poli-cymaking process. In counterterrorism policy it is hard for the observer or the pub-lic to know whether all options were considered during a highly secretive internal decision-making process. Nevertheless, it is clear that the American government is sensitive to this requirement.

President Reagan's public justification for the bombing of Libya was explicit in this regard. He explained, "We always seek peaceful avenues before resorting to the use of force—and we did. We tried quiet diplomacy, public condemnation, economic sanctions, and demonstrations of military force. None succeeded."

The Clinton administration also said that force was a last resort in 1998, and there were frequent references to having no choice.[32] Bill Richardson, U.S. Am-bassador to the UN, claimed that the United States acted only after efforts to con-vince Sudan and Afghanistan to cease cooperation with bin Laden had failed.[33] Other options that were tried, which did not prevent the attack on the embassies, included persuading Saudi Arabia and then Sudan to expel bin Laden (he was expelled from Sudan in 1996 after which he traveled to Afghanistan). The Clinton administration convinced the UN to implement sanctions against the Taliban and called repeatedly for them to turn over bin Laden. Law enforcement had also been tried extensively. From at least 1996 on the CIA had tracked the al Qaeda network, and intelligence investigations had produced numerous indictments and arrests.

Sanctions, law enforcement efforts, and limited military strikes failed to prevent the September 11 attacks, and they no longer appeared timely in light of a continued threat of unacceptable harm. Nevertheless, before launching combat operations in Afghanistan, the Bush administration again asked the Taliban to surrender bin Laden, offering several eleventh hour "last chances." The government used Pakistan as an intermediary, to the extent even of sending a delegation of Pakistani religious leaders to persuade their counterparts to comply. Although one could argue that the Taliban should have been given more time, the American public and the international community accepted that force was a last resort.

The need to use force to rescue hostages seems to have passed, but it would be unwise to assume that the hostage seizures will not be repeated. Hijackings, after all, were thought to be a thing of the past before September 11. One alternative to the use of force in rescuing hostages was making concessions to terrorist demands, a policy the United States has rejected in principle since 1973. However, from the perspective of moral philosophy, Martin Hughes criticized the claim that governments should never negotiate with terrorists. He denied that negotiations confer legitimacy on the opponent or imply submission to dictation. In his view, there is no domino effect: Ransoming some victims does not endanger others.[34] Lapan and Sandler agreed that the conventional wisdom that states should not negotiate does not withstand theoretical scrutiny. They conclude that states should not commit themselves in advance to a no-negotiation strategy. Their findings suggest that "when governmental declarations are not completely credible and uncertainty characterizes the government's costs of not negotiating, then never negotiating is likely to be time inconsistent and not a plausible policy."[35] Reuben Miller found that between 1968 and 1977 governments were reluctant to comply with the demand that prisoners be released but they acceded to less threatening demands such as ransom or publicity.[36] Governments also tended to compromise or negotiate rather than comply directly.

Another general alternative to the use of force against terrorism is preventive security, which has much to recommend it. However, analysts have noted a substitution or displacement effect, which makes the policy more problematic in terms of the normative criterion of reasonable hope, discussed below. When new technologies or policies are applied to prevent specific kinds of terrorist events, terrorists transfer their efforts to new but related targets.[37] Installing metal detectors in airports, for example, apparently decreased hijackings in the 1970s but produced an increase in other forms of hostage seizures, such as kidnappings, and in assassinations.[38] Thus enhanced airport security in the post–September 11 period may have the unintended consequence of deflecting terrorism into other areas.

PROPORTIONALITY AND REASONABLE HOPE

O'Brien explained that the use of force has to be proportionate to the need to achieve the just cause and that "the proportionality of initial and continuing recourse to force must be judged in the light of the probability of success."[39] In normative terms, the use of force must be expected to do more good than harm and to be effective in accomplishing its purpose. Note that what is asked here is what decision makers anticipate at the time of choosing to use force. A disparity between intention and result does not matter if it could not have been expected.

Frederic Kirgis, representing the American Society of International Law, suggested that the proportionality aspect of self-defense becomes relevant when the necessity test has been met.[40] It can have two meanings. Either the intensity of the defending state's use of force must match that of the aggressor, which is a difficult standard to meet in the case of terrorism, or it must be designed to do nothing more than defend against a reasonably perceived threat. Schmitt agrees that the proportionality principle does not mean equivalency.[41] Defending oneself from terrorism may require a greater magnitude of force than the attacker had to use, especially since terrorism is always a form of surprise attack. Proportionality means that the defending state must use sufficient force to cause the terrorist to desist. The response is thus limited to the amount of force required to defeat an ongoing attack or prevent an imminent one.

Questions of proportionality were raised in 1986 with regard to Libya. The war in Afghanistan could be challenged on these grounds, but the harm inflicted on the United States was so great that proportionality did not become an issue for the public. There was also a reasonable expectation that ground combat would work when limited bombings from the air had not worked.

In light of the requirement of a reasonable hope of success, it is interesting that before September 11, there was a disparity between the expectations of the American government that deterrence and preemption would work and research findings from the scholarly community. In general, theoretical studies of the effectiveness of the use of military force against terrorism were skeptical. In an edited volume, David Charters criticized American policy as based on a biased analysis that overestimated the threat to the state. In his view, the use of military force to retaliate against terrorist incidents produced no visible deterrence: "The political and moral costs of reprisals were usually greater than their deterrent or attrition effects."[42] Other analysts also concluded that retaliation neither deterred future terrorism nor provoked escalation. Propositions tested on Israeli data indicated that "whatever effect reprisals may have in deterring future attacks or causing a 'spiral' of counterattacks is but a short-term phenomenon lasting no more than nine months, in the case of Israel."[43] Similarly, Enders, Sandler, and Cauley found that retaliatory raids imposed short-run costs with no long-term benefits.[44] The subsequent research of Enders and Sandler supported this proposition, especially in the case of the Reagan administration.[45] Shaikh argued that retaliation is effective only if based on subsequent apprehension and prosecution of terrorists.[46]

Some public criticism of the bombing of Libya was also based on the charge of ineffectiveness. Richard Falk contended, "There is little evidence to suggest that any of the Reagan inner circle believed that such an air strike would abate terrorist activity. On the contrary, as with the public, most expected a rise in terrorist incidents to ensue, and this has indeed happened."[47] Libyan agents were responsible for the bombing of Pan Am 103 in 1988, presumably in retaliation for the 1986 air attacks. Similarly, even at the time many observers doubted that the 1998 strikes would do more than temporarily set back Osama bin Laden's network. CIA Director George Tenet warned shortly afterward that bin Laden was planning more attacks against American targets, and subsequent events proved him right. Credible terrorist plots were discovered on the eve of the millennium; in October 2000, the *U.S.S. Cole* was bombed; and in September 2001, the country suffered the most deadly terrorist attack in its history.

Even after the initiation of the "war on terrorism," the American government was still attracted to the idea of deterrence. The Defense Advanced Research Projects Agency commissioned two studies of the effectiveness of deterrence as a response to terrorism.[48] Neither concluded that deterrence was likely to be successful.

Related to the proportionality requirement is the principle of noncombatant immunity, found in the *jus in bello* discussion of just war theory. As Adam Roberts has pointed out, the principles relating to the right to resort to force (*jus ad bellum*) are distinct from the requirements applicable to the actual use of force in military operations.[49] However, in practice the two are often confused, especially since the way in which force is employed will affect judgments as to its original justifiability. Roberts adds that "in antiterrorist campaigns in particular, a basis for engaging in military operations is often a perception that there is a definite moral distinction between the types of actions engaged in by terrorists and those engaged in by their adversaries. . . ."[50] Avoiding civilian casualties is critical to that distinction because the essence of terrorism is targeting civilians.

The political dimension of the principle is also important. The American public and international opinion are sensitive to the issue of noncombatant immunity. The 1986 raid on Libya was criticized on the grounds of causing excessive civilian casualties. President Clinton apparently based his decision on target selection in Khartoum on the premise that the plant would be unoccupied during the attack. A second target was taken off the list because of the risk of civilian casualties.[51] The war in Afghanistan prompted criticism of indiscriminate use of cluster bombs and other nonprecision munitions.

CONCLUSIONS

Before September 11, the American government defined and treated terrorism simultaneously as crime and national security threat. The use of military force was rare. A "war" against terrorism was not contemplated. American ambivalence was a result of the contradictory nature of terrorism as well as uncertainties about the effectiveness of different policies. These troublesome issues were not resolved by the adoption of the metaphor of a "war on terrorism" or completion of the military campaign in Afghanistan. Al Qaeda survived the war in Afghanistan, and similar transnational challengers may emerge in the future. Decisions about using force to combat terrorism will continue to be based on considerations of both justice and political expediency, but the two interests need not be incompatible. Self-defense will be offered as the central justification for using force, and we can expect the scope of the principle to be widened as threats to security become more and more elusive. Preemptive use of force, in particular, is likely to become more common.

For the future, a grave concern is the prospect of terrorism using chemical or biological weapons. Reducing that danger is one of the reasons offered by the Bush administration for war against Iraq. One reason for the relaxation of standards of proof in Sudan in 1998 was the fear that al Qaeda might acquire chemical weapons. If a state or a nonstate actor should resort to terrorism using "weapons of mass destruction" (WMD), would a military response be justified? What type of force would be proportional? Richard K. Betts has argued that conventional military retaliation might not suffice against such an attack and that responding in kind would be appropriate.[52] It is critical that policy makers and the public consider the moral implications of using force in advance of the emergency that would call for such a momentous decision. They must be prepared to resist the temptation to exact revenge rather than follow the principles of justice.

NOTES

1. Abraham D. Sofaer, "Terrorism and the Law," *Foreign Affairs* 64, no. 5 (summer 1986), pp. 901–922.
2. "Terrorism and the Modern World," U.S. Department of State Current Policy No. 629, October 25, 1984.
3. *Public Report of the Vice President's Task Force on Combating Terrorism* (Washington, D.C.: U.S. Government Printing Office, February 1986).
4. Statement before the Subcommittee on Africa, Senate Foreign Relations Committee, May 15, 1997.
5. In Seymour M. Hersh, "Annals of National Security: The Missiles of August," *The New Yorker*, 12 October 1998, p. 37.
6. Remarks by the President to the Opening Session of the 53rd United Nations General Assembly, New York, 1998.
7. Madeleine K. Albright, "The Testing of American Foreign Policy," *Foreign Affairs* 77, no. 6 (November/December 1998), pp. 50–64.
8. For a review of American policy before September 11 see David Tucker, *Skirmishes at the Edge of Empire: The United States and International Terrorism* (Westport, CT: Praeger, 1997).
9. See Martha Crenshaw, "Terrorism," in *The United States and Coercive Diplomacy*, ed. Robert J. Art and Patrick M. Cronin (Washington, D.C.: United States Institute of Peace Press, 2003) and "Terrorism, Strategies, and Grand Strategies," in *The Campaign against International Terrorism*, ed. Audrey Kurth Cronin and James M. Ludes (Washington, D.C.: Georgetown University Press, 2003).
10. Two sources worth mentioning from the period before September 11 are Mona Fixdal and Dan Smith, "Humanitarian Intervention and Just War," *Mershon International Studies Review* 42 (November 1998), pp. 283–312 and Paul Gilbert, *Terrorism, Security and Nationality: An Introductory Study in Applied Political Philosophy* (London: Routledge, 1994). See also William V. O'Brien, *Law and Morality in Israel's War with the PLO* (New York: Routledge, 1991). After September 11, consult Michael N. Schmitt, "Counter-Terrorism and the Use of Force in International Law," *Marshall Center Papers, no. 5* (George C. Marshall European Center for Security Studies, Garmisch-Partenkirchen, Germany: November 2002) and "Just War Tradition and the New War

on Terrorism" (a Pew Forum on Religion & Public Life Discussion, October 2001, with Jean Bethke Elshtain, Stanley M. Hauerwas, and James Turner Johnson. Available at <www.pewforum.org>). See also Adam Roberts, "Counter-terrorism, Armed Force and the Laws of War," *Survival* 44, no. 1 (spring 2002), pp. 7–32.

11. See Schmitt, p. 51.

12. See the argument by Ronald Steel, "In the Company of Terrorists," *New York Times*, 23 August 1998. Sudan and Afghanistan, in his view, were accomplices, not bystanders, and thus legitimate targets.

13. See Antonio Cassese, *Terrorism, Politics and Law: The* Achille Lauro *Affair* (Princeton: Princeton University Press, 1989).

14. Cassese, p. 129.

15. See Zbigniew Brzezinski, *Power and Principle* (New York: Farrar Straus Giroux, 1983).

16. See Gilbert, pp. 8–9 and also Chapters 4 and 11.

17. O'Brien, 1991, p. 320.

18. See p. 66.

19. See Pew Forum on Religion & Public Life Discussion, 2001.

20. From a pragmatic perspective, policy analyst Brian Jenkins also cautions against seeking revenge. See *Countering Al Qaeda* (Santa Monica, CA: Rand Corporation, 2002.)

21. Interview on ABC-TV *This Week*, August 23, 1998.

22. See p. 9.

23. Address by President Reagan to the nation, 14 April 1986, text in *Selected Documents No. 24*, Bureau of Public Affairs, U.S. Department of State.

24. E. P. Thompson et al., *Mad Dogs: The U.S. Raids on Libya* (London: Pluto Press, 1986), p. 3.

25. In an interview on CBS-TV *Nightly News with Dan Rather*, August 21, 1998.

26. James Risen, "To Bomb Sudan Plant, or Not: A Year Later, Debates Rankle," *New York Times*, 27 October 1999; Tim Weiner and Steven Lee Myers, "Flaws in U.S. Account Raise Questions on Strike in Sudan," *New York Times*, 29 August 1998; and Tim Weiner and James Risen, "Decision to Strike Factory in Sudan Based on Surmise," *New York Times*, 21 September 1998. See also Paul Pillar, *Terrorism and U.S. Foreign Policy*. See also James Risen and David Johnston, "Experts Find No Arms Chemicals at Bombed Sudan Plant," *New York Times*, 9 February 1999.

27. "Chemical Weapons in the Sudan: Allegations and Evidence," *The Nonproliferation Review* VI, no. 1 (fall, 1998).

28. Pillar, pp. 107–109.

29. See *Financial Times*, August 22–23, 1998.

30. See Seymour M. Hersh, "The Missiles of August," *New Yorker*, 12 October 1998, p. 34.

31. See Schmitt, especially pp. 22 and 71.

32. See Dan Rather interview with Secretary of State Albright on CBS *Nightly News*, August 21, 1998.

33. See Frederic L. Kirgis, "Cruise Missile Strikes in Afghanistan and Sudan," *American Society of International Law Insight* (August 1998).

34. Martin Hughes, "Terror and Negotiation," *Terrorism and Political Violence* 2 (1990), pp. 72–82.

35. Harvey E. Lapan and Todd Sandler, "To Bargain or Not to Bargain: That Is the Question," *AEA Papers and Proceedings* 78 (1988), p. 16.

36. Reuben Miller, "Acts of International Terrorism: Governments' Responses and Policies," *Comparative Political Studies* 19 (1986), pp. 385–414.

37. Walter Enders, Todd Sandler, and Joe Cauley, "UN Conventions, Technology and Retaliation in the Fight Against Terrorism: An Econometric Evaluation," *Terrorism and Political Violence* 2 (1990), pp. 83–105.

38. See Jon Cauley and Eric Iksoon Im, "Intervention Policy Analysis of Skyjackings and Other Terrorist Incidents," *AEA Papers and Proceedings* 78 (1988), pp. 27–31.

39. O'Brien, 1991, p. 297.

40. See Frederic L. Kirgis, "Cruise Missile Strikes in Afghanistan and Sudan," *American Society of International Law Insight* (August 1998). Schmitt (2002) adds, "Whereas necessity asks whether the use of force is appropriate, proportionality asks how much may be applied" (p. 29).

41. Schmitt, p. 20.

42. David Charters, ed., *The Deadly Sin of Terrorism: Its Effect on Democracy and Civil Liberty in Six Countries* (Westport, CT: Greenwood Press, 1994), p. 220.

43. Bryan Brophy-Baermann and John A. C. Conybeare, "Retaliating against Terrorism: Rational Expectations and the Optimality of Rules versus Discretion," *American Journal of Political Science* 38 (1994), p. 209.

44. Walter Enders, Todd Sandler and Joe Cauley, "UN Conventions, Technology and Retaliation in the Fight Against Terrorism: An Econometric Evaluation," *Terrorism and Political Violence* 2 (1990), pp. 83–105.
45. Walter Enders and Todd Sandler, "The Effectiveness of Anti-Terrorism Policies: A Vector-Autogression-Intervention Analysis," *American Political Science Review* 87 (1993), pp. 829–844.
46. Ayaz R. Shaikh, "A Theoretic Approach to Transnational Terrorism." *The Georgetown Law Journal* 80 (1992), pp. 2, 131–132, 174.
47. "Rethinking Counter-terrorism," in Thompson et al., p. 129.
48. See Paul K. Davis and Brian Michael Jenkins, *Deterrence & Influence in Counterterrorism* (Santa Monica: The Rand Corporation, 2002) and *Discouraging Terrorism: Some Implications of 9/11*, ed. Neil Smelser and Faith Mitchell for the National Research Council of the National Academies of Science (Washington, D.C.: National Academy Press, 2002).
49. Roberts, p. 9. The focus of his article is on *jus in bello*. See also Schmitt, pp. 21–22.
50. Roberts, p. 9.
51. James Risen, "To Bomb Sudan Plant, or Not: A Year Later, Debates Rankle," *New York Times*, 27 October 1999.
52. Richard K. Betts, "The New Threat of Mass Destruction," *Foreign Affairs* 77 (January/February 1998), p. 31.

FROM JUST WAR TO JUST PEACE

CHARLES W. KEGLEY, JR.

University of South Carolina

GREGORY A. RAYMOND

Bosie State University

Far less thought has gone into how to craft a just peace than into how to wage a just war. Yet the policy dilemma faced by every political leader fortunate enough to bask in the glow of a hard-earned military victory is how to forge a durable peace settlement. It "is easy to patch up a peace which will last for thirty years," warned British Prime Minister David Lloyd George at the end of World War I. "What is difficult, however, is to draw up a peace which will not provoke a fresh struggle when those who have had practical experience of what war means have passed away."[1]

How victors treat the vanquished when a war ends has far-reaching implications for the durability of the peace settlement. Peace treaties can be drafted in ways that either dampen or inflame the underlying disagreement between the former belligerents. Reaching a peace agreement is far more difficult than desiring it; sustaining peace once it has been attained is even more demanding. Battlefield success, no matter how impressive, does not automatically yield a durable peace settlement. The geopolitical landscape is littered with military victories that were never converted into stable international orders. As one student of war termination has observed, prudent victories "are but small islands engulfed by an ocean of imprudence, like small specks of rationality afloat in a sea of insanity."[2]

MORAL DILEMMAS AT WAR'S END

How, at the close of a war, should the winning side deal with the defeated? Policymakers confronting this question often find themselves caught in the ineradicable tension between two schools of thought. One school councils leniency: Victors should

This chapter is adapted from Charles W. Kegley and Gregory A. Raymond, *From War to Peace: Fateful Decisions in International Politics* (Boston: Bedford/St. Martin's and Belmont, CA: Wadsworth, 2002).

be magnanimous to extinguish any desire for revenge by the vanquished. Another school calls for sterner measures: Victors should be harsh to ensure that the enemy's defeat is irreversible. The first approach seeks stability by building trust between adversaries; the second, by eliminating an adversary's capacity to mount a future military challenge. Throughout the ages, philosophers and theologians, novelists and playwrights, as well as journalists and social scientists have debated the relative merits of compassionate versus punitive peace settlements.

What makes it difficult to choose between these contending approaches to building a postwar peace are the complex trade-offs between short-term security and long-term reconciliation that policymakers face at war's end. Imposed settlements always look seductive. Yet while they may temporarily reduce the prospects that the defeated will retaliate, people harboring an acute sense of injustice do not easily forget suffering at the hands of others. History is replete with examples of settlements that provoked a new round of hostilities by creating a sense of injustice among those on the losing side. Peace, in these situations, never endures; it is an interlude when one side or the other longs for revenge, and neither can overcome the rancor of their collective past to restore amicable relations.

Thus the victor in search of a lasting accord with the vanquished must somehow blend demands for security from domestic constituencies with policies the former enemy accepts as fitting. It must be able to quash challenges to the new international order while developing procedures that allow complaints to be aired and peaceful change to occur. The obstacles to these goals are numerous: Some victors have not gone far enough to protect their security, humiliating the defeated without weakening their capability to retaliate; others have gone too far, plundering the defeated in fits of avarice and rage. The challenge for victors is to ascertain which intermediate approach to peace between the extremes of a lenient and harsh settlement will most dampen the conditions that might ignite another round of warfare between the same belligerents.

What follows are twelve policy prescriptions that sketch out an approach to peacemaking that abstains from hope-for-the-best beneficence without embracing heavy-handed oppression. Leniency and harsh treatment are polar extremes on a continuum of possible peace settlements. Rather than conceiving of the victor's choice in dichotomous terms, these prescriptions embody a more nuanced approach to dealing with the defeated.

TWELVE PRESCRIPTIONS FOR A JUST PEACE

The role of emotions in decision making has generally been neglected by contemporary students of international security. Yet, as suggested by recent neurological research, deep-seated emotions are central to decision making, narrowing some options and eliminating others.[3]

Different emotions are brought into play by the manner in which a war begins and how it is conducted. For example, victors who have been targets of brutal, unprovoked aggression will have to grapple with feelings of treachery and betrayal, something unlikely to color the postwar policies of victors who initiated wars for opportunistic reasons. Regardless of how a war may have started and whether one was fighting to defend or overthrow the status quo, the longer the duration and the greater the costs, the more angry emotions will constrict the range of choices available to victor and vanquished alike. Mirror imaging, the propensity of each side in a conflict to see in its own actions only rectitude and in those of the adversary only malice, reduces the prospects for leniency by the winner and acquiescence by the loser. In such an atmosphere of mutual distrust, victors face difficult choices in sorting out short-term desires from long-term interests. Even from an advantaged position in which the enemy surrendered unconditionally, the victor still must decide what kind of peace agreement would enhance security. Should the peace be lenient or punitive? Can it combine elements of conciliation with retribution? How will the prostrate adversary respond? What countermoves are likely once the loser recovers from defeat? Military triumph solves certain problems but creates new ones. Given the far-reaching repercussions that result from how victors deal with the defeated, what steps can be taken to solidify a durable peace settlement?

Prescription 1

Carefully Define Interests and Priorities When Making Decisions about War and Peace   It would seem prudent for states to specify their goals and carefully calculate the costs, risks, and benefits of alternative courses of action when formulating their foreign policies. Especially in the realm of national security, where the choices can spell the difference between life and death, states have enormous incentives to engage in long-range planning. This requires clarifying values, specifying objectives, and differentiating vital interests from those that are secondary.

Unfortunately, many states have not engaged in the kind of systematic, rigorous analyses necessary to meet these criteria. In a puzzling world where accurate, timely information is scarce, it is difficult to reach a clear consensus on national objectives. This trade-off is abundantly clear in the realm of peacemaking, when victors in war must reconcile their natural desire for retribution against the equally pressing need for reconciliation. As one diplomat has noted:

> A nation often does not recognize its own self-interest. One of the most vexing problems is to determine what is best for their nation. A related difficulty is to ascertain when a moth-eaten policy that once was viable is no longer valid. The international kaleidoscope is constantly changing; old formulas must be adjusted to new facts . . . [unfortunately] nations that drift with events may become their victims. Those nations that refuse to become the master of events, especially when they can do so, may wind up being their slaves. Not only that, but such chronic drifters permit others to dictate their foreign policy for them.
>
> Improvisation is risky procedure. Policies should be formed in advance of the emergency, not just after disaster strikes. A statesman should strive for a long-range major gain (sometimes with incidental losses) rather than a short-term minor gain. The United States was notoriously shortsighted during World War I and World

War II; it fought for quick military victory without proper regard for long-range consequences. Too many Americans believe that once they have triumphed in the battlefield, all their troubles will be over. This attitude explains the psychology of "Whip the bullies and bring the boys home."[4]

Peacemaking is a complicated art whose success often hinges on being able to see long-term interests. Passion, however, obscures our time horizon. Just as Virgil's Aeneas ignored Anchises' advice about mercy (*clementia*) when he killed Turnus in a fit of rage at the conclusion of the Trojan war against the Latins, national leaders sometimes find it difficult to subordinate their private desire for revenge to the public good that would result from a sober assessment of how new, unanticipated problems may arise from the way immediate problems are solved.

PRESCRIPTION 2

Military Strategy in War Fighting Should Be Coordinated with the Political Strategy for Peacemaking Victory is not an end in itself. Military forces should be deployed for national purposes, not for promoting the interests of the military doing the fighting. However, this principle is sometimes overlooked, and that exacerbates the problem of making peace.

At the root of the danger is the difficulty of separating military objectives from basic national goals. Although people tend to see a country's foreign policy as the product of a single calculating intelligence, in fact most governments are amalgams of large, semiautonomous bureaucratic organizations that have their own interests and hold different conceptions of national security. Since policy is often formulated by a small group of senior officials, each of whom may occupy a leadership position within one of these organizations, it can be difficult orchestrate words and deeds in a coherent program that will be implemented faithfully by subordinates.[5] Fearing that bureaucratic politics contaminate military decisions, the armed forces sometimes are given substantial leeway in shaping the conduct of the war. Yet when crucial military and political decisions are compartmentalized, battlefield triumphs may not advance vital political aims. As one observer of this problem has noted, "Making peace is not a military operation, and even when a military response is unavoidable, tactical considerations ought to be tempered by greater political goals."[6]

How wars are fought and won influences how peace agreements are designed and maintained. Without a mechanism to integrate the conduct of war with planning for peace, questions of grand strategy can devolve to questions of operational art. In such circumstances, insufficient attention is devoted to the geopolitics of military victory. Where and when an adversary is forced to lay down its arms can have long-term political consequences. Consider the case of the German Dolchstoss legend, the stab-in-the-back interpretation of Germany's defeat in World War I. At the end of the war, the German army was still in France. Given that a civilian government surrendered to the Western allies, and no allied offensive ever reached Germany, disgruntled German officers later said that their army had not been defeated. Rather, it was betrayed by traitors who had negotiated a treaty of shame. This association between the allegedly perfidious Weimar Republic and the humiliating Treaty of Versailles haunted German political life for the next 14 years.[7] Adolf Hitler made it a staple in his bombastic appeals to the German masses. To prevent a similar reinterpretation of history from souring the peace after World War II, the United States and Great Britain called for the 'unconditional surrender' of the Axis powers at the 1943 Casablanca conference.

Harmonizing military and political strategy does not mean politicians should consider themselves field commanders. Just as military leaders may be inattentive to how their actions affect the contours of the postwar settlement, political leaders ignorant of military matters may interfere with the conduct of crucial operations. According to one scholar, Winston Churchill's "meddling in the military affairs of the Middle East Command in 1940–1941 contributed to four separate yet connected disasters: the Greek expedition, the fall of Crete, Rommel's recapture of Cyrenaica, and the fall of Singapore."[8] Backseat driving by impatient political leaders may lead to assaults being launched too soon or in the wrong place. During the 1982 war between Argentina and Great Britain over the Falklands Islands, for example, British General Julian Thompson was ordered by his political superiors in London to seize an Argentinian position at Goose Green, despite its lack of military significance and serious logistical problems in mounting the attack.[9] The purpose of coordinating political and military strategy is to ensure that the process of war termination facilitates postwar peace building. Although political leaders decide war aims, they must avoid the temptation to micromanage the war effort, and never lose sight of their responsibility for seeing that military action should service the political goal of making peace.

PRESCRIPTION 3

Planning for the Postwar Era Must Begin Early   The eve of victory is not the time to begin formulating plans for dealing with the many complicated problems that arise when wars end. Decisions must be made on the evacuation of wounded soldiers, the exchange of prisoners of war, the release of interned civilians, the repatriation of displaced persons, and the restitution of property. National leaders must also wrestle with questions pertaining to how many troops should be demobilized, how to absorb them into the labor force, and how to compensate those who have borne the costs of fighting. In some instances, they may have to confront additional challenges, including stationing occupation forces in conquered territory, retiring war-related debts, rebuilding damaged infrastructure, and converting armaments industries to the production of consumer goods. The nature of a war determines the complexity of these issues. Generally speaking, the longer the fighting continues and the greater the number of belligerents involved, the more difficult management of these issues becomes.[10]

Regardless of whether a war is terminated by a series of piecemeal agreements while the fighting drags on or through a comprehensive settlement after a truce, the bargaining position of victors erodes over time. As the United States discovered after the Persian Gulf War, and what was repeatedly reinforced for the next decade as an intractable Saddam Hussein hardened his resolve and plotted revenge, whatever is not exacted from the adversary during the shock of defeat becomes far more difficult to attain later.[11]

Unfortunately, postwar policies rarely emerge from deliberative plans; they unfold incrementally through a tyranny of small decisions, owing more to impulse than design. Lacking a grand strategy for the world of their making, victors usually improvise and muddle through the immediate aftermath of the war. "Few indeed are the occasions on which any statesman sees his objective clearly before him and marches toward it with undeviating stride," observes Harold Nicolson.[12] Most decisions "are like Topsy—they just grow." Indeed, there "may be no policy at all but simply a drift with events."[13]

To prevent policy drift, victors need to project what is likely to occur at the end of the war, anticipate the potential obstacles to a lasting peace settlement, and design a plan for surmounting them. Planning means forecasting the range of plausible futures, setting clear goals for attaining a specific desired future, and recommending actions for realizing that future. The sooner a formal attempt is undertaken to accomplish these tasks, the greater the chances that decision makers will be alerted to peacemaking opportunities they might otherwise miss.

PRESCRIPTION 4

Know the Character of Your Allies and Your Adversaries   A common cause for the breakdown of peace and onset of war is that one or more of the participants failed to appreciate the character of their opponents, attributing to them interests and objectives at variance with their actual intentions. History is littered with numerous examples of such miscalculations. Consider the misjudgments made in the twentieth century that contributed to the outbreak of both world wars. For example, German leaders went to war in 1914 and again in 1939 because, in part, they misread the isolationist impulses of the United States and Great Britain, and assumed that they would stay on the sidelines to preserve peace for themselves; moreover, the Germans underestimated the strength and resolve of the democracies and their willingness, once endangered, to fight for principle. After early setbacks, the democracies allied in World War I and World War II, and finally triumphed.

Of course, democratic states also can misread the potentially belligerent motives of others. Adolf Hitler, for example, lulled many democracies into a false sense of security when he negotiated a series of nonaggression pacts with neighboring countries, as did Joseph Stalin of the Soviet Union. Ironically, Hitler signed a nonaggression pact with Stalin in 1939, who only discovered his miscalculations two years later, when to his shock Hitler attacked the Soviet Union, its "ally" in the nonaggression agreement. Neither Stalin nor the Western European democracies read Hitler accurately. A practitioner of realpolitik, to Hitler diplomacy and treaties were merely a means to prepare for war.

When wars end, the same kinds of misperceptions about the character of a defeated adversary may doom the prospects for a durable peace. Rapprochement—a relaxation of tensions and restoration of friendly relations—may follow peace negotiations and calm fears of renewed aggression, but it is no guarantee of harmony. Victory is likely to produce a precarious peace if the vanquished is ruled by someone whose philosophy impels them to redefine justice for themselves. Often, warned Carl von Clausewitz in 1832, "the conquered nation sees [peace] as only a passing evil, to be repaired in after times."[14] This is especially true of dictatorships, which, on the whole, have a demonstrably poor record of abiding by peace settlements. Despots can be vindictive—an attribute that can easily be ignored by a peace-loving country that, after defeating its enemy in battle, mistakenly projects its own values onto the vanquished. That appears to have been the case in the Persian Gulf War. At the start, Saddam Hussein totally misjudged U.S. intentions, initially thinking that the United States would not fight, and then assuming that U.S. forces would collapse because they could not take casualties. Similarly, the United States misread Hussein's character and aims after the war when Americans mistakenly assumed that the leader of war-ravaged Iraq had learned his lesson and changed heart. Yet more than a decade after the war, the Iraqi dictator was still plotting revenge.

Modern history attests to the capacity of democratic states to keep peace with one another. Because free governments tend to be pacific, encouraging the transition of nondemocratic states to democracies is a viable method of promoting global security. The Wilsonian adage of "making the world safe for democracy" should be taken seriously as a path to peace since states that make their foreign policy decisions through democratic procedures can be expected to avoid fighting each other and adhere to peace accords negotiated with nondemocracies.

PRESCRIPTION 5

Prepare the Public for the Transition from War to Peace   Nationalistic fervor, so important for mobilizing the population for war, can become an obstacle to concluding a reasonable peace. Political leaders frequently stoke the fires of xenophobia on the home front to encourage sacrifice for the war effort. Denigrating the enemy's character is among the most common techniques to fuel these flames. Rhetorical appeals containing derogatory assertions about an enemy's character are a form of "ethotic" argument.[15] Typically, the thrust of these arguments during a war is to emphasize something diabolical about the character of the opponent in order to arouse a strong negative response. After highlighting these traits, an attempt is made to transfer the negative response to a conclusion about the intentions, actions, and motivations of the opponent.[16] Ethotic arguments appeal to the well-documented tendency of people to attribute their own behavior to situational factors while attributing the same behavior to an adversary's dispositional characteristics.[17] For example, if the leader of a particular country authorizes the strategic bombing of an enemy city, he might plead that he was driven to it by the exigencies of military necessity. However, when a rival engages in the same behavior, the leader probably would explain it by referring to his counterpart's inherent character flaws. Given that most people habitually overestimate the importance of dispositional causes when explaining the behavior of others, it is not surprising that ethotic arguments are common, politically acceptable, and persuasive during wartime.

Another reason for the effectiveness of ethotic arguments is the tendency of people to make facile connections between current problems and certain past events that they have personally or vicariously experienced. Research in cognitive psychology has found evidence that people are "classifiers" who attempt to understand the world by matching what is presently occurring with experiences that are stored in the form of memory schemata.[18] Simply put, schematic reasoning involves comparing the current situation with prototypes in one's memory. Among the types of schemata that influence decision making are stereotypical images that represent the character traits of vividly recalled or easily imagined individuals—the ruthless gangster, the sadistic bully, and so on. Despite the fact that an adversary may bear only a superficial resemblance to one of these "stock" characters, when little is known about someone our expectations will be shaped by presumed similarities to these stereotypes.

Finally, ethotic arguments are compelling because they allow people to evade responsibility. Combatants fall back on negative stereotypes and other discrediting devices to reduce guilt over their own repugnant acts by projecting blame on the enemy. Since the enemy allegedly is unscrupulous, one's own unethical behaviors are interpreted as preemptive measures.[19] According to the old saw, sometimes you have to fight fire with fire, and this way of thinking easily leads to the conviction that the end justifies the means, regardless of how evil are those means.

Heavy doses of ethotic argumentation have a dangerous side effect. When the war ends, the public may have little empathy for the losing side and expect to receive what it believes are justifiable spoils from the victory over a sinister enemy. For example, when it was learned that Russia refused to pay an indemnity or cede territory at the end of the Russo–Japanese War of 1904–1905, the *Asahi Shimbun*, a Japanese newspaper, printed the peace terms in a black frame, above a picture of a weeping soldier's skeleton. In response to this and similar editorials in other newspapers, tens of thousands of Japanese demonstrators clashed with police and set fire to government buildings on September 5 and 6, 1905, prompting the government to declare martial law and prohibit further criticism of the treaty.[20] Accentuating a diabolical image of the enemy may rally the populace when morale is low, but it will distort the peace settlement unless public expectations regarding the fruits of victory are attenuated before the fighting halts. Wartime adversaries may have to face unpleasant truths about themselves and their enemies. They must both give up the self-righteous belief that all virtue resided in their own behavior and that all blame can be ascribed to the enemy. Praise for an opponent's valor, differentiating between those who fought with honor and those who committed war crimes, and reminding one's own citizens of the plight of victims on both sides are critical in reversing the effects of wartime propaganda that denigrates the enemy's character.

PRESCRIPTION 6

Victors Should Not Ignore the Passion for Vengeance   A passion for vengeance resides at the very core of our sense of justice. The moral vocabulary we use when discussing how to deal with perpetrators of grievous offenses is permeated with metaphors about debt ("repaying a wrong") and balance ("getting even") that underscore the central place of vengeance in our conception of punishment.[21] From the ghost of Clytemnestra who implores the Furies to avenge her murder by Orestes to the ghost of Hamlet's father who demands Hamlet avenge his murder by Claudius, playwrights through the ages have fascinated us with tales of wrathful anger. Although revenge themes are still common in film and literature today, we usually regard vengeance as the "sick vestige of a more primitive stage of human development," something that "falls within the province of detectives and other specialists in abnormal psychology."[22] Yet it is difficult to deny the satisfaction most humans feel when those guilty of some moral outrage receive their comeuppance, regardless of whether the penalty deters others from engaging in offensive conduct. Indeed, we often speak of "poetic justice" when miscreants who have evaded formal punishment experience a misfortune that nullifies ill-gotten gains.

The need for vengeance derives from powerful emotions that peacemakers ignore at great risk. It generally arises in the aftermath of premeditated campaigns of aggression that violate international humanitarian norms, such as the those undertaken by the Axis powers in World War II. If the victims of these campaigns believe that wrongdoers failed to receive their just deserts, a sense of closure is never reached and private acts of retaliation are likely to follow.[23] Evil must be condemned and its perpetrators held responsible for their appalling deeds. The issue for victors is not whether angry emotions that demand punishment for wrongs are irrational and therefore inappropriate for consideration when crafting a peace settlement, but rather when and how it is reasonable to satisfy these demands.

PRESCRIPTION 7

Avoid Taking Revenge, but Seek Retributive Punishment for the Culpably Guilty   To assert that a passion for vengeance is sometimes warranted is not to advocate wanton vindictiveness. Unrestrained vengeance has the potential to degenerate into an endless blood feud. In the culture of the vendetta, retaliation for an injury involves more than "an eye for an eye, a tooth for a tooth."[24] It is "an overpowering and consuming fire that burns away every other thought" and creates "the wildest, sweetest kind of drunkenness."[25] Under such a code of conduct, revenge is a duty. "He who cannot revenge himself is weak," proclaims an old Italian proverb. "He who will not is contemptible."

The dangers of spiteful, measureless retaliation lead many theorists to differentiate between revenge and retribution. Revenge is an attempt "to impose suffering upon those who have made one suffer, because they have made one suffer."[26]

It is a personal act—a self-righteous returning of wrong for wrong in which the avenger seeks pleasure from the suffering inflicted on the culprit. In Homer's *Iliad*, Achilles embodies the concept of revenge when he turns his wrath toward Hector, the Trojan warrior who slew his friend Patroclos. "Lions and men make no truce, wolves and lambs have no friendship—they hate each other for ever," Achilles tells his opponent. "So there can be no love between you and me; and there shall be no truce for us." After killing Hector and mutilating his body, Achilles declares: "Fare thee well, Patroclos. . . . See now I am fulfilling all that I promised! I said I would drag Hector to this place and give him to the dogs to devour raw; and in front of your pyre I would cut the throats of twelve noble sons of the Trojans, in payment for your death."[27]

Retribution lacks the resentful, vindictive spirit of revenge; it avenges a moral transgression dispassionately, without personal rancor. In contrast to the paroxysm of violence shown by Achilles, retribution has limits.[28] Since revenge has no objective limits, it is normally restricted by social norms that specify what constitutes an affront, who is obliged to respond, what means may be used, when it can occur, and what will be done to those who fail to live up to their obligations. In some societies, these norms transform revenge into ritualized acts of violence that extinguish smoldering disagreements before they ignite into full-scale fighting.[29] More typically, acts of revenge "overpay" rather than "even the score," thereby adding new injuries that reinforce old hatreds.[30] Retributive justice attempts to halt this escalatory momentum by taking jury-like activity out of private hands, distinguishing between crimes and their punishment, and placing limits on the penalties wrongdoers pay.

Two basic schools of thought exist on the nature of retributive justice. The maximalist school, represented by Immanuel Kant, holds that there is a duty to punish anyone who is guilty and culpable for wrongdoing, and that the punishment should be equal to the seriousness of the offense.[31] Minimalism, the second school of thought, also expresses moral indignation over the behavior of the culpable. However, it asserts that punishment should be relative to the seriousness of the offense and, unlike in a strict liability system, allows for mitigating circumstances that can partially or completely absolve the offender.

For victors seeking a durable peace, a minimalist conception of retributive justice offers several important benefits. First, by holding specific individuals accountable for any war crimes or crimes against humanity that they may have committed, it defuses the possibility that charges of collective guilt will be leveled against an entire defeated nation, as happened to Germany following World War I. Second, avoiding collective condemnation facilitates the normalization of relations between victor and vanquished after the war. Third, by showing that international humanitarian law cannot be violated with impunity, it helps those who were victimized bring closure to the experience. Finally, by eschewing revenge in favor of retributive justice through a fair and impartial judicial process (ideally through an international tribunal), reconciliation and the pursuit of restorative justice can begin.

PRESCRIPTION 8

Victors Should Forgive the Forgivable, but Not Forget   Reconciliation is a process of developing a mutually conciliatory accommodation between former enemies.[32] It is a dynamic, sequential process that requires actions by those who have suffered wrongs as well as by those who have committed them. The former consists of forgiving; the latter, apologizing. Although it is common to hear references to forgiveness and apology in our everyday conversations, rarely does anyone seriously reflect on their precise meaning. Because both are complex, multidimensional concepts, let us briefly discuss each in turn.

Perhaps the most systematic contemporary work on the elusive concept of forgiveness has been done by Donald Shriver.[33] Genuine forgiveness, he explains, has four dimensions. First, forgiveness begins with a memory of past evils suffused with a moral judgment of injustice. Second, forgiveness entails forbearance: Past wrongs are neither overlooked nor excused, but punishment is not reduced to revenge. Third, forgiveness includes empathy for the enemy; that is, a recognition of the other side's humanity. Finally, genuine forgiveness is restorative; it seeks to repair fractured human relationships and promote social healing.

For social healing to occur, wrongdoers must shoulder the responsibility for apologizing. Like forgiveness, a sincere apology entails several things. First, it involves feelings of sorrow and regret for the injurious act.[34] Second, it expresses shame over what was done and repudiates that kind of behavior.[35] Third, it contains an avowal henceforth to conduct oneself in the proper way.[36] Finally, it includes a gesture of penance to atone for the transgression. In certain societies, apologies inaugurate a process of lustration. Rather than just stigmatizing the offender, the members of these societies follow their denunciations with a highly visible ritual of reacceptance.[37] In this way, the wrongdoer is reintegrated into the fold instead of remaining an outcast, forever condemned to the margins of public life. Public ceremonies of reconciliation, such as the ancient practice observed by some Native Americans of burying war axes, can help reverse relations among former adversaries.

Apology and forgiveness can jointly soothe raw postwar feelings, but not necessarily in every situation. No victor can force the vanquished to have feelings of sorrow and remorse for injurious acts. Even when someone has suffered directly from the misdeeds of a truly repentant person, deep introspection normally is required before the relationship can be repaired. Forgiving under ordinary circumstances is difficult. What happens when the injustice is far greater in scope and magnitude? Are certain offenses of such moral gravity and some perpetrators at such moral fault that apology is an empty gesture and forgiveness beyond human reach? Does anyone have the moral agency to forgive massive atrocities committed against others? How should we respond to existential evil? Consider the plight of Simon, a Jewish internee in a Nazi concentration camp.[38] One day he encountered a mortally wounded SS officer who asked forgiveness for the many heinous crimes he committed against other Jews. Did Simon have the power or the right to forgive him for his unspeakable acts? Perhaps there are some deeds so horrific that recompense for the victims and forgiveness for the perpetrators are outside of the victors' human capability.[39]

Prescription 9

A Dictated Peace Is a Precarious Peace; Victors Should Involve the Vanquished in Settlement Negotiations   History judges a state as a winner in war if it can force the enemy to surrender. But winners can ultimately lose the peace if they fail to include the defeated at the conference table. There are many perils to the art of peacemaking. Perhaps none is as perilous as summoning the courage and skill to negotiate the terms of surrender with an enemy.

A classic example of the dangers of imposing a settlement is provided by the harsh treatment forced upon France in 1871 at the conclusion of the Franco-Prussian War. The prostrate French were instructed about the terms of the peace treaty and were not given much of a chance to modify the settlement. Their thirst for revenge over this humiliation "was a prime combustible leading to the global conflagration of 1914–1918. The Germans forgot one of their own proverbs: 'Revenge does not long remain unrevenged.'"[40]

Victors should avoid treating the grievances of the defeated as if they were simply outrageous bargaining tactics. The losing side in a war may believe it has legitimate complaints and a right to express them. When victors deny that perceived right and proclaim that they alone can define justice, they deprive the defeated of a chance to express ideas about what constitutes a fair peace settlement. Not only does this cause a loss of face, but also it removes any stake the defeated might have had in upholding the settlement. Even concessions by the victor on issues of low priority can assuage an adversary. As Roger Fisher and William Ury point out, giving the other side a small role in drafting the settlement creates a sense of ownership: "An outcome in which the other side gets absolutely nothing is worse for you than one which leaves them mollified."[41]

Showing disrespect to an adversary by precluding their participation in discussion about peace terms is risky for another reason besides the likelihood that insulting treatment will evoke future efforts to vindicate a wounded sense of honor. It is also bad policy because it overlooks the possibility that yesterday's enemy may be needed as tomorrow's friend. Peace settlements must look forward rather than backward. Victors should be aware of the interests underlying their opponents' stated position and look for opportunities to work toward achieving superordinate goals that neither side could achieve alone.[42] Shared interests may not be immediately obvious, but there will almost always be features in a peace settlement where victors can satisfy some interest of the other side without damaging a significant interest of their own.[43]

In sum, victors in search of a durable peace settlement should apply the Golden Rule in diplomacy, treating the vanquished the way they would wish themselves to be treated were they in the same position. So long as one is not dealing with an utterly ruthless, depraved opponent, restraint and a readiness for conciliation can evoke gratitude and set in motion a positive spiral of tension-reducing reciprocation. Victors who couple firmness regarding their own interests with fairness toward the interests of others encourage defeated powers to work within the postwar system. Nowhere is this more important than in resolving outstanding territorial issues. A fair disposition of territorial claims, coupled with simple, unambiguous, and prominent line of demarcation, are critical to building a lasting peace.

PRESCRIPTION 10

Beware of Allies Whose Interest in the Peace Negotiations Centers on Gaining the Spoils of Victory   Military alliances are formal agreements between sovereign states that coordinate member behavior under certain specified contingencies. Coordination may range from a detailed list of armed forces that will be furnished by each party to the broader requirement of consultation should a serious dispute occur. In addition to differing according to the level of coordination, alliances also vary in terms of the target and duration of their accords. The target of an alliance may be left implicit or may be identified as a single country, a group of states, or a geographic region. Alliance duration may be limited to a relatively short period of time or constructed to last indefinitely.

Rarely are alliances formed just to express friendship or some vague ideological affiliation. They are constructed for clear, calculated advantage. In the first place, alliances help states acquire benefits that might not have been attained by acting unilaterally. In the second place, they reduce the costs associated with foreign policy undertakings by spreading them among several partners. If the perceived benefits exceed the costs, and if the costs are politically sustainable, states worried about their security will join alliances despite the uneven burdens they necessitate and the unequal returns they provide.

It is always uncertain whether an alliance will serve the purposes for which it was originally created. Will it deter external attacks? If not, will the members uphold their treaty commitments when faced with the possibility of war? And if they do, will the alliance be able to defeat the aggressors? Fighting in concert with allies is a challenge. Enormous amounts of time and energy must be invested in resolving interallied disagreements on strategy. Even when a consensus exists, friction may still arise over the priorities assigned to specific theatres of the war. Further complicating matters, units from various countries—trained under different philosophies, armed with different weapons, and configured for different missions—must somehow work in tandem, occasionally in the midst of petty rivalries among allied commanders. As one observer of military partnerships has put it, alliances are "like a house built by jealous carpenters with no boss and with many different plans for the design of the building."[44]

Alliances, in other words, are rickety constructions whose structural integrity diminishes when the common external threat that brought them into being recedes. With victory in sight, aggressively self-interested members of large wartime coalitions will likely be tempted by the chance for booty and begin jockeying for a peace settlement that furthers their own selfish aims. At this point it is crucial for those states with aspirations of building a durable peace settlement to use the waning days of the war to unite behind a collective peace plan. If major issues are left unresolved until a formal peace conference, the most determined ally will end up in possession of important assets that then can be removed only through a perilous confrontation.[45]

The success of a multilateral peace conference depends on the victors' capacity to transcend the desire for short-term relative gains and embrace the goal of avoiding mutual loss. Perhaps no statesman was better at framing the settlement process in these terms than Austria's Metternich. At the Congress of Vienna he was able to control events by defining their moral framework. Keenly aware of the importance of reducing the grandiose claims put forth by others—rather than simply promoting his own—Klemens von Metternich made concessions appear as sacrifices to a common cause. The legitimacy of a peace settlement, he always said, rests on acceptance, not imposition.[46]

PRESCRIPTION 11

Victors Should Be Prepared to Use Military Force after the War Ends
Thomas Schelling has written, "It takes at least as much skill to end a war properly as to begin one to advantage."[47] Losers may still possess bargaining assets, even when they have no hope of winning a war. Not only can they struggle on and extract a price from the winner by making victory more costly, they may, like Saddam Hussein following the Persian Gulf War, be able to undermine postwar stability. The durability of a peace settlement hinges on the victor's ability to (1) anticipate how dissatisfied parties may challenge new security arrangements, and (2) develop effective contingency plans for arresting these challenges. Ironically, "military victory is often a prelude to violence, not the end of it," notes Schelling.[48] The successful victor generally holds the threat of more pain to come in reserve as a way of inducing the vanquished to accommodate itself to defeat. Conciliation is unlikely to succeed without the backing of a credible deterrent.

By itself, restraint in victory may not be enough to diffuse the losers' desire for revenge. Occasionally restraint toward the vanquished must be combined with a convincing use of military force against someone else. Take, for instance, relations between Prussia and Austria after the Seven Weeks War. As early as December 1866, Bismarck had sought a rapprochement with Austria, but was rebuffed. With Prussia's shocking victory over France at the Battle of Sedan, attitudes in Vienna began to change. Austrian Foreign Minister Friedrich Ferdinand Baron Beust, an ardent opponent of Bismarck, concluded that it was now in Austria's interest to distance itself from the French. In a memorandum written on May 18, 1871, Beust stated that Austria was detrimentally affected by the French loss at Sedan in two ways. First, Prussia could exert its immense military power against Austria directly. Second, it could interfere indirectly with Austria by manipulating German nationalist sentiments within Austria's multinational empire. Given the leverage Berlin would have over Austria, he recommended seeking an accommodation with Prussia.[49]

PRESCRIPTION 12

The Vanquished Have Responsibilities in Making Peace Winners in war have the power to exercise their will. As a result, they have received most of the praise when peace settlements succeeded and most of the blame when they failed. Indeed, it is tempting to believe that the responsibilities for making peace rest exclusively with the choices of victors. That temptation should be overcome, however, because the actions of the defeated can influence the peace plans of the victors.

Losers, like winners, must also make hard choices. Should they resent their loss and strive to undermine the new postwar order? Or should they adjust to the painful turn of events and work within the new order? The choice is difficult even when the loser is guilty of wrongdoing; it becomes agonizing when the loser is innocent. How should the vanquished respond when it was responsible for the war? Conversely, what should it do when the winner provoked the showdown and then violated prevailing codes of military conduct? What should it do when blame is relatively equal? The answers depend in large measure on whether the war effort was regarded by the loser as being worth the costs. Wars perceived as not having been worth their costs engender a domestic political environment where accommodationists rather than defiant hard-liners prevail. According to John Vasquez, a repeat of war between the same two parties is less likely when accommodationists govern political life within the country that has lost the war.[50]

Defeated nations are always in poor bargaining positions. Yet they are not without power. In certain circumstances, a principled posture by accommodationists within the defeated country can influence how victors behave once the fighting ends. Assuming the loser is not annihilated (like Carthage after the Third Punic War), the victor must confront a series of questions about the role of its former enemy in the postwar world. Can the vanquished be trusted? Do they intend to stand by the peace agreement? Will they recoil into battle at the first opportunity to avenge their losses? Uncertainty over the answers to these questions can plague a victor, leading it to expend scarce resources for contingencies it would prefer to avoid.

Consider the following scenario: What would a victor do if a defeated country accepted its part of the blame for the war's onset and its accommodationist government sought to work dutifully within the new international order? A pacific response by the subjugated can sometimes disarm the conqueror. Losing parties can win by practicing "moral jujitsu," in the terminology of Richard B. Gregg. Jujitsu is an Oriental martial art that throws the powerful off balance by countering its attack. In Gregg's conception, a repentant former enemy can encourage the victor to be merciful by throwing him off moral balance:

> He suddenly and unexpectedly loses the moral support which the usual violent resistance of most victims would render him. He plunges forward, as it were, into a new world of values. He feels insecure because of the novelty of the situation and his ignorance of how to handle it. He loses his poise and self-confidence. . . . [In this way, the vanquished party] uses the leverage of a superior wisdom to subdue the rough direct force of his opponent.[51]

Suffering may be a viable strategy for a state defeated in war. Principles can produce power. "Most advocates of principled nonviolence believe that unmerited suffering is the most forceful way to affect an opponent's conscience." Self-imposed suffering and "the willing acceptance of sanctions imposed for noncooperation are considered most effective for bringing about a change of heart in one's opponents."[52] As the twentieth century's leading prophet of this philosophy, Mahatma Gandhi, explained,

> Things of fundamental importance to the people are not secured by reason alone, but have to be purchased with their suffering. Suffering is the law of human beings; war is the law of the jungle. But suffering is infinitely more powerful than the law of the jungle for converting the opponent and opening his ears, which are otherwise shut, to the voice of reason.[53]

To heed his advice about encouraging compassion through *satyagraha* (or "truth force") is to ask the loser in war to respond in an unusual way. Disarming the victor by appealing to its morality is not easy. Tempers flare in the heat of battle, and enemies often dehumanize each other as accusations fly back and forth. Memories of war continue to smolder long after a truce is struck, threatening to ignite once again into an inferno of hatred. But if the defeated dutifully serves the victor after the war, and if it can identify itself with principles the victor accepts as just, it may be able to embarrass the victor into living up to its own beliefs about fair play. Of course, such a strategy assumes that the victor believes in fair play and is not committed to a policy of genocide.[54]

JUSTICE AND RECONCILIATION

Achieving a just and lasting peace between former adversaries is difficult in international politics because mistrust is endemic among sovereign states in an anarchic environment. Without a higher authority possessing the legitimacy and coercive capability to preserve peace, states must fend for themselves while struggling with multiple fears: the fear of attack by enemies; the fear of exploitation by allies; and the fear of being victimized by an unfair treaty. These fears peak as war clouds gather, but scarcely dissipate when the fighting ends. As the belligerents face the task of rebuilding their relationship, insecurity persists. The parties to every war face uncertainty as they look to the future.

The chronic suspicion infecting world politics does not auger well for building a lasting peace. Entrenched doubts about promises voiced by a former foe inhibits mutually beneficial collaboration and encourages defensive noncooperation. Yet, building peace requires building trust, even among states that have few reasons to have confidence in one another. At war's end, the victor must consider actions that seem counterintuitive, such as reconciling with an adversary previously perceived as without scruples.

How can bitter adversaries overcome the rancor of their collective past and trust one another? Admitting injury and injustice are essential to the healing process. Peacemaking is not merely a matter of letting bygones be bygones. Reconciliation depends on a sincere effort to set the record straight through repentance and to build a new record through restitution.[55] It also depends on victors showing mercy to the defeated. Although mercy is a virtue that can conflict with the demands of justice, it nonetheless serves as a potential source of influence for the victor as well as a source of constraint for the vanquished. Recipients of magnanimity are placed in a position of social indebtedness. The greater their feeling of indebtedness, the greater their subsequent attempts to reduce it. Over time, this kind of exchange relationship is thought to create obligations that generate reciprocity.[56]

Empathy is also crucial for finding the common ground needed for reconciliation.[57] The architect of a peace settlement "must be able to comprehend the innermost interests of the vanquished and to empathetically assess the particular world of the defeated if he is to serve his own interests."[58] Victors must overcome what has been called "compassion fatigue" and the vanquished must move beyond recrimination. Both parties need to see how their fates are intertwined. This requires that there be some general agreement as to the wrongs committed during the war, a consideration of the impact that those wrongs have had, and attempt to atone for them.[59] As one scholar has put it:

> To achieve a comprehensive mutual accommodative relationship requires that significant members of the antagonistic parties combine a minimal level of [understanding of each other's] view and actions. First, the injured and the perpetrators openly acknowledge that reality of the terrible acts that were committed. Second, the injured are provided with prospects for security and well-being. Third, those who experienced injustices receive redress in some measure. Finally, the injured accept with compassion those who committed injurious conduct as well as acknowledge each other's suffering. The injured and the perpetrators of injury may refer to individuals, groups, organizations, peoples, or countries. The injured and the perpetrators are not to be regarded as mutually exclusive categories.[60]

In conclusion, when we think about making peace, we must think about justice. The end of a war requires calculations to be made about the allocation of benefits and burdens, rewards and punishment. These are ethical choices, not legal or military ones. While scholars rightly devote enormous effort to studying the causes of war, complementary research efforts on how states make peace lag far behind. As Thomas Gregor and Clayton Robarchek remind us, "The real puzzle for social scientists is not war and violence, but a more unusual phenomenon: peace."[61]

NOTES

1. David Lloyd George, "Final Draft of the Fontainbleau Memorandum," as reprinted in Martin Gilbert, *The Roots of Appeasement* (New York: Plume Books, 1966), p. 189.
2. Nissan Oren, "Prudence in Victory" in *Termination of Wars: Processes, Procedures and Aftermaths* (Jerusalem, Israel: Magnes Press, 1982), p. 153.
3. Antonio Damasio, *Descartes' Error: Emotion, Reason, and the Human Brain* (New York: G. P. Putnam's Sons, 1994), pp. 173–174; Also see Keith Devlin, *Goodbye Descartes: The End of Logic and the Search for a New Cosmology of Mind* (New York: John Wiley Sons, 1997).

4. Thomas Bailey, *The Art of Diplomacy* (New York: Appleton-Century-Crofts, 1968), p. 96.

5. See Wallace Thies, *When Governments Collide: Coercion and Diplomacy in the Vietnam Conflict, 1964–1968* (Berkeley: University of California, 1980), pp. 376–383.

6. Amos Oz, "Israel's Wrath, Iran's Sweet Grapes," *New York Times*, 25 April 1996, p. A17.

7. On September 29, 1918, General Erich Ludendorff, who had assumed dictatorial powers over the war effort, informed the kaiser that Germany's military position on the western front was untenable and that he must seek immediate peace negotiations. Ludendorff called for the creation of a new democratic government, apparently so the military would not have to admit defeat and sue for peace. The purpose in pointing out that the way World War I ended gave reactionaries an opportunity to propagate a stab-in-the-back myth is not to suggest that the allied powers should have refused the peace overtures and fought on until they could seize German territory. With some 10 million men killed and twice as many wounded, it was important to bring the fighting to a close as soon as possible. This case illustrates the proposition that the geographic position of victorious troops has political consequences for the postwar period. Of course, stab-in-the-back myths can surface even when the territory of the losing side is occupied. Following the Franco-Prussian War, for example, Captain Alfred Dreyfus, a Jewish officer in the French army, was falsely convicted of treason in a shameful effort to suggest that the war had been lost due espionage rather than military failure.

8. Geoffry Regan, *Great Military Disasters* (New York: M. Evans and Company, 1987), p. 131.

9. Max Hastings and Simon Jenkins, *The Battle for the Falklands* (New York: Norton, 1983), p. 362.

10. Robert E. Randle, *The Origins of Peace* (New York: Free Press, 1973), pp. 36–52, 478–480.

11. Henry Kissinger, *Diplomacy* (New York: Simon & Schuster, 1994), p. 257.

12. Harold Nicolson, *The Congress of Vienna* (New York: Viking, 1946), p. 19.

13. T. B. Millar, "On Writing about Foreign Policy" in *International Politics and Foreign Policy*, ed. James N. Roseneau (New York: Free Press, 1969), p. 61.

14. Cited in Bailey, op. cit., p. 261.

15. The term "ethotic" is derived from Aristotle's discussion of *ethos* (character) in deliberative rhetoric. An example can be found in his discussion of Dionysius's request for a bodyguard: Because in the past Peisistratus, Theagenes, and other schemers sought bodyguards as part of their master plans to become despots (and presumably because Dionysius and the others are alike in certain important character traits), Dionysius should not be trusted since he probably has the same purpose in mind. For an analysis that applies Aristotle's example to foreign policy, see Gregory Raymond, "The Use of Ethotic Argument in Foreign Policy," in *Proceedings of the Second International Conference on Argumentation*, ed. Frans H. Van Eemeren et al. (Amsterdam: Stichting Internationala Centrum voor de Studie van Argumentatie en Taalbeheersiung, 1991), pp. 1306–1040.

16. Alan Brinton, "Ethotic Argument," *History of Philosophy Quarterly* 3 (July 1986), pp. 245–258.

17. Richard Nisbet and Lee Ross, *Human Inference* (Englewood Cliffs, NJ: Prentice Hall, 1980).

18. Deborah Welch Larson, *Origins of Containment* (Princeton: Princeton University Press, 1985), pp. 50–57.

19. Hubert Blalock, *Power and Conflict: Toward a General Theory* (Newbury Park, CA: Sage, 1989), p. 138. An illustration of this point can be found in David Hume, *A Treatise on Human Nature*, ed. Henry D. A. Ken (New York: Hafner Publisher, 1948), p. 188. If "a civilized nation" was in a conflict with barbarians "who observed no rules even of war, the former must also suspend their observance of them . . . and must render every action or recounter as bloody as possible."

20. Ben-Ami Shillony, "The Japanese Experience" in *Termination of Wars: Processes, Procedures and Aftermaths*, ed. Nissan Oren (Jerusalem, Israel: Hebrew University, 1982), pp. 91–101.

21. Robert Solomon, "Justice and a Passion for Vengeance" in *What is Justice?*, ed. Robert C. Solomon and Mark C. Murphy (New York: Oxford University Press, 1990), pp. 299–300.

22. Susan Jacoby, *Wild Justice: The Evolution of Revenge* (New York: Harper & Row, 1983), p. 17. An example of the view that vengeance and justice are antithetical can be found in the criticisms Senator Robert A. Taft (R-Ohio) made of the Nuremberg and Tokyo war crimes trials at the end of World War II. In a speech delivered at Kenyon College, he asserted that a trial of the vanquished by the victors is animated by a "spirit of vengeance" and cannot be impartial. See Robert A. Taft, "Equal Justice under Law: The Heritage of the English-Speaking Peoples and Their Responsibility," *Vital Speeches* 13 (November 1, 1946).

23. Reflecting on the "accumulated passion" and "demand for retribution that rose like a plaintive chant from all the desolated lands" in the aftermath of the Second World War, Herbert Wechsler defended the International Military Tribunal at Nuremberg on the grounds that a failure by the Allied powers to proceed would have forsaken those who had suffered at the hands of the Nazi regime. "Who can doubt," he asked rhetorically, "that indiscriminate violence, a bloodbath beyond the power of

control, would have followed an announcement by the responsible governments that they were unwilling to proceed?" Herbert Wechsler, "The Issue of the Nuremberg Trial" in *From Nuremberg to My Lai*, ed. Jay W. Baird (Lexington, MA: Heath, 1972), p. 126.

24. Exod. 21:24–25; Lev. 24:17–20.
25. Miloven Djilas, *Land Without Justice* (London: Methnen, 1958), pp. 105–107.
26. Jon Elster, "The Norms of Revenge" *Ethics* 100 (July 1990), p. 862.
27. Homer, *The Iliad*, trans. W. H. D. Rouse (Edinburgh: Thomas Nelson and Sons, 1938), pp. 260, 265–266.
28. Robert Nozick, "Retribution and Revenge," in *What is Justice?*, ed. Robert C. Soloman and Mark C. Murphy (Oxford: Oxford University Press, 1990), pp. 281–283. Some of these limits derive from an acceptance of the distinction between intentional and unintentional wrong.
29. Victor Kiernan, *The Dual in European History* (Oxford: Oxford University Press, 1989), p. 21.
30. Elizabeth Wolgast, *The Grammar of Justice* (Ithaca: Cornell University Press, 1987). For an analysis of the social dynamics created by a code of revenge, see Pietro Marongiu and Graeme Newman, *Vengeance* (Toronga, NJ: Rowman and Littlefield, 1987).
31. The distinction between maximalist and minimalist schools of retribution is made by Martin P. Golding, *Philosophy of Law* (Englewood Cliffs, NJ: Prentice Hall, 1975), p. 85.
32. Louis Kriesberg, *Constructive Conflicts: From Escalation to Resolution* (Lanham: Rowman and Littlefield, 1998).
33. Donald Shriver, Jr., *An Ethic for Enemies: Forgiveness in Politics* (New York: Oxford University Press, 1995), pp. 6–9.
34. N. Tavuchis, *Mea Culpa: A Sociology of Apology and Reconciliation* (Stanford: Stanford University Press, 1991), p. 31.
35. Thomas Scheff, *Bloody Revenge: Emotions, Nationalism and War* (Boulder, CO: Westview, 1994), p. 135.
36. E. Goffman, *Relations in Public* (New York, Harper, 1971), p. 113.
37. John Braithwaite, *Crime Shame and Reintegration* (Cambridge: Cambridge University Press, 1989).
38. Simon Wiesenthal, *The Sunflower* (New York: Schoken, 1976).
39. See Deuteronomy 32:35.
40. Bailey, op. cit., p. 267.
41. Roger Fisher and William Ury, *Getting to Yes* (Boston: Houghton Mifflin, 1981), p. 75.
42. M. Sherif and C. W. Sherif, *Groups in Harmony and Tension* (New York: Harper & Row, 1953).
43. Roger Fisher, Elizabeth Kopelman, and Andrea Kupfer Schneider, *Beyond Machiavelli: Tools for Coping with Conflict* (Cambridge, MA: Harvard University Press, 1994), p. 241.
44. Edward Vose Gulick, *Europe's Classic Balance of Power* (Ithaca: Cornell University Press, 1955), p. 86.
45. Kissinger, op. cit., p. 405.
46. Henry Kissinger, *A World Restored* (Boston: Houghton Mifflin, 1973), pp. 21, 312.
47. Thomas Schelling, *Arms and Influence* (New Haven: Yale University Press, 1966), p. 128.
48. Ibid., p. 12.
49. John Orme, "The Unexpected Origins of Peace: Three Case Studies," *Political Science Quarterly* 111 (spring 1996), p. 110.
50. John Vasquez, *The War Puzzle* (Cambridge, MA: Cambridge University Press, 1993), pp. 202, 208–210. Accommodationists are defined as "individuals who have a personal predisposition (due to beliefs they hold) that finds the use of force, especially war, repugnant, and advocates a foreign policy that will avoid war through compromise, negotiation, and the creation of rules and norms for non-violent conflict resolution."
51. Richard B. Gregg, *The Power of Non-Violence*, rev. ed. (New York: Schocken Books, 1966), p. 52.
52. Heidi Burgess and Guy Burgess, "Justice without Violence: Theoretical Synthesis" in *Justice Without Violence*, ed. Paul Wehr, Heidi Burgess, and Guy Burgess (Boulder: Lynne Rienner Press, 1994), p. 14.
53. Cited in Gregg, op. cit., p. 150.
54. Obviously, pacific responses are not viable against everyone. The sack of Hamanu in the seventh century B.C.E. by the Assyrian leader Assurbanipal is one of many examples that testify to the inability of a vanquished people to prevent their utter destruction by a brutal conqueror. Even rulers who labored to integrate diverse populations into unified states occasionally responded to military adversaries with unmitigated fury. The sixteenth century Mughal Emperor Akbar, for example, was so enraged by the resistance of the Rajput fortress of Chitor, that after overrunning the stronghold his forces massacred thousands of people.

55. Lyn S. Graybill, "South Africa's Truth and Reconciliation Commission: Ethical and Theological Perspectives," *Ethics & International Affairs* 12 (1998), pp. 43–79.
56. Ralph Dimuccio, "The Study of Appeasement in International Relations," *Journal of Peace Research* (March 1998), p. 250.
57. Oren, 1982, op. cit., pp. 150–151.
58. Michael Ignalieff, *The Warrior's Honor* (New York: Metropolitan, 1998).
59. Graybill, op. cit., p. 49.
60. Louis Kriesberg, "Reconciliation: Conceptual and Empirical Issues" (paper presented at the annual meeting of the International Studies Association, Minneapolis, MN, 1998), p. 5.
61. Thomas Gregor and Clayton A. Robarchek, "Two Paths to Peace: Semai and Mehinaku Nonviolence" in *A Natural History of Peace*, ed. Thomas Gregor (Nashville: University of Tennessee Press, 1996), p. 160.

FROM MORAL NORM TO CRIMINAL CODE

THE LAW OF ARMED CONFLICT
AND THE RESTRAINT OF CONTEMPORARY WARFARE

JAMES TURNER JOHNSON

Rutgers University

This chapter examines the contemporary law of armed conflict, that portion of international law that sets limits on the conduct of forces engaged in armed conflict. I focus on two issues: first, the relation of this portion of international law to moral conceptions of the restraints that should be observed on harm done in armed conflict, especially the historical connections among the positive law, the customary law, and just war tradition; second, how, beginning a half-century ago, developments in the law of armed conflict have extended its scope and reshaped it as a form of criminal code and the implications of the law thus recast for contemporary and future armed conflict.

The first issue requires a theoretical, historical, and comparative analysis. Looking backwards, there is the problem of how well the international law on armed conflicts encapsulates and carries forward the concerns of the moral tradition of just war, in which it is historically based. The issue here is the moral adequacy of the established international law limits in just war terms. Looking forward, there is a rather different problem: how the law of armed conflicts relates to conceptions of the justified limits of war in the moral traditions of other cultures. The contemporary face of the question of the relation of the law to the morality of armed conflicts is one particular element in the larger problem of cultural relativity—in extreme terms, whether there is a "clash of civilizations"—in the present-day world.

The second group of issues arises from the ongoing effort to fit international legal restraints on armed conflict to the actual nature of warfare—the often sharp contrast between war as it should be conducted according to the law of armed conflicts and war as it actually has been—and is being—carried on across the spectrum of contemporary armed conflicts. Whatever the success of the law in restraining past warfare, contemporary armed conflicts have posed a major challenge to the system of restraint defined in the law. The treatment of noncombatants in contemporary conflicts has been a particular problem. Major provisions of the law aim to protect noncombatants and the structures of noncombatant life, prohibiting direct, intentional attacks on certain classes of people, on undefended population centers, and on certain kinds of public buildings such as schools, hospitals, and buildings dedicated to cultural purposes and religion. Yet direct, intentional targeting of noncombatants has been rife in contemporary armed conflict. Further, though the law prohibits attacks on undefended population centers, scorched-earth destruction of population centers has been a characteristic feature of the conflicts in Bosnia and Kosovo and has also been widespread in the Russian military effort to subdue Chechnya. While the law seeks to protect schools, hospitals, and buildings dedicated to culture and religion—as well as the people inside them—from direct, intentional attack, the conflicts in the former Yugoslavia have provided multiple examples of intentional destruction of such buildings, and conflict in Rwanda has added examples of persons being slaughtered despite their being inside the walls of such legally protected places. So the central questions are, in simple terms, whether the law is up to the task of restraining the conduct of contemporary armed conflicts, and what may be done to increase its effectiveness.

Providing an adequate answer to these questions is what the effort to define the law of armed conflicts as a form of criminal code is about. This effort includes three chief elements: first, the reshaping of the law itself to broaden its coverage, to specify the idea of "war crimes," and to apply the law to individuals rather than states; second, the emergence of the idea that third-party armed intervention is justified as a means of response to violations of the law; and third, the increasing use of court proceedings as a means of investigating war crimes, trying individuals as war criminals, and imposing punishment.

All of these continue to evolve, but the increasing role of court proceedings in recent years has been particularly striking. Originally international law held states responsible for the conduct of their armed forces and left it up to the states how to enforce the requirements of the law, whether through courts-martial or by other means. The Nuremberg and Tokyo trials after World War II were the first examples of international tribunals to try individuals for their conduct during war, not only or mainly as violators of the existing laws of war but also as violators of "crimes against humanity." For more than four decades these were the only examples of such trials, but the creation of special courts under international auspices to bring individuals to justice for their conduct during armed conflict was renewed with the establishment of the International Criminal Tribunal for the Former Yugoslavia (ICTY) in 1993 and that for Rwanda (ICTR) in 1994. By the end of the 1990s momentum had built for the creation of a permanent International Criminal Court, and currently the Statute of the ICC has been ratified by more than half the nations needed for this court to become established.[1] Yet for various reasons the remainder of the process of creating the ICC is likely to be measured in years, and perhaps decades; the United States in particular remains powerfully opposed to the court as currently defined. Elsewhere, though, there has been significant development, especially in the very active work of the ICTY and in the use of domestic courts in various countries to seek redress for war crimes and punishment of war criminals.

In the case of the ICTY the most striking development has been the delivery of former Yugoslav head of state Slobodan Milosevic to the tribunal by the present Yugoslav government. Milosevic had been indicted by the Court in 1999, during the conflict over Kosovo, on charges that his security forces had committed war crimes in that province. He is the first former head of state to be delivered by a government to face an international war crimes court.[2] Two elements in this case are especially interesting. First is the debate within the Yugoslav government itself over whether to try Milosevic in a Yugoslav court, a move that, if it had been carried out, could have been argued to preempt international jurisdiction in the matter. This is an issue important not only for the jurisdiction of the ICTY but also for the ICC, whose statute includes a similar provision. The second element in this case is Milosevic's defense, denial of the court's jurisdiction as a violation of the rights of sovereignty.[3] The question of sovereignty, its rights, and the protections due to it are central in much of the effort to deal with contemporary armed conflict, focusing the problem of enforcing international norms within a state's borders against the wishes of the state's government. Once again, this is a central issue in the debate over the ICC.

Even apart from the delivery of Milosevic, the ICTY has been increasingly successful in its efforts to achieve the surrender of persons it has indicted. That it has actively sought to pursue its investigations without bias is illustrated by a second striking case, the investigation of the NATO bombing campaign against Yugoslavia over the Kosovo conflict. One frequent claim against war crimes tribunals is that they dispense "victor's justice" and ignore wrong conduct on the part of the victorious forces. The ICTY prosecutorial review of the complaints against NATO actions provides a powerful example to the contrary.[4] Establishing a basis in general issues and applicable international law, the review examined five specific incidents raised in the complaints. Part of its process was to pose questions relating to the allegations being investigated to the NATO forces (including, prominently, those of the United States), and to receive answers, including, in the case of the United States, a formal response from the U.S. Army Judge Advocate General's Office. Like the case of Milosevic, this one is interesting not only because of what it shows of the ICTY's procedures and the scope of its jurisdiction, but also as a precedent for the interaction between individual governments and the ICC, if the ICC becomes a reality.

Finally, there is the recent use of domestic courts in various countries to address war crimes and punish war criminals. The older story in this regard has been that of civil suits designed to gain redress and payment of compensation for wartime actions of defendants, such as unlawful confiscation of property, use of slave labor, and participation in actions leading to loss of life. The more recent story is the use of domestic courts for criminal prosecutions for crimes of war. Two recent cases stand out: the effort by the Spanish government to extradite from the United Kingdom former Chilean head of state General Augusto Pinochet, to bring him to trial in Spain for his responsibility in the deaths of Spanish citizens in Chile as a result of actions of his government; and the trial and conviction in a Belgian criminal court of four Rwandans, including two nuns, for their involvement in the mass killings in Rwanda in 1994. This latter trial proceeded on the basis of Belgian laws adopted in 1993 codifying the provisions of the Geneva Conventions as part of the domestic code of law. The four Rwandans had been residents of Belgium when arrested.[5] These two cases are different in nature and in their conclusions; what they have in common is that they show that the move to transform the rules of war into a criminal code has expressions in domestic law as well as in international law.

THE POSITIVE LAW OF ARMED CONFLICTS

The law of armed conflicts, as it exists today, incorporates the various Geneva and Hague Conventions and other relevant international declarations, treaties, and certain provisions setting limits on the conduct of forces engaged in an armed conflict.[6] As positive law, made up of the formal agreements of states, it is a relatively recent phenomenon, dating back only to the first Geneva Convention of 1864. Most of the development of such law, indeed, has taken place in the past hundred years, beginning with the multilateral declarations of the Hague Conference of 1899. Twentieth-century landmarks of its growth include the Hague Conventions of 1907, updates to the Geneva Conventions in 1906, 1929, 1949, and (through Protocols referring to the 1949 Conventions) 1977, agreements aimed at eliminating chemical, biological, and nuclear weapons, other agreements aimed at limiting certain uses of conventional weapons and at protecting cultural property during an armed conflict, and the development of the idea of war crimes and of procedures for prosecution of war criminals. In general terms, the positive law thus defined has had two main thrusts: to prohibit direct, intentional harm to civilians and other classes of protected persons (the particular focus of the Geneva Conventions), and to rule out the use of certain means of war deemed to be disproportionate and/or indiscriminate in their effects (the particular focus of the Hague rules, supplemented by some other agreements).

The term "law of war" was in general use up until the 1970s, and the specific reference of the positive law was to international conflicts formally declared as wars and, after the 1949 Geneva Conventions, other international armed conflicts not formally recognized as wars by one or both adversaries.[7] The 1977 Geneva Protocols, though, extended the coverage of the old "law of war" in two regards: first, by strengthening the application of the law to international armed conflicts not formally of the status of wars; second, by explicitly including noninternational armed conflicts within the scope of the law.[8] The "law of armed conflicts" has since been the proper usage, though "war" and "armed conflict" are interchangeable so long as the former is understood as having the broader meaning of the latter.

Since World War II, the surrounding context, scope, and applicability of the law of armed conflicts have been altered and expanded in two other major ways. The first of these has been toward broadening the concept of what is protected against violation, going beyond the specific provisions of the various conventions, declarations, and other agreements to encompass fundamental human rights and obligations of "humanity." The second has involved two related changes: a shift toward conceiving violations of the law of war according to the model of criminal law, that is, as "war

crimes," and toward holding individuals involved in such violations personally responsible for them, as "war criminals." These two developments overlap both in their
origins and in their effects. Both trace to the Nuremberg and Tokyo tribunals at the
end of World War II, but both have seen further evolution in the statutes of the ICTY,
the ICTR, and the ICC.

The idea that there are fundamental human rights that ought never to be violated, even in the conditions of war, first appears formally with the concept of "crimes
against humanity" at the Nuremberg trials and has subsequently been developed, beginning with the Universal Declaration on Human Rights in 1948, in the form of
international human rights law defining specific human rights and providing for
their protection. While the law of armed conflicts and human rights law have their
own particular histories and have generated specific bodies of literature and precedent, they also share a considerable area of overlap. In contemporary usage, they are
often treated as two aspects of one body of law termed international humanitarian
law, as in the Statute of the International Tribunal for Rwanda, where the compe-
tence of the tribunal is defined as extending to "the power to prosecute persons responsible for serious violations of international humanitarian law," including
genocide, crimes against humanity, and violations of the law of armed conflicts
(specifically Article 3 common to the Geneva Conventions of 1949 and of Additional Protocol II, that extend these Conventions to noninternational armed conflicts).[9] Similar language is found in the Statute of the International Tribunal for the
Former Yugoslavia, where the particular forms of international humanitarian law
identified are the 1949 Geneva Conventions, the "laws or customs of war," genocide
and crimes against humanity.[10]

The importance of the ideas, now increasingly commonplace, that violation of
the rules on conduct in armed conflicts constitutes a "war crime," and that individuals guilty of such violations may be prosecuted, convicted, and punished under international auspices for such crimes, may best be grasped by considering what these
concepts replaced. The older standard is well summarized in this passage from 1907
Hague Convention IV:

> A belligerent party which violates the provisions of the said Regulations shall, if the
> case demands, be liable to pay compensation. It shall be responsible for all acts com-
> mitted by persons forming part of its armed forces.[11]

That is, on the older normative understanding, the laws of war applied to states, not
to individuals, and violations, if they occurred, were to be set right by compensation
paid by one state to another, not by the criminal prosecution and punishment of individuals who had perpetrated the violations. Any punishment of such individuals
was left to the states involved, who had the power to decide whether or not to punish, and if so, what punishment to exact. The Nuremberg and Tokyo trials took a new
view, one reflected in the contemporary war crimes tribunals for Rwanda and the
former Yugoslavia and in the Statute of the International Criminal Court. The old
standard understanding, though, still retains considerable vitality, as shown by the

fact that the Rwanda and former Yugoslavia trials are the only war crimes tribunals that have been held under international auspices since those following World War II and by the line of legal argument the United States has raised against the ICC proposal as it currently stands. There are also other problems—political, theoretical, and practical, as illustrated in different ways by the cases briefly discussed previously— with the concept of violations of the rules of armed conflict as war crimes for which individuals may be held responsible in an international forum; yet it clearly has great importance for how the law of armed conflicts is conceived today.

The result of these developments is that the positive law of armed conflicts, as it stands today, is different in important respects from the law of war as it stood during World War II or even at the time of the Geneva Conventions of 1949. One major difference is in jurisdiction: not only over international conflicts having the legal status of wars, but also over other armed conflicts between and among states and also armed conflicts internal to states. Also different is the development of a concept of the law of armed conflicts as a form of criminal law applicable to individuals and making them liable to trial and punishment under international agency—a change that, however importantly active in the present world, still lies somewhat uneasily, with unresolved tensions, within the law alongside the older, and still present, understanding that the law on armed conflicts applies to states and is to be punished by damages, with criminal prosecutions of individuals, if any, to be left up to the states involved. The third major change is the assimilation of the law of armed conflicts together with human rights law into international humanitarian law, a development that dramatically extends the scope and nature of the rules that apply in armed conflicts beyond the specific rules and protections laid out in the positive law of armed conflicts.

Positive international law, however, is unlike positive domestic law. Domestic law is promulgated by the legislative power of government, while positive international law is the result of agreements among states. Domestic law can be enforced by government power, but the enforcement of international law depends on the states themselves, operating collectively or at times in smaller groups or even individually. Thus in international law it is of major importance to know as exactly as possible what states have actually agreed to be the law: whether a particular state has signed and ratified a particular convention, declaration, or other instrument, and what formal reservations, if any, were made at the time of signing. External compulsion as a form of enforcement, particularly compulsion by military intervention or actions by international courts, is in tension with the understanding of sovereignty consensually accepted in international law. The West's role in such enforcement raises issues of cultural imperialism. Further, there is a clear double standard between more and less powerful nations. China does not have to fear intervention or war crimes trials over its takeover of Tibet; Russia does not have to fear them over the conduct of its forces in Chechnya. Beyond these considerations is the matter of how states actually behave. For understanding what international law provides is not simply a question of using the positive law to measure compliance, but rather to an important degree just the opposite: What the law actually is must be measured by examining the behavior of states. Hence the concept of customary international law, which is the law that can be read through the collective record of state behavior, and which may or may not correspond closely or directly with what is provided in positive international law.

International law has its origins in customary law in two respects. The concept of international law arose when all that existed was customary law. This is why James Brown Scott could speak of "the Spanish origin of international law" in the work of Vitoria and his contemporaries,[12] or why the work of Grotius has been frequently cited as the beginning of the modern conception of international law—though Vitoria, Grotius, and other early modern thinkers were not involved with the making of positive law but were theorists working to understand, interpret, and regularize for their own eras a broad yet consensual tradition of moral reflection and customary behavior—the tradition of just war. This tradition[13] developed historically as a cultural consensus that included elements from canon law and secular law, theology and philosophy, the code of chivalry, the practice of warfare, and the customs of relations among sovereigns. The customary law as known by the early modern theorists of international law was an expression of the legal aspect of this broader tradition. Thus the route from moral norm to criminal code in the law of war begins with just war tradition, understood thus broadly, and runs through customary international law to the development of positive international law over the past century and a half.

The positive law of armed conflicts originated only with the Geneva Conventions of 1864 and 1906 and with the Hague Conferences of 1899 and 1907, but these all had deep roots in the customary law. It is clear from the language of the early agreements defining the law of war that the framers understood this and saw their task as putting the contents of that customary tradition in positive form: Typical is the preamble to the 1907 Hague Convention IV, which states the objective of the Convention to be defining "the general laws and customs of war . . . with greater precision" and "confining them within such limits as would mitigate their severity as far as possible."[14] The positive rules thus defined were not understood as created *de novo* out of the agreement of the states signatory to the Convention; rather they concretized and gave more "precision" to what was already well established in custom, while setting limits to some of the more extreme behaviors of states during war.

Yet the effort to define the customary rules in positive international law by the agreement of states is an important development. Where there is ambiguity, the agreement of a state to a particular formulation subjects it to that formulation. Where the particular customs of one culture have dominated in a specific formulation of international law, the agreement of a state from a different cultural background means the acceptance of that formulation. Historically, much of positive international law, and by no means least the law of war, developed out of the customary law of the West; yet agreement to the positive law, regardless of cultural background, implies willingness to be bound by it. This bears importantly on the question of cultural relativity posed at the beginning of this paper and will be discussed in more detail in the following sections.

THE LAW OF ARMED CONFLICT
AND WESTERN MORAL TRADITION ON RESTRAINT IN WAR

Historically the roots of the law of armed conflict, as we have just seen, are in the broader tradition of just war. Indeed, the law of armed conflicts as it has developed over the past century and a half has become one of the major carriers of that broader tradition in the contemporary world, alongside other streams including theological ethics, moral and political philosophy, military codes of conduct, and the actual behavior of belligerents. Not all of historical just war tradition is moral in the narrow sense, as comprising self-conscious, disciplined moral reflection; yet it is all moral in a broader sense, as a repository of values, principles, assumptions about right and wrong behavior, and proper and improper purposes of armed conflict. Hence to assess the moral scope and adequacy of contemporary international law on armed conflicts—or, for that matter, any of the other contemporary streams carrying elements of that tradition, all of which have been historically shaped—requires judging it by reference to the broader historical tradition of just war.

It is useful to begin by thinking briefly about the terms we can use in carrying out this comparative assessment. It has become commonplace in recent moral discussion, following Paul Ramsey's lead, to think of the just war idea of right conduct in war by means of two moral principles, discrimination and proportionality.[15] These are not, however, terms found earlier in the historical just war tradition—nor is the term "noncombatant" or the idea of "noncombatant immunity,"—the latter being frequently used in recent discourse as interchangeable with the principle of discrimination. Neither are any of these terms found in the international instruments defining the law of armed conflicts. If we use them in carrying out a moral assessment of the law of armed conflicts, we need to recognize that in doing so we are working at a level of abstraction higher than that found in both the law of armed conflicts and historical just war tradition, and that a translation is necessary. It is not wrong to use these terms, and in fact they are quite useful, but the specificity of the law of armed conflicts and the historical just war tradition are also valuable in their own rights. These general terms of moral analysis should never obscure the actual way the historical tradition and the positive law have described what they are about.

What both just war tradition and the law of armed conflicts have sought to achieve is not a theoretical definition of noncombatancy or the principle of discrimination but something much more concrete. In the first place, this is protection from harm for certain classes of persons. The earliest formal statements that fed into the developing just war *jus in bello* date to the tenth century and were canons adopted by various conferences of bishops seeking to establish a "peace of God" to limit the conduct of men under arms at that time. These canons typically prohibited, on pain of excommunication, violence against church property, priests, bishops, monks and nuns, and pilgrims, as well as peasants and townspeople going about their daily business. Later refinements added the property of the latter groups and the persons and property of travelers happening to pass through a war zone.[16] Such was the content of the normative listing in the canon law of the early thirteenth century. By the end of the

Middle Ages a somewhat different listing, coming from the sphere of the chivalric code and the *loi d'armes*, the customs of knightly war, had expanded the categories of persons who should not be the object of attack in war to include women, children, the aged, the infirm, the mentally impaired, and in general all persons not of the knightly class who were not individually engaged in bearing arms or other involvement in war. This was where the concept we have come to call noncombatancy lay at the time of the writers Honoré Bonet and Christine de Pisan during the Hundred Years War; it was the concept inherited by Vitoria, Grotius, and their contemporaries and passed down in subsequent conceptions of the *jus in bello*, the law of war.[17] When there was any justification given for these lists, it was typically a very general reference to what is required by justness or fairness: Such people as those listed do not take part in war, and so they should not have war made against them. This approach to limiting the conduct of war has a direct parallel in the definition of classes of protected persons in the modern law of armed conflicts.

The just war *jus in bello*, as it first coalesced during the Middle Ages, also drew on two other ways of approaching limitation of violence. One was the Augustinian requirement of right intention. While this concept became formally part of the *jus ad bellum*, that part of the tradition having to do with the decision to resort to force, it clearly also bore on the intentionality behind the conduct of individuals engaged in fighting justified wars. As summarized by Thomas Aquinas, in a form that was to become progressively more influential in later moral theology, the Augustinian idea of right intention meant two distinct things: first, negatively, the avoidance of wrong intentions; second, positively, the purpose and goal of achieving peace at the end of war through the practice of just war. The former was summarized by Augustine in a memorable passage quoted by Aquinas:

> What is evil in war? It is not the deaths of some that will soon die anyway. The passion for inflicting harm, the cruel thirst for vengeance, an unpacific and relentless spirit, the fever of revolt, the lust of power, and such like things, all these are rightly condemned in war.[18]

What is interesting in Augustine's list of evil, and thus proscribed, intentions is that they are described by reference to the behaviors they produce: bullying, self-aggrandizement at the cost of others, and so on. It is not by any means a distant reach to associate this conception of intentions—and thus behaviors—to be avoided in just war with the contemporaneous lists made by the canonists and chivalric writers of persons not to be attacked and property not to be molested or seized.

The purpose of achieving peace in just war is also central in this further passage from Augustine quoted by Aquinas:

> We do not seek peace in order to be at war, but we go to war that we may have peace. Be peaceful, therefore, in warring, so that you may vanquish those whom you war against, and bring them to the prosperity of peace.[19]

Right practice in war is thus understood as essential to the achievement of peace.

The remaining approach to the restraint of war that fed into the early development of just war tradition during this period was the effort to prohibit the use of certain weapons: siege machines, the crossbow, and the longbow. This was an approach undertaken specifically through churchly canons, beginning with the Second Lateran Council in 1139, but with strong support from norms found in chivalry. The canons give no reasoning for their prohibiting the use of these weapons. Looking back, though, we can see that in the context of the warfare of the period these were precisely the weapons whose use tended to cause forms of damage contrary to the conceptions of restraint already in place. Siege weapons could not discriminate between persons and property allowed to be attacked and those not to be attacked. Crossbows and bows and arrows were more likely to cause death (through infection) than temporary incapacitation, and moreover, on the battlefield they were used in volleys to shower indiscriminate destruction on an enemy force. In short, by the standards of the time all three kinds of banned weapons were both indiscriminate and disproportionate. From the chivalric perspective such weapons added a further dangerous dimension, since the men who fought with these kinds of weapons were mercenaries specially trained in their use, not men of the knightly class, and had not been socialized into the chivalric concept of virtuous war.

These were all medieval developments; yet they have direct analogies in the modern positive law of armed conflicts. The effort to ban siege machines is recalled in contemporary positive-law efforts to limit the effects of bombardment,[20] though the medieval approach was to ban the weapons themselves, while the positive-law approach has been to identify certain kinds of targets as off-limits. Another analogy may be seen between the medieval weapons bans and contemporary legal proscription of weapons of mass destruction, those types of weapons today recognized as inherently indiscriminate and disproportionate in their effects.[21] Similarly, the effort to prevent the disproportionate damage caused by crossbow bolts and arrows in medieval warfare is recalled in the effort to ban the use of expanding bullets in the 1899 Hague Declaration III.[22] Finally, as to the question of the mercenaries who employed the weapons named in the medieval bans, this twelfth- and thirteenth-century effort to keep such people out of the practice of war anticipates the later concern, during the nineteenth and early twentieth centuries, to find some way to deal with partisan bands who fought without being subject to military order and discipline and often without respect to the established laws and customs of war.[23] The various kinds of irregular forces typical of contemporary armed conflict raise the same problem, but thus far no comprehensive solution is in sight.

The effort to restrain war by limiting those who may take part in it—defining those outside the limits to be not soldiers but criminals—deserves a somewhat closer look. Medieval just war thinking, from the standpoints of both church and chivalry, sought to restrict the practice of arms—as well as the harm done in that practice—to a relatively narrow class of people, those who had received socialization as knights and who thus had internalized in the form of virtue the rules laid down in canon law and the code of chivalry. By the early modern period, when armies of knights had been replaced by much larger forces of common men, codes of military discipline arose as a way to impose external restraint on the conduct of war by this new class of soldier, who had not benefited from socialization into the virtues of knightly behavior under arms.[24] There are direct historical as well as thematic links between the best and most complete of the nineteenth-century military codes of conduct, the U.S. Army's General Orders No. 100 of 1863,[25] compiled during the Civil War under the direction of the international lawyer Francis Lieber, backwards to the earlier normative tradition of just war and forward to the early development of the positive international law of war. Codes of military discipline and rules of engagement still function to restrain the conduct of soldiers during armed conflicts, only now the relationship to the positive international law of armed conflicts flows the other way from the case of Lieber, with national codes shaped in accord with the provisions of the international law.

What, though, of persons in arms who operate without such a code, whether because their nation or rebel movement has not given them any such rules restricting their conduct, or because the movement for which they are fighting is not coherent or well organized enough to be able to establish and enforce rules of conduct, or because they are in fact only self-constituted bands of people, often no more than children, who happen to come into possession of weapons and use them as dictated only by their own interests or pleasures? A look at contemporary armed conflicts reveals widespread examples of all these phenomena. This poses a serious problem for the application of the law of armed conflicts today, but it is not a moral problem with the extent of the law; rather it is a practical problem with how to give the law actual restraining force in such conflicts.

In noting parallels between formative just war tradition and the positive law of armed conflicts I am not trying to make the twentieth and early twenty-first centuries sound identical with the twelfth. Rather I mean to stress an opposite point: that despite the commonality of purpose and approach, to set morally acceptable restrictions on the destructiveness of war in any given time requires close attention to the context and to the face of war in that time. Weapons' limits as a means of restraining war become archaic when the particular weapons themselves fall out of use. The people who make war more terrible because their purpose is ultimately to kill and to profit from it change from one time to another. The problem of banning mercenaries from warfare during the Middle Ages was different from that addressed by the rules on partisans laid out in the nineteenth and early twentieth centuries, and both these problems were very different from how to deal with the boy-soldiers of contemporary African armed conflicts or the death squads of the Bosnian conflict and Latin American civil wars. The law of armed conflicts carries the major thrust of the moral tradition of the just war *jus in bello*. Indeed, in contemporary armed conflicts it is in many respects more like moral tradition than law, because the means of enforcement rightly associated with good law are inadequate or entirely lacking. But it requires regular updating to deal with changes in the face of war.

When we think broadly about the contemporary law of armed conflicts in comparison with the just war *jus in bello*, we must recognize a fundamental underlying commonality; yet spelling out exactly what this means in the form of restraints on the practice of war must necessarily take account of the empirical face of war in any given period. How, for example, do we think today about who ought not to be directly, intentionally harmed in war? The list of protected persons laid out in Geneva law is not identical in detail with the list given in the canonical *De Treuga et Pace* in the thirteenth century. One of the most complete twentieth-century lists is that given by John Ford, S.J., in his 1944 article on strategic bombing, a list that includes shoemakers, dairymen, telephone girls, reporters, and other contemporary occupations.[26] But no list is any good if it does not address the specific nature of armed conflict in its own time. The existing law of armed conflicts has been framed over the past century first in terms of the formally declared wars between states, and since the 1977 Geneva protocols more broadly it has been adapted to the conditions of interstate conflicts that are not formally wars as well as intrastate conflicts that were earlier consensually understood to be outside the purview of international law. Perhaps the contemporary face of armed conflict is sufficiently different to warrant further development in the law to express the fundamental purposes underlying both the law and the broader moral tradition of restraint in war.

Thinking morally about the adequacy of the law of armed conflicts, however, raises a different kind of issue as well. No matter how carefully the law is framed and how scrupulously it is kept up to date (both matters that, in actuality, seldom reach the optimum), it is still only law, and law by its nature deals with behavior far better than with intent. Judged with respect to the broader just war tradition, international law on armed conflicts does not reflect all of that tradition. When just war tradition coalesced as a culture-wide consensus in the Middle Ages, it drew on theological conceptions of morality in war as expressions of virtue, the knightly code of conduct, and the empirical practice of ruling as well as canon and civil law; this gave the conception of just war a richness and texture that increased its contemporaneous relevance as well as its historical staying power. The law alone, then and now, represents only part of the whole. To restore the full richness and texture will require a continuing dialogue with the other carriers of the tradition: moral philosophers and theologians, theorists and practitioners of government, and the professional military.

Finally, there is the question of how we ought morally to think of the process by which the law of armed conflict comes into being, is sustained, and is enforced in actual conflicts. That it depends on the agreement of states for all these elements in the process is both a strength and a weakness, both practically and morally. States, by their nature, have an obligation to be selfish, that is, to serve the good of their own citizens. This is, of course, the fundamental insight of realism. The particular texture of the law of armed conflicts reflects this reality in many ways, where the need for broad international consensus slows change in the law and differences in perception of national interest make for uneven application. These are weaknesses, to be sure. On the other hand, at best the requirement that states agree to the provisions of the law and honor those provisions in armed conflict makes for a fundamentally strong structure: government by the consent of those governed. But as has gradually become apparent in recent years, for such democratic forms to function well, there needs to be a civil society knitted together by complex commonalities and shared purposes. Such a common base existed for the law of war so long as it was being shaped by the countries of the West, who shared a common history and culture; one is arguably less present now, even though the institutional structures of international order are more fully developed. This requires more thought and work and leads us to the following section.

THE LAW OF ARMED CONFLICTS AND CONFLICTS ACROSS CULTURES

Tied closely to the pattern of warfare directed against noncombatants that has been characteristic across the spectrum of contemporary armed conflict is another pattern: a tendency to define such conflicts in terms of fundamental cultural differences between the adversaries. This claim takes different forms, is rooted in different factors, and may be significant for only one of the parties to a particular conflict; yet it leads to a conception of the entire population of the opposing side as enemies worthy of attack, whether they are functionally engaged in the fighting or simply trying to live out their everyday lives despite the fighting. This way of thinking of armed conflict raises a fundamental challenge to the law of armed conflicts: Tied as it is to an inheritance from Western culture, framed as it is in terms of conflicts over political differences, how can it be held to matter in conflicts inflamed by cultural differences between adversaries, especially when one or both of them may be from a totally different culture from that of the West?

The form of the challenge may be explicit or implicit: a denial of the law itself as illegitimate, or a refusal to accept the law's binding power. An example of the explicit challenge is provided in this observation by Ann Mayer for the specific case of the religion and culture of Islam:

> Accepting the authority of international law means superseding Islamic international law, which has its own specific rules on questions of war and peace, but doing this offends the supremacy of Islamic law. . . . Furthermore, the origin of international law in Europe means that for at least some Muslims, acknowledging its authority is perceived as entailing a victory for Western culture at the expense of Islamic culture.[27]

An example of the implicit form of the challenge is supplied by this passage from the Serb nationalist writer Milan Kommenic, referring to the conflict between ethnic Serbs and Albanians over Kosovo:

> We do not seek mercy from you, don't you seek it from us. You have never given it to us, and we no longer have the right to give it to you. . . . We have long ago eaten up the moldy pretzel of internationalism that falsely joins us in brotherhood and falsely unites us.[28]

The implicit challenge does not have to be spelled out in words. Deeds themselves—direct, intentional attacks on the adversary's noncombatant population as a way of winning the struggle against the adversary—provide the most widespread example of implicit challenge to the law of armed conflicts.

Should denials of the legitimacy of the law or refusal to accept its binding power in some kinds of situations be allowed to stand as the last word on the applicability of the law of armed conflicts to contemporary conflicts? I think not. Rather, three different kinds of response can be made to these challenges.

The first response, against the argument that wars across major cultural divides cannot by their nature be restrained by a law historically rooted in the moral traditions of one particular culture, is to observe that this makes far more of cultural differences than is warranted. The ideas of restraint in war encoded in international law, whatever their historical relation to the moral traditions in western culture, in fact have a broad resonance in the moral traditions of other major cultures as well. Several examples of such resonance, including the Hindu tradition concerning the *Kshatriya* or warrior caste, the Japanese tradition of *bushido*, and the ancient Chinese conception of the "gentleman warrior," are provided by James A. Aho's study of the relation of religious mythology and war.[29] In terms of Islamic traditions, John Kelsay has convincingly drawn attention to the rules of war between the *dar al-Islam* and non-Muslim societies as laid out in classical Islam and their provisions for mitigation of harm to noncombatants,[30] while Khaled Abou el Fadl has done the same for wars of rebellion within the Islamic world as treated by that portion of Islamic law known as *akham al-bughat*.[31] It is demeaning to other cultures—as well as factually incorrect—to suggest that the restraints on conduct in war encoded in the law of armed conflicts are somehow unique to Western culture and not paralleled in other major cultures of the world. In other words, there is a good deal more consensus as to the proper limits of conduct in war across cultures than is admitted by the apostles of cultural difference as a fomenter of conflict. In formal terms, consensus to the provisions of the law of war exists in the agreement of states to those provisions. But even if it is granted that this consensus is not universally well developed—as in the form of an international equivalent of a domestic civil society—there remains another path to agreement, that of reciprocal interaction. Indeed, much of the actual effect of international law, including the law of armed conflicts, depends on this, as nations modulate their conduct by considering what others will do in response. While there remains a place for the exercise of hegemonic power in enforcing the law of armed conflicts, the strength of the law does not depend on such power alone but also draws from consensus across political and cultural divides and from modulated reciprocities where consensus is weak.

A second line of response to the challenges posed to the law of armed conflicts by cultural differences is that despite such differences, the various agreements defining the law of war and the broader body of international humanitarian law have been, in most major respects, agreed to by all states either explicitly or in the context of membership in the United Nations. This is more than empty form; such agreement entails acceptance of responsibility to abide by this law and enforce it, as well as opening the door to externally imposed punishment and coercion if the responsibility is neglected or flouted. While the previous argument was that the challenge to the law of armed conflicts posed by cultural difference does not hold up on substantive grounds, this argument is positivist: The challenge does not hold up because the positive law as it exists includes the responsibility to abide by it.

A third and final argument against the challenges described previously is that the breakdown in respect for the requirements of international law in contemporary armed conflict does not really follow from cultural differences between adversaries but is no more than willful violation of the law, covered by invocation of such differences, for the purpose of gaining advantage over the enemy. One point in support of this judgment is that even despite claims of culturally rooted difference, adversaries in many of the worst contemporary conflicts share a common culture, and the claims of difference may serve only to provide convenient cover for other aims. This is Judith Miller's argument about the role of religion in the Arab-Israeli conflict;[32] one also thinks of the deep commonalities shared by the adversaries in Northern Ireland, Somalia, Rwanda, and even Bosnia, where despite Serb references to the Muslims as "Turks," the two sides share a common ethnicity, spoken language, and much of the fabric of everyday life as it existed prior to the onset of the fighting.

A somewhat different approach to this same argument is to consider the nature of the forces characteristically involved in contemporary armed conflicts, the chaotic conditions often present, and the absence of accountability that is manifest in many different ways in the conduct of the armed forces in such conflicts. The emergence of war against noncombatants as a characteristic feature of contemporary armed conflicts often correlates with the presence of self-constituted armed bands, often composed of individuals who have no personal ties to the larger society; the child-soldiers of the conflict in Sierra Leone provide an example. Sometimes the correlation is with the utter breakdown of the state, as in Somalia. In other cases the correlation is with the relatively small size or military weakness of one adversary relative to another, so that the weaker party chooses to attack noncombatant instead of military targets because they could not stand up to a military defense; this is generally the case with terrorism, as exemplified by the acts of the IRA in Northern Ireland and such groups as Hamas in the Arab-Israeli conflict. In all these kinds of cases, cultural differences between the adversaries are not the primary or direct cause of the violence against noncombatants; rather that violence arises from the other reasons noted.

In short, the clash-of-cultures argument against the relevance of the law of armed conflicts in contemporary conflicts is not convincing. That the law has not always or with any regularity worked well to control the conduct of armed forces in such conflicts is granted; yet this is not somehow an inevitable result of the presence of claims of cultural difference between adversaries often found in such conflicts. Rather we are returned to the more basic question: how to use the law of armed conflicts to end the familiar presence of atrocity and mitigate the harm done in such conflicts.

MAKING THE LAW OF ARMED CONFLICTS WORK: THE PROBLEM OF ENFORCEMENT IN CONTEMPORARY CONFLICTS

The law of armed conflicts, as it has taken shape since World War II, has an extremely broad range. Beginning with the 1949 Geneva Conventions it has claimed authority over not only declared wars but other forms of serious international conflict,[33] and beginning with the 1977 Geneva Protocol II it has extended its scope to domestic conflicts as well, provided only that in the domestic arena it does not apply to "situations of internal disturbances and tensions, such as riots, isolated and specific acts of violence and other acts of a similar nature."[34] It is arguable that measures for enforcement of this law have only recently begun to draw close to matching the implications of this broad reach claimed for the law.

The 1949 Geneva Conventions assumed the old standard for enforcement: As provided by common Article 2, it was the duty of the signatory powers, if engaged in an armed conflict, to abide by the terms of the Conventions, even in cases in which one party to a conflict was not a signatory. No provisions for enforcement extended to non-signatory powers; they had not agreed to the Conventions and were not bound by them. An "impartial humanitarian body, such as the International Committee of the Red Cross,"[35] might offer its services in helping to carry out the provisions of the Conventions, but the parties to a conflict were not required to accept such services.

Such a model for enforcement had not worked well earlier, as underscored by the necessity of war crimes trials after World War II; nonetheless, maintaining sovereignty precluded anything further. And as noted earlier, the whole fabric of international law prior to that time had depended on self-enforcement by states in respect of the principle *pacta sunt servanda*: Agreements, once entered into, must be observed. This was backed up by the granting of the right of reciprocity: If one party did not observe the conditions of an international agreement in its dealing with others, then they were not obliged to observe the agreement in dealing with the first party. But in the case of the law of armed conflicts common Article 2 of the 1949 Geneva Conventions undercut the threat of reciprocity by binding signatories to observe the conditions of the Conventions even when in a conflict with an adversary that had not agreed to the Conventions. But would this system for enforcement actually work in time of conflict? In the post-1949 environment, World War II had provided a kind of vaccination against international wars, and the Cold War provided a further check against major conflicts that might involve the superpowers, their allies, and client states; thus none of these erupted to test the postwar system for enforcement of the rules for fighting. In the many insurgency wars of the 1950s, 1960s, and 1970s, though, these rules were often asymmetrically or otherwise unevenly observed, completely ignored, or manipulated for propaganda purposes.

A not entirely logical but all too common response to a failure in enforcement of existing law is to toughen the law. This was the effect of the 1977 Geneva Protocols, which explicitly clarified that all sorts of civil wars, including insurgency conflicts, were covered by the newly renamed law of armed conflicts,[36] expanded the implications of the limits by explicitly referring to the requirements of international human rights law,[37] and implicitly laid on all parties to a conflict the duty to abide by the provisions of the law.[38]

The 1977 Protocols also, however, set in place new provisions relating to monitoring the conduct of the fighting and enforcing the limits imposed by the law. Thus early in Protocol I we encounter this statement: "The High Contracting Parties undertake to respect *and to ensure respect* for this Protocol in all circumstances."[39] A new mechanism for implementing this responsibility was established: The requirement that each party to a conflict "shall without delay designate a Protecting Power for the purpose of applying the Convention and this Protocol" and permit the designated power to do its job.[40] A further step was to reshape the law as a criminal code by making clear its application to individuals, not just states, and by providing for penal prosecutions of individual violators.[41] Yet some of the force of these new provisions for enforcement was diminished by an explicit statement of the principle of nonintervention.[42]

It is thus not without irony that in contemporary armed conflicts, intervention, whether diplomatic or by means of sanctions or by armed force, has become a principal means of preventing or halting violations of the law of armed conflicts and of providing a context within which penal prosecution of violators can meaningfully proceed. Intervention, in short, in contemporary armed conflicts takes a place similar to that of the police in domestic society. The "protecting powers" mechanism is today in total disarray; for third-party states to seek "to ensure respect" for the law requires that they interpose themselves into nascent or ongoing conflicts. The issue is the authority by which they do so, and this is accordingly an area in which customary law, along with interpretation of the positive law, has been rapidly developing. As noted earlier, the positive-law prohibition of intervention had never succeeded in doing away with the customary-law allowance of "sphere-of-interest" interventions by regional hegemons; in contemporary context such rationalization of intervention has become increasingly respectable, so that it is widely regarded as a failure of statecraft when, for example, the OSCE or NATO fails to react, or reacts too late, to warfare against noncombatants in Bosnia or Kosovo. (The relation to the sphere-of-interest exception to intervention is confirmed rather than denied by Russian and Chinese opposition to NATO's Kosovo action.) More broadly, the onus is on the major powers to act even when the violations are taking place in a conflict outside their traditional spheres of interest; thus the United States was drawn into the conflict in Somalia and has repeatedly been faulted for not intervening militarily to prevent the 1994 Rwandan genocide, and the Western powers were collectively criticized for failure to act militarily to halt the fighting in Sierra Leone.[43]

A three-tier system seems to have emerged for understanding authority for justified intervention to stop violations of international humanitarian law, including the law of armed conflicts and human rights law: Best is the authority established by a Security Council resolution, typically based on Article 7 of the United Nations Charter, declaring the situation to be one that poses a threat to international peace and security; next best is a multilateral action, whose authority comes from the degree of consensus demonstrated by the multilateral cooperation; and in cases of extreme emergency, unilateral action or action by a small number of states who may or may not be coordinating their efforts, and who may indeed be acting against the objections of other states. Bryan Hehir, among others, has argued that to be justified, interventions must be undertaken multilaterally.[44] Morally speaking, there is nothing inherent in multilateralcy that makes it superior to unilateral action in all cases, and in terms of the contemporary development of international law, multilateralcy is not the only option.

The new tolerance for intervention—and even preference for it, in cases of egregious violations of international humanitarian law—does not sit well alongside the doctrine that every state is equal in its sovereign inviolability.[45] (As noted earlier, the sovereignty doctrine also is in tension with the claims to jurisdiction of international criminal courts.) This doctrine, though, has never achieved in practice what it claims in theory. Not all states are equal in fact. It is quite one thing to apply the new attitude toward intervention to remedy violations of international law when the state in question is relatively powerless; larger, more powerful states represent an entirely different situation, where the principle of sovereign inviolability is backed up by the power to repel intervention and the likelihood that intervention would lead to major war. A further practical limitation on the use of intervention to respond to violations of the law of armed conflicts is that it is very costly in terms of the forces required, and there are simply not enough forces to intervene in every conflict characterized by such violations. Despite these problems, intervention has emerged as a major tool for enforcement of the law of armed conflicts in the contemporary world.

The still-in-process development of an international court system to punish violators of the law as war criminals represents a further effort to enhance the rule of international law in contemporary armed conflicts. It completes the triad of law-police-courts found in domestic society. The first step in this direction of transforming the law into a criminal code was the shift in international law, noted earlier, away from regarding states as the responsible parties and toward holding individuals accountable for violations of the rules for conduct during armed conflict. Intervention by force to stop such violations and perhaps to apprehend violators represents a second step. Yet without an international criminal court to try violators, it remained for the various states to decide whether and how to treat them in given cases. Where violations followed from state policy, there was no likelihood of domestic trials and punishment; in particular, there was no possibility of bringing the officials—up to the head of state—responsible for such policy to justice without a radical change in government. The key, then, to enforcing individual accountability under international law related to armed conflicts has been the creation of war crimes tribunals under international auspices: the tribunals for the former Yugoslavia and Rwanda and the effort to establish a permanent International Criminal Court. With the idea thus established that wrongful behavior in an armed conflict may be investigated and punished as criminal, national courts have a new freedom to pursue war crimes prosecutions according to their own laws, as illustrated by the case of the Belgian trial of Rwandan expatriates and that of General Pinochet mentioned previously.

Defining acts against international law during a conflict as criminal acts incurring liability for prosecution and punishment provides a powerful enforcement tool that bears on conduct during a conflict in different ways at three different stages. First, before an armed conflict breaks out, the concept of war crimes carries the assumption that the values it seeks to protect are sufficiently important and universal that they will be recognized by potential parties to such conflict, so that such actors will organize and control their efforts accordingly. Criminal behavior at this stage would be decisions to plan the armed struggle in ways that violate the established rules and the values underlying them. Second, during an armed conflict the concept of war crimes embodies the assumption that the leadership (political and military) of the parties to the conflict will exert control over their armed forces so as to ensure compliance with the internationally recognized standards for belligerents (international humanitarian law, including the law of armed conflicts) and that individual combatants will act according to these standards. Criminal behavior at this stage lies in acts of omission and commission in violation of the established standards. Third, after the conclusion of an armed conflict the concept of war crimes assumes a continuing effort, at both the domestic and international levels, to identify war crimes, determine the persons responsible for them, and bring these persons to justice before an impartial court.

That the institutionalization of courts to carry through such proceedings is still relatively new and not fully developed means that as yet their ability to deter war crimes from being committed in fact remains untested. The ICTY and ICTR investigations and trials all have to do with acts already committed, and there is no sign that the existence and work of these *ad hoc* tribunals have had any deterrent effect on other contemporary conflicts. Nonetheless, taken all together, these three sorts of effects at different stages relative to an armed conflict argue that the institution of international war crimes proceedings will prove an effective tool for enforcing international law on the conduct of armed conflict and thus imposing restraint on how such conflicts are fought.

The rationale behind the concept of war crimes trials, like that of the laws seeking to regulate the conduct of armed conflict, goes deeper, however; this rationale is closely connected to the conviction that the observance of restraint during a conflict makes it easier to establish peaceful relations between the parties once the fighting is over. If the rights of noncombatants are violated, or if disproportionate destruction is inflicted on the enemy, or if means *mala in se* are employed, or if human rights of the enemy are systematically violated, then it will be more difficult or impossible to reach genuine peace between the parties to the conflict. As Augustine put it, the achievement of genuine peace implies that belligerents "be peaceful in warring." Keeping the conduct of conflict restrained is a first step toward resolving the conflict peacefully. The reason is not only that the observance of restraint minimizes the deep sense of wrong and hatred that unrestrained war fighting can cause; it is also that keeping the fighting under restraint requires cooperation between the conflicting parties and helps to build the habits of reciprocal interaction needed for a negotiated settlement to the conflict and postconflict cooperation.

Despite the powerful advantage in enforcement offered by the institutionalization of international war crimes proceedings, there remain serious objections to such proceedings. Some concerns relate to two principles that occupied prominent places in early statements of the law of war, both identified previously: the principle of sovereignty and the principle that it is the responsibility of individual belligerents to enforce compliance with the law and punish violators. Arguments based on both principles have been made in the case of Slobodan Milosevic's indictment by the ICTY, as noted earlier. Concern to maintain these principles reflects the earlier, and still fundamental, conception of international law as the product of agreements among sovereign states. A different kind of concern arises from a basic clash between goals typically pursued by different sorts of third parties in any given contemporary conflict: on the one hand, to stop the fighting by achieving a negotiated settlement; on the other hand, to restrain the conduct of the fighting and punish atrocities. It is difficult, and perhaps inherently contradictory, to press war crimes investigations, indictments, and trials when doing so may target the very people whose leadership and agreement must be had in order to reach a negotiated end to the conflict. (It is not without irony that at the time of the Dayton accords then-Yugoslav President Milosevic was treated as a valuable partner in the process, while today, when the peace is established and he is no longer head of state, he is detained under indictment by the ICTY.) A related issue is that war crimes prosecutions may leave one or both sides in a conflict leaderless after the end of the conflict and thus unable to organize politically for reconstructing peaceful society. A third problem, illustrated by the cases of Radovan Karadzic and Ratko Mladic in Bosnia, is that leaders indicted as war criminals may nonetheless retain considerable power in their own communities, so that arresting them may prove impossible in practical terms, and trying to do so may reignite the armed conflict.

In moral terms, though, there remains much to be said for holding individuals directly responsible for their personal involvement in acts violating the standards laid out in international law bearing on armed conflict. Indeed, in historical perspective doing so is no innovation; it is rather a return to the normative understanding that underlies international law, an understanding that existed for centuries before positive international law began to put its provisions in the form of constraints binding on states. The means of institutionalizing the enforcement of these transnational standards has varied over time. For a period during the Middle Ages the church sought to discipline—and punish where necessary—individuals who engaged in unacceptable conduct during wars; later the chivalric community took on this role. At the dawn of the modern period the enforcement of the standards for right conduct in war shifted, first, to national sovereigns, and then after the development of the state system, to the states. Yet the standards themselves remained above the state system, and even as the positive law of war began to take shape around the idea that states should be held accountable for their soldiers' unacceptable conduct during war, the standards themselves were reaffirmed as transnational. Holding states responsible for behavior according to the law of war was only a means of enforcement. When states fail in this responsibility—as has been, for various reasons, characteristic in contemporary armed conflict—there is good reason to fall back on the earlier normative model of a transnational institution that seeks to ensure that individual participants in armed conflicts are held to standards of discipline in their conduct as fighters and punished for violating these standards. War crimes proceedings constitute one important way—though attention should also be given to other possibilities—to institutionalize this deep understanding of the rules for conduct in armed conflict as rising above individual states, to ensure respect for these rules as laid down in international law before a conflict as well as during it. After the end of a conflict there is a further moral reason for supporting war crimes proceedings: They help to reestablish a system of justice in a war-torn society and thus constitute an important step toward the rebuilding of that society as one governed by just law. In Augustinian terms, war crimes proceedings not only help to ensure that participants in a conflict are "peaceful in warring," but that the ultimate purpose of the restoration of peace is achieved.

For the present the existence and work of the ICTY and the ICTR argue that the idea of the courts and of the criminalization of international law on armed conflicts have won out. It is still too early to tell, though, whether the theoretical, practical, and political concerns arguing against the institutionalization of war crimes trials might yet prevail in the shaping of international law and the behavior of states in the future, or whether the institutionalization process begun in the international tribunals for Rwanda and the former Yugoslavia and the effort to establish an International Criminal Court will ultimately win out, not only in the provisions of positive international law but in the customary practices of states, or whether some intermediate state of affairs will result. It is also not clear how the use of domestic courts to address crimes of war will develop—whether this is a trend that will grow more robust and widespread on its own, or whether it needs to be encouraged, in one way or another, by the existence and operation of international courts. If international courts have jurisdiction unless domestic courts take action first, this provides a significant spur for such domestic action. But the exact nature of the relation between domestic and international courts in treating crimes of war is one of the important issues remaining to be worked out. Important moral issues are embedded in the arguments on both sides of the issue of international criminal courts. Indeed, the institutionalization of war crimes proceedings will succeed only if the concerns that argue against it, whether moral, political, or practical, are somehow satisfied.

The future role of intervention, both in itself and as an element in an overall judicial process, as a means of enforcing international law on the conduct of armed conflict also remains somewhat uncertain. Ultimately both intervention and war crimes trials are dependent on the contemporaneous empirical shape of the international order, and this could change to their detriment. In the present and the foreseeable future, though, military intervention provides the police power that an effective war crimes institution requires. If one favors war crimes prosecutions but opposes military intervention, then some means must be found to replace interventionary military force with some other form of international police power—a prospect that is very controverted and remains at present only on a distant horizon.

NOTES

1. When I wrote the original version of this paper for presentation in early 1999 supporters of the ICC were convinced of its likely success as the institutional next step along the path marked by the Nuremberg and Tokyo tribunals and those for the former Yugoslavia and Rwanda.
2. See also "Milosevic Is Given to U.N. for Trial in War-Crime Case," *New York Times*, 29 June 2001, pp. A-1, A-12.
3. See also "At Arraignment, Milosevic Scorns His U.N. Accusers," pp. A1, A6, and "Milosevic Brings Air of Scorn to Tribunal," *New York Times*, 4 July 2001, p. A-7.

FROM MORAL NORM TO CRIMINAL CODE   89

4. International Criminal Tribunal for the Former Yugoslavia, *Final Report to the Prosecutor by the Committee Established to Review the NATO Bombing Campaign Against the Federal Republic of Yugoslavia*.
5. See also "Mother Superior Guilty in Rwanda Killings," *New York Times*, 9 June 2001, p. A-4.
6. Standard collections of documents defining the law of armed conflicts include Leon Friedman, ed., *The Law of War: A Documentary History*, 2 vols. (New York: Random House, 1972); Adam Roberts and Richard Guelff, eds., *Documents on the Laws of War*, 2nd ed. (Oxford: Clarendon Press, 1989); and Dietrich Schindler and Jiri Toman, eds., *The Laws of Armed Conflicts: A Collection of Conventions, Resolutions, and Other Documents* (Leiden: A. W. Sijthoff; Geneva: Henry Dunant Institute, 1973).
7. For a summary of how such law related to civil conflicts see Thomas W. Farer, "The Laws of War 25 Years after Nuremberg," *International Conciliation*, no. 583 (May 1971), pp. 30–31.
8. See Protocol I, Preamble and Article 1, and Protocol II, Article 1, in Roberts and Guelff, *Documents*, pp. 389–390, 449–450.
9. U.N. Doc. S/RES/935 (1994), Annex, *Statute of the International Tribunal for Rwanda*, Preamble and Articles 1–4.
10. U.N. Doc. No. S/25704 & Add. 1 (1993), Annex, *Statute of the International Tribunal*, Preamble and Articles 1–5.
11. 1907 Hague Convention IV Respecting the Laws and Customs of War on Land, Article 3; Roberts and Guelff, *Documents*, p. 46.
12. James Brown Scott, *The Spanish Origin of International Law. Part 1: Francisco de Vitoria and His Law of Nations* (Oxford: Clarendon Press; London: Humphrey Milford, 1934).
13. See particularly James Turner Johnson, *Ideology, Reason, and the Limitation of War* (Princeton and London: Princeton University Press, 1975) and *Just War Tradition and the Restraint of War* (Princeton and Guildford, Surrey: Princeton University Press, 1981).
14. Roberts and Guelff, *Documents*, p. 45.
15. This point is found throughout Ramsey's writing; see, for example, Paul Ramsey, *The Just War: Force and Political Responsibility* (Lanham: Rowman and Littlefield, 2002).
16. On the "peace of God" see also James Turner Johnson, *The Quest for Peace* (Princeton and Guildford, Surrey: Princeton University Press, 1987), pp. 79–86. More generally on the medieval canon law development of the idea of noncombatant immunity see Johnson. *Ideology, Reason, and the Limitation of War*, pp. 35–38, 43–46.
17. See also Johnson, *Just War Tradition*, pp. 131–150.
18. Augustine, *Contra Faustum* xxii, 74, cited in Thomas Aquinas, *Summa Theologica*, II/II, Q. 40, Art. 1, vol. II (New York: Benziger Brothers, Inc., 1947), p. 1360.
19. Augustine, *Letter to Boniface*, cited in Aquinas, *Summa Theologica*.
20. For example, 1907 Hague Convention IV, Annex (Regulations), Articles 25, 27 (Roberts and Guelff, *Documents*, p. 53); 1923 Hague Draft Rules of Aerial Warfare, Articles 22–26 (Roberts and Guelff, *Documents*, pp. 126–128).
21. For example, the 1971 Convention on Biological Weapons; Friedman, *The Law of War*, pp. 767–771.
22. Roberts and Guelff, *Documents*, p. 40.
23. See, for example, Francis Lieber, *Guerrilla Parties: Considered with Reference to the Laws and Usages of War* (New York: D. van Nostrand, 1862), and 1907 Hague Convention IV, Article 1 (Roberts and Guelff, *Documents*, p. 48).
24. See also Johnson, *Just War Tradition*, pp. 179–178.
25. *Instructions for the Government of the Armies of the United States in the Field* U.S. War Department, General Orders No. 100 (New York: D. van Nostrand, 1863).
26. John C. Ford, S. J., "The Morality of Obliteration Bombing," *Theological Studies* 3 (September 1944), pp. 261–309.
27. Ann Elizabeth Mayer, "War and Peace in the Islamic Tradition and in International Law," Chapter 8 in *Just War and Jihad*, ed. John Kelsay and James Turner Johnson (New York: Greenwood Press, 1991), p. 199.
28. Cited in Michael Sells, "Religion, History, and Genocide in Bosnia-Herzegovina," Chapter 1 in *Religion and Justice in the War Over Bosnia*, ed. G. Scott Davis (New York and London: Routledge, 1996), p. 34.
29. James A. Aho, *Religious Mythology and the Art of War* (Westport, CT: Greenwood Press, 1981).
30. John Kelsay, "Islam and the Distinction Between Combatants and Noncombatants," Chapter 9 in *Cross, Crescent, and Sword*, ed. James Turner Johnson and John Kelsay (New York: Greenwood Press, 1990).

31. Khaled Abou El Fadl, *"Akham al-Bughat:* Irregular Warfare and the Law of Rebellion in Islam," Chapter 7 in Johnson and Kelsay, *Cross, Crescent, and Sword.*
32. Judith Miller, *God Has Ninety-Nine Names* (New York: Simon & Schuster, 1996).
33. 1949 Geneva Conventions, Common Article 2 (Roberts and Guelff, *Documents,* pp. 171–172, 194–195, 216–217, 273–274).
34. 1977 Geneva Protocol II, Article 1.2 (Roberts and Guelff, *Documents,* p. 450).
35. 1949 Geneva Conventions, Common Article 3 (Roberts and Guelff, *Documents,* pp. 172, 195, 217, 273).
36. 1977 Geneva Protocol I, Article 1, and Protocol II, Article 1 (Roberts and Guelff, *Documents,* pp. 390, 449–450).
37. 1977 Geneva Protocol II, Preamble (Roberts and Guelff, *Documents,* p. 449).
38. 1977 Geneva Protocol I, Article 1, and Protocol II, Article 1 (Roberts and Guelff, *Documents,* pp. 390, 449–450).
39. 1977 Protocol I, Article 1.1, emphasis added (Roberts and Guelff, *Documents,* p. 390).
40. 1977 Geneva Protocol I, Article 5.2 (Roberts and Guelff, *Documents,* p. 391).
41. 1977 Geneva Protocol II, Article 6 (Roberts and Guelff, *Documents,* pp. 453–454).
42. 1977 Geneva Protocol II, Article 3 (Roberts and Guelff, *Documents,* p. 450).
43. See, for example, Elizabeth Rubin, "Saving Sierra Leone, At a Price," *New York Times,* 4 February 1999, p. A-27.
44. J. Bryan Hehir, "Intervention: From Theories to Cases," *Ethics & International Affairs* 9 (1995), pp. 9–10. Hehir explicitly rejects unilateral intervention as against the "presumption against war" he posits as basic to just war theory: "To maintain the presumption, the expansion of the category of just cause for intervention should be accompanied by a corresponding prohibition of the right of individual states to intervene" (p. 9; the "presumption against war" is posited on p. 7). See, in response, James Turner Johnson, "The Broken Tradition," *The National Interest,* no. 45 (fall 1996), pp. 27–36; James Turner Johnson, *Morality and Contemporary Warfare* (New Haven and London: Yale University Press, 1999), pp. 35–36.
45. Indeed, it is arguable that the traditional doctrine of sovereignty has effectively lost power to prevent humanitarian intervention. See also Thomas G. Weiss and Jarat Chopra, "Sovereignty Is No Longer Sacrosanct: Codifying Humanitarian Intervention," *Ethics & International Affairs* 6 (1992), pp. 95–117.

WHAT'S LIVING AND WHAT'S DEAD IN NUCLEAR ETHICS

STEVEN LEE

Hobart and William Smith Colleges

If we look back over the past twenty years, we find a rich and wide-ranging debate over nuclear ethics. Spurred by the 1983 pastoral letter of the U.S. Catholic bishops, the debate engaged the general public and the military, as well as the academy, to an extent unprecedented in the nuclear age. Despite the vigor and breadth of the debate, however, it broke little new ground. Most of the major issues had already been addressed in the previous great nuclear debate, that of the late 1960s. Central to both debates were discussions of the moral acceptability of a strategic posture based on mutual assured destruction (MAD), the relative moral and strategic merits of counter-value and counterforce targeting, and the moral implications of strategic defense. Between the times of the two debates, much had changed technologically in nuclear weapons and their delivery systems—yet the moral issues remained the same. These moral issues arose with the advent of nuclear technology and its development in the first twenty years of the nuclear age, but they remained largely unaltered in the face of further technological innovation.

Since the 1980s, of course, the nuclear world has changed radically, not in its technological dimensions, but in its political dimensions. The Cold War is long over. How does this change the moral debate?[1] It is time to ask, from our vantage point more than a decade past the end of the Cold War, what's living and what's dead in the Cold War ethical debate over nuclear weapons?

During the 1990s, the moral issues surrounding nuclear weapons policy all but disappeared as a matter of public discussion. With the end of the Cold War, nuclear complacency replaced nuclear angst, and nuclear weapons in general, and nuclear ethics in particular, were little discussed. But nuclear weapons have not gone away, so the question remains, what should our moral concerns be with nuclear weapons after the Cold War? How much of the Cold War moral debate is still relevant and how much of it needs to be recast? With the end of the Cold War, what has nuclear ethics become?

With the new century, we do indeed have a renewed debate over nuclear weapons policy. Like the 1980s debate, it is occurring partly as a result of the proposals of a Republican president to substantially revamp U.S. nuclear policy, including the building of extensive ballistic missile defenses. So, now we are able, like those in the 1980s, to connect our abstract moral analysis of nuclear weapons to policy initiatives under active consideration.

What changes in nuclear strategic posture has President Bush proposed? In remarks at the National Defense University delivered in May of 2001, the president proposed the building of missile defenses and a reduction in the number of nuclear weapons.[2]

> We need new concepts of deterrence that rely on both offensive and defensive forces. Deterrence can no longer be based solely on the threat of nuclear retaliation. Defenses can strengthen deterrence by reducing the incentive for proliferation. . . . I am committed to achieving a credible deterrent with the lowest possible number of nuclear weapons consistent with our national security needs.

The building of defenses, he acknowledges, would require abandoning the 1972 Anti-Ballistic Missile Treaty. This new approach to nuclear security "reflects a clear and clean break from the past, and especially from the adversarial legacy of the Cold War."

The administration has not cast these proposed changes overtly in moral terms, in contrast with the Reagan administration's proposals two decades earlier. But the same moral rationale that was explicit then is implicit now. We must move away from the old concept of deterrence based on mutual threats of annihilation, in part, because it is immoral to make such threats. So the moral issues are again engaged, at least implicitly.

HOW THE NUCLEAR WORLD HAS CHANGED

There are four important differences between then and now.

1. First and most importantly, the Cold War hostility between the superpowers has substantially disappeared with the dissolution of the Soviet Union and the coming into existence of a post-communist Russian state. Whereas there are now regional nuclear rivalries, such as that between India and Pakistan, there is no longer a global nuclear rivalry. This means that the threat of a global nuclear war, for the time at least, has largely disappeared. Another aspect of the end of Cold War hostility is that Russia has been greatly weakened by its political transformation and the United States now stands as the lone superpower.

2. Second, the most important military threats the United States now faces are different from those of the Cold War. For one, the main danger from nuclear weapons is probably an increased likelihood of nuclear proliferation and nuclear terrorism. If a nuclear weapon is used in the next decade, its user is most likely to be either a new state proliferator or a terrorist organization. The end

of the Cold War has not only brought the dangers of proliferation and terrorism to the fore (they had, after all, been there all along), but it has exacerbated them. The anti-proliferation discipline that the superpowers exercised over
other states has weakened and the breakup of the Soviet Union has made nuclear materials and complete weapons potentially available for theft or sale on
the black market.

3. A third important difference between then and now is the apparent range of feasible nuclear policies. Radical reductions in nuclear arsenals, or even complete
nuclear disarmament, are now perceived, in a political sense, as real possibilities. Amidst the tensions of the Cold War, radical reductions or complete disarmament were utopian dreams. Now their realization can at least be imagined.
Many share the view that nuclear weapons, having kept the Cold War cold, have
done their job, so that now we should get rid of them. Of course, the bomb remains deeply entrenched in our political and military cultures. But the ratio-
nalizations for keeping it have lost much of their force.[3]

4. Fourth, the technology involved in weapons systems has advanced considerably.
Most significantly, advances in the areas of computing, miniaturization, remote
sensing, and information processing, at the basis of what has been dubbed the
revolution in military affairs, may have important implications for the development of new modes of nuclear weapons policy.

THE COLD WAR DEBATE

In order to determine whether and how nuclear ethics has changed we need to review the Cold War debate.[4] The most fundamental way to characterize the understanding reached about nuclear ethics in the Cold War is that deterrence presents a
profound moral paradox. The morally paradoxical nature of nuclear deterrence can
be expressed in terms of three tenets.

1. First, the use of nuclear weapons in war is morally unacceptable, due to the
great devastation nuclear weapons would likely cause to noncombatants and to
civilian social structures. The great likelihood of this harm is due to physical
differences between the effects of nuclear and conventional weapons. Nuclear
weapons have not only much greater blast effects, they also have other novel effects, such as radioactive fallout, that spread their destruction over a much wider
area. In addition, there is a serious risk of escalation from the use of a few weapons
to the use of many. This argument follows from just war theory focusing in particular on the principle of discrimination.

2. The second tenet concerns nuclear deterrence. Like nuclear use, nuclear deterrence under the regime of MAD is morally unacceptable. The morally unacceptability of use implies the moral unacceptability of the threat to use, under
the principle that it is morally wrong to intend to do what it is morally wrong
to do. The assumption behind this implication is that the threat to use nuclear
weapons must involve the conditional intention to do so. To be effective, the
nuclear threat cannot be a bluff. An essential feature of just war theory is that
intentions are subject to moral assessment, as are the actions. Because, under

a regime of MAD, part of what is threatened, and so conditionally intended, is the destruction of the opponent's society, the threat is not morally acceptable. This argument, then, is a further application of the just war principle of discrimination. Moreover, the immorality of the threat can be argued on grounds other than the principle of discrimination. For example, the threats involved under a MAD regime are seen to be morally unacceptable when understood as policies of hostage-holding on a vast scale.[5]

Most of those who dissented from this tenet did so because they dissented from the first tenet as well. They accepted both the implication from the immorality of use to the immorality of the threat to use and the principle of discrimination but argued that nuclear use need not contravene the principle. They imagined, for example, a limited nuclear war, one where the nuclear targets were limited to military installations outside of urban areas. But, given that large numbers of nuclear weapons were targeted on urban areas (an essential feature of MAD) and that the likelihood of keeping a nuclear war limited to isolated military targets was probably not high, any use of nuclear weapons would have carried with it a morally unacceptable risk of escalation that would have brought about the deaths of vast numbers of civilians.

3. The third tenet, like the second, concerns deterrence. While nuclear deterrence, under the second tenet, was morally unacceptable, it was, at the same time, under the conditions of the Cold War, morally required. To begin to appreciate the positive moral status of nuclear deterrence, consider another aspect of just war theory. While the *jus in bello* principle of discrimination prohibits nuclear deterrence, along the lines of the argument just sketched, the *jus ad bellum* principle allowing military self-defense seem to permit it.

    Moreover, from a consequentialist (or utilitarian) moral perspective, the practice of nuclear deterrence is not merely permissible, but morally required. For the consequentialist, we are obligated to adopt the policy that brings about the highest level of human well-being. Given the hostile superpowers of the Cold War, each vulnerable to destruction by the other, continuing a policy of nuclear deterrence could reasonably be seen by each of them as necessary to avoid nuclear attack at the hands of the other, an attack that would not only cause great suffering in the nation attacked but also would be a disaster on a global scale. Thus, comparing the consequences of maintaining the policy of nuclear deterrence with those of abandoning it, the implication was that continuing with nuclear deterrence was morally required.

These considerations were often cast in terms of the notion of strategic stability. Roughly speaking, a military situation between two adversaries has strategic stability when it minimizes the risk of war between them. A military situation is stable when there is little temptation for aggression on either side and when the various kinds of shocks that might arise in the relationship between the opponents are unlikely to lead to war between them. The argument, then, is that if one side greatly reduced or eliminated its nuclear weapons, then the result would be great instability, making nuclear war more likely. Clearly, the moral imperative for the consequentialist is to maximize stability. Thus, we have the moral paradox. From one moral perspective (the just war principle of discrimination) the Cold War policy of nuclear deterrence was morally impossible. From another moral perspective (consequentialism), nuclear deterrence, assuming that its abandonment (by one side) would greatly increase instability, was morally required. The conflict nuclear weapons generated between these moral perspectives ran deep, and, with the moral stakes so high on each side, seemed intractable. Nuclear weapons put morality at war with itself.

This was new. The morally paradoxical nature of nuclear deterrence makes nuclear weapons morally novel in comparison with other weapons, aptly called "conventional." No other kind of weapon had ever generated this kind of moral conflict. Conventional weapons systems can be used in morally permissible ways and do not involve the risk of escalation to societal destruction. Conventional deterrence is not morally problematic in the way that nuclear deterrence is, because conventional deterrence can be practiced in a morally acceptable manner.

MAD generated the moral paradox. MAD is a situation in which military opponents each have a capability to destroy the society of the other even after receiving a surprise attack. Nuclear weapons make such a situation possible for the first time in history. MAD is an objective state of military affairs, not a doctrine or strategy. It is the context in which strategy must be made. MAD is the source of the moral paradox because of two of its features. First, nuclear weapons make possible societal destruction, something that, from one moral perspective, must not even be threatened. Second, given that one's opponent can destroy one's society, nuclear weapons, from another perspective, morally require that one threaten the opponent with such destruction, as necessary to minimize the risk of nuclear war.

Another important feature of MAD is the impossibility of effective defense against nuclear attack. Deterrence is necessary because defense is impossible. With nuclear weapons, deterrence replaced defense as the only effective mode of national security. Traditionally, the chief purpose of military policy was to develop a capacity to deny the opponent any gains it might seek through aggression. This was the chief source of stability under conventional weapons. But, under a regime of MAD, such denial is no longer possible, and security must be sought through the threat of retaliatory punishment, which, in the case of nuclear weapons, is an immoral threat to destroy the opponent's society.

In the age of MAD, stability must be sought through deterrence by threat of punishment, rather than through defense and a capacity for denial. At the same time, peace has become a much more morally valuable commodity, given the consequences for human well-being of nuclear war. Peace requires stability, and the moral argument for nuclear deterrence is based on the claim that it is essential to maintain stability. In a situation of MAD, the best way to preserve peace, and avoid an unimaginable human catastrophe, is to maintain nuclear deterrence, a policy that involves morally unacceptable threats.

If the moral paradox is a function of MAD, then the way to escape it is to get beyond MAD. During the Cold War, some theorists argued that we could achieve a *technological obviation* of the MAD relationship. They rejected the claim that defenses against nuclear attack could not be effective. With effective defenses against nuclear attack, one side would take away the other side's capacity for assured destruction, and the MAD relationship would no longer hold. The argument was that technological obviation could be achieved either through defenses alone or through defenses combined with effective counterforce capabilities, nuclear weapons with the accuracy to destroy much of the nuclear capability of the other side. The hope for the defenses was embodied in Reagan's Strategic Defense Initiative, popularly known as "Star Wars."

But the hope behind the idea of technological obviation was as utopian as proposals for complete nuclear disarmament. To eliminate the other side's capacity for assured destruction, even a nation with effective counterforce capability would require defenses that were near-perfect, given the destructive power of even a few nuclear weapons. The offense dominance of nuclear weapons was so overwhelming that no foreseeable technological breakthrough could overcome it.[6]

Thus, the main conclusion of the Cold War moral debate, on my reading, is that nuclear deterrence was morally paradoxical, as implied by the three tenets, and that there was no feasible way to avoid this paradox. It should be noted that this paradox, as a moral paradox, was a practical rather than a merely theoretical matter. It affected our collective moral life because it seemed to preclude our acting in a morally acceptable way. Thus, there was during the Cold War a special urgency in our efforts to solve the paradox and a great frustration in our inability to do so.

NUCLEAR ETHICS IN THE NEW CENTURY

Given the differences between our nuclear world and that of the Cold War, what should we say about nuclear ethics today? Four points deserve consideration, especially in relation to the paradox identified above: (1) the end of the superpower military rivalry; (2) the new military threats we appear to face; (3) the belief that complete nuclear disarmament may now be a feasible policy option; and (4) the advances in technology.

END OF THE SUPERPOWER RIVALRY

The military hostility that characterized the Cold War relationship between the superpowers is gone. Does that mean that the United States and Russia are no longer in a MAD relationship? Two elements are necessary for a MAD relationship. First, two states must each have the military capacity to destroy the other's society even after a surprise attack, and, second, they must be military opponents. While the United States and Russia clearly satisfy the first condition, their mildly friendly relations at this time suggests that they may not satisfy the second.

There is room for dispute here. Imagine a scale of hostility between nuclear powers, at one end of which is the United States and Britain, and at the other end of which is the United States and the Soviet Union during the height of the Cold War. The current affinity between the United States and Russia would put their relationship somewhere in the middle of this scale. There is considerably more conflict of interest between the United States and Russia than there is between the United States and Britain. In addition, the political instability of Russia at the moment contains the risk of a rapid reversion to something like the old level of hostility between it and the United States. So, are the United States and Russia military opponents? Are they in a MAD relationship? There is no clear answer to this question. There are clear cases of nuclear powers who are not military opponents, such as the United States and Britain, and clear cases of nuclear powers who were, such as the United States and the former Soviet Union. And there are cases in between.

If two nuclear powers are not military opponents, they have no need to deter each other, so they do not possess nuclear weapons for the sake of making threats against each other. Hence, in terms of their relationship to each other at least, their possession of nuclear weapons does not run afoul of the principle of discrimination and is morally acceptable. Mere possession of nuclear weapons is not by itself immoral, if the weapons are not being used to make threats against civilian targets. But once nuclear powers begin to perceive each other as military opponents, each will, as a result of that perception, intend for its nuclear weapons to be recognized by the other as a retaliatory threat, whether or not that threat is made explicit.

For the sake of the current argument, then, we cannot say definitely whether or not the United States and Russia are in a MAD relationship. So, let us consider both possibilities. If the two nations are military opponents, and so in a MAD relationship, then the end of the Cold War has not changed things morally—the moral paradox remains. If so, nuclear ethics today is not substantially different from nuclear ethics during the Cold War.

But what if the United States and Russia are not currently military opponents, and so are not in a MAD relationship, as many observers would maintain? Because the moral paradox depends on MAD, it would seem that the paradox is gone as well. The dissolution of the Soviet Union resulted in the dissolution of the paradox. Nuclear ethics today would then be fundamentally different from nuclear ethics during the Cold War. But this judgment is too quick. The moral paradox is built into MAD, and MAD is a universal relationship, not a particular relationship. MAD is an abstract relation that has multiple potential instances. The military relationship between the United States and the Soviet Union was one such instance. That instance existed for a time and now has ended. But the potential is there for other instances of the MAD relationship to come into being. All that is required is two nuclear powers with a level of hostility between them sufficient for them to be military opponents. This may be or become the case with the United States and China, for example.

The moral paradox lies in the potential of MAD to be instantiated and not in the vagaries of its instantiation in the Soviet/American relationship. That relationship is an historical, cultural phenomenon and as such it is unique. But MAD is merely one element in the mix of elements that was the Cold War. MAD can be repeated in other historical situations. What we made of MAD culturally, as exhibited, for example, in the film *Dr. Strangelove*, was unique, but MAD itself is an objective state of military capabilities between hostile nuclear powers. It has a reality beyond the cultural forms in which it may be embodied at different times. It is repeatable. Certain political and military conditions must be satisfied for an instance of MAD to exist. But once they are, it does.

If the United States and Russia are not currently military opponents, MAD is now latent rather than manifest, at least in their relationship. But, even so, in the potential for MAD to reappear lies the continuing presence of the moral paradox. Nothing since the end of the Cold War has changed this. So, the most that can be said about nuclear ethics today is that the end of the Cold War has brought about a temporary resolution of the moral paradox. Because MAD can return, the end of the cold war has not brought a permanent solution of the paradox.

NEW MILITARY THREATS

The second change in our nuclear world is the new military threats we appear to face, specifically nuclear proliferation and nuclear terrorism.[7] These have been a problem for decades, and the moral issues they raise are not new, though they appear now with a new vigor. Because the acquisition of nuclear weapons is now easier, the problem is getting more attention. One issue is whether it is morally permissible for a nonnuclear state (or a terrorist group) to acquire nuclear weapons. Given the moral unacceptability of either using nuclear weapons or practicing deterrence with them, the answer seems to be no.[8] Of course, if a potential state proliferator is facing a military opponent with nuclear weapons, it would face the moral paradox directly, a moral demand that it acquire nuclear weapons along with the moral demand that it not do so. But all nuclear powers were once nuclear proliferators, and the moral demands regarding acquisition are on par with the moral demands regarding abandonment or deacquisition.

Another moral issue raised by proliferation is how far a state is allowed to go to keep another state (or terrorist group) from acquiring nuclear weapons. What are the moral limits of antiproliferation efforts? In the case of terrorist groups, these limits would be quite wide, but what about potential state proliferators? We may assume that the moral limits regarding interference with a potential state proliferator would be set by the moral limits, more generally, of one state's interference with the internal affairs of another state. There may, however, be greater moral latitude for antiproliferation interference, given the regional and global threat that nuclear weapons pose. In addition, there are two other circumstances that would make a broader range of antiproliferation interference morally justifiable. First, the interference may be multilateral, for example, through the United Nations, rather than unilateral. Second, the interference may be something that the state has indirectly consented to, for example, by being a signatory of the Nuclear Non-Proliferation Treaty (NPT).

A third moral issue, though, may limit allowable interference to stop proliferation. This is the issue of fairness, often raised by India prior to its series of nuclear tests in the late 1990s. One way to pose the issue is to ask to what extent hypocrisy limits a nation's moral freedom of action. The hypocrisy in question is that of the nuclear powers who hold on to nuclear weapons but demand that other states not acquire them. Is it fair of the nuclear powers to make such demands, and, if not, does this imply that, without getting rid of their own, they are not morally entitled to interfere to keep other states from acquiring them? The moral argument against such inter-ference is bolstered by the fact that the nuclear states hold on to their own despite hav-ing promised, in Article VI of the NPT not to do so. Beyond the issue of fairness, there is the matter of effectiveness. The nuclear powers' holding on to their own nu-clear weapons may make their antiproliferation efforts much more difficult.

In any case, because the moral problems of proliferation existed during the Cold War and because new proliferators face the same moral problem faced by the old pro-liferators (the current nuclear powers), the moral debate regarding proliferation is the same now as it was during the Cold War.

NUCLEAR DISARMAMENT

The third change in our nuclear world is the perception, new since the end of the Cold War, that complete nuclear disarmament (CND) is a real possibility. Because the Cold War is over, nuclear weapons are no longer seen as necessary. There may no longer be an overriding reason for keeping them, and the realization that this is the case may make their abandonment politically feasible. At the same time, there is a sense of urgency about the need to move quickly toward nuclear disarmament, based on the belief that the current window of opportunity may be narrow. Interna-tional tensions may rise over the next several years to the point that there is again a MAD regime.

The feasibility of CND seems to entail that nuclear ethics now is fundamental-ly different than it was during the Cold War, for it appears that CND would solve the moral paradox. If nations had no nuclear weapons, they would not be making nuclear threats, so the moral objection to their military policies would vanish. During the Cold War, the paradox seemed intractable because the two principal proposed so-lutions, technological obviation and the elimination of nuclear weapons, were not real, that is feasible, solutions. They were utopian, one for technological reasons and the other for political reasons; hence neither was available to solve the paradox. The possibility of eliminating nuclear weapons seems no longer utopian. This would alter the nuclear ethics debate fundamentally, refocusing it from a theoretical concern about whether the moral paradox had an achievable solution to a practical concern bringing a solution about. If no nation had nuclear weapons, then MAD would not again become instantiated, even if military hostility arose between former nuclear powers. MAD would, of course, remain a possibility, but one that in the absence of nuclear weapons could not be realized.[9]

On the contrary, however, the possibility of CND no more changes the funda-mentals of the ethical debate than does the possibility, now realized, of warmer re-lations between the nuclear powers. The absence of nuclear weapons would provide no more of a permanent solution to the moral paradox than does the absence of hos-tility between nuclear powers. The instantiation of MAD requires nuclear weapons in the hands of hostile powers. If the hostility goes away or the weapons go away, that instance of MAD ceases to be, but another instance will come to be if either the hostility or the weapons return. The truth of the cliches that nuclear weapons cannot be "disinvented" or that the nuclear genie cannot be put back in the bottle testify to this.

But there is a deeper point to be made about the moral implications of the possibility of the elimination of nuclear weapons. The absence of nuclear weapons might not, by itself, provide even a temporary resolution to the moral paradox, in the way that the lack of hostility does. The abandonment of nuclear weapons may be less of a moral advance than is commonly thought. This is because nuclear war would remain a continuing possibility under CND. Nuclear weapons could be rebuilt after they had all been dismantled. Thus, the logical features structuring the deterrence relationship of hostile nuclear powers would, in some respects, continue to structure that relationship after their nuclear disarmament. Each would still need a policy to deter nuclear war. As a result, nuclear threats would, in one sense, survive the abandonment of nuclear weapons. Because the risk of nuclear war would continue to exist, a policy for managing that risk would still be needed.

The risk of nuclear war in a world in which nuclear powers had abandoned their nuclear weapons would result from the possibility of the weapons being rebuilt. So, in managing that risk, a state would, as Jonathan Schell argues, seek to deter its opponent from rebuilding, and this would be achieved, at least in part, by the nation's having the capacity to follow suit and to rebuild its own nuclear weapons.[10] In this rebuilding capacity would lie a threat to rebuild them, and this threat, a threat to make a nuclear threat, would itself be a nuclear threat of sorts. Schell refers to this policy as "weaponless deterrence." Because the weapons could be rebuilt, they would continue to cast their shadow over a world in which they had been eliminated. The strategic logic of nuclear deterrence would remain in force, structuring the military policies of the hostile erstwhile nuclear powers.

The argument is that if nuclear deterrence, in the form of weaponless deterrence, would survive the abandonment of nuclear weapons, then the abandonment would not even temporarily resolve the moral paradox. The paradox is a creature of nuclear deterrence, and so if deterrence remained, so would the paradox, whether the deterrence is practiced with weapons or without. Because weaponless deterrence is a form of deterrence, it would mimic not only the strategic logic of deterrence with weapons, but its moral logic as well. In other words, since it may be appropriate to regard the situation after abandonment of nuclear weapons as itself a form of nuclear deterrence, the moral paradox would remain as well.

The question comes down to how effective a form of deterrence weaponless deterrence would be. Would weaponless deterrence lead to more or less stability? Would it or would it not greatly increase the risk of nuclear war? If weaponless deterrence is as effective or more effective than deterrence with weapons, then abandonment would resolve the paradox by bringing military policy into accord with the principle of discrimination. But if weaponless deterrence is significantly less effective, the paradox would remain: We would be required to abandon the weapons to bring policy into line with the principle of discrimination, but required to retain them on consequentialist grounds.

Which form of deterrence has greater stability? Schell claims that weaponless deterrence has greater stability.[11] Its stability benefit is that it lengthens the "nuclear fuse," the lead time needed to wage nuclear war, the time that would transpire between the decision to wage a nuclear war and the commencement of the nuclear destruction. The chief virtue of a longer lead time is that it would allow a greater opportunity for decisions that would halt the process before it led to catastrophe. The result would be "a stability that we cannot even dream of in our present world of huge nuclear arsenals."[12] A longer lead time is indeed an important gain, but there is more to stability than the length of the nuclear fuse.

The advantage Schell claims for weaponless deterrence is primarily the advantage of avoiding accidental nuclear war. The longer lead time would greatly reduce or eliminate the possibility of a run-away escalatory process in which nuclear weapons would be used without authorization by central authorities. (We may refer to this virtue of weaponless deterrence as *accidental-war stability*.) But how would weaponless deterrence fare in terms a more familiar kind of stability, namely, *crisis stability*? Crisis stability is the ability of a deterrence posture to resist a slide into war in a crisis. The extent of crisis stability is the extent to which a deterrence posture can create a firm belief in the mind of the opponent that striking first would not be advantageous under any circumstances. In the case of deterrence with weapons, crisis stability is due to mutual vulnerability. The absence of mutual vulnerability when each side has few or no nuclear weapons leads many commentators to argue that the attempt to abandon nuclear weapons would lead to serious crisis instability. The concern is that in a crisis, such as an imminent or actual conventional war, the nations would rush to rebuild their nuclear weapons, the way in 1914 the combatants on World War I rushed to mobilize. They might do so either out of the belief that the first nation to have the weapons would be able to use them to great advantage or out of fear that the opponent, acting on this belief, would be hurrying to rebuild its own weapons.

The degree of crisis stability, since it is based on the strength of each side's belief that a first strike would not be to its advantage, is a function of the strength of its perception that a first strike against its opponent would be met by devastating retaliation. This perception would inevitably be stronger when the nation has an existing assured destruction capability than when it has no nuclear arsenal. The reason is that the potential for retaliation lodged in a rebuilding capacity is more easily destroyed than the potential for retaliation lodged in existing weapons. First, it is inherently easier to reduce the vulnerability of existing weapons than to reduce the vulnerability of a rebuilding capacity, if only because the weapons are much smaller and more easily hidden than the large-scale industrial facilities that would constitute the rebuilding capacity. Second, the opponent would have more time to destroy the potential when it resides in a rebuilding capacity than when it resides in actual weapons. In a condition of mutual assured destruction, the opponent would have time for only one attack before the retaliatory attack would be launched, but under weaponless deterrence it may have time for a number of attacks before the weapons could be rebuilt and a retaliatory strike could be launched. Thus, crisis stability is much weaker under weaponless deterrence.

There is a third kind of stability, *noncrisis stability*. This kind of stability concerns the likelihood that war could result from an escalatory process that begins by one side challenging the interests of the other in some relatively small way, some limited form of aggression. Noncrisis stability results from the opponent's fear that such a challenge to the nation's interests could result in things getting out of hand and escalating to mutual destruction. But this fear would not be as strong in the case of weaponless deterrence, due to the long series of steps involved in the rebuilding process before retaliation could occur. Given the extra steps, the opponent is more likely to believe that the escalatory process initiated by its aggression could be arrested prior to its own destruction. This belief is less likely under mutual assured destruction, where the process from initial aggression to destruction could be very short. The weaker the fear of inevitable escalation, the weaker noncrisis stability. Thus, lengthening the nuclear fuse through the abolition of nuclear weapons, while it has an advantage in terms of accidental-war stability, has serious disadvantages in terms of crisis and noncrisis stability. Nuclear war might be more likely in a world of hostile or potentially hostile nations where nuclear weapons had been abandoned.

This rough comparison provides at least some reason for thinking that nuclear deterrence with weapons is to be preferred over weaponless deterrence on consequentialist grounds. If so, then the abandonment of nuclear weapons would not resolve the moral paradox, even temporarily. The conflict between the two moral perspectives would remain. The principle of discrimination would continue to favor abandonment of the weapons and the consequentialist perspective would continue to favor their retention.

ADVANCES IN TECHNOLOGY

During the Cold War, a ballistic missile defense that would be sufficiently effective (even in conjunction with counterforce weapons) to put an end to the condition of MAD was not technologically feasible. There is little reason to think that that has changed, despite the technological advances over the past two decades. Of course, missile defenses might be adopted for other strategic purposes, but they would put an end to the paradox and alter the fundamentals of the moral debate only if they could put an end to MAD. Because of the near-perfection that would be required of a defensive system for it to be able to remove the other side's capacity for assured destruction, it seems clear that the technological advances that have been made are not up to the job. This is especially clear in the light of the ability of the offense to adopt countermeasures to thwart the defenses. Here, too, then, the paradox still holds and moral debate remains primarily unchanged.

But, while defenses cannot overcome the condition of MAD, they have important moral consequences given what would be inevitably deployed within a MAD condition. Extensive defenses that are less than near-perfect, as defenses would certainly be, are morally objectionable because they would decrease stability, especially crisis stability. If nuclear adversaries have extensive defenses, and a crisis occurs, each side may fear that the other side is contemplating a first strike. Each side may believe that its defenses create a significant advantage from striking first, or believe that the other side is thinking this. Either belief could, in a crisis, make it much more likely that one or the other side would initiate war. Defenses could make war more likely.

So where does this all leave us? What is living and what is dead in nuclear ethics? The end of the Cold War has changed nothing fundamental about nuclear ethics. The most basic feature of nuclear ethics, the moral paradox, remains unsolved. The paradox is inherent in the weapons themselves, not in any particular geopolitical situation. The end of the Cold War may have provided a temporary resolution of the paradox with the ending of the MAD relationship between the United States and the former Soviet Union. But, the paradox is waiting to reemerge with the coming again of military hostility between nuclear powers. It is there in the weapons and in our knowledge of how to construct them.

The end of the Cold War should help us to realize the fuller moral implications of our nuclear situation. From a moral point of view, the historical arrival of MAD in the early '60s radically changed international politics. Once MAD came into being, nuclear ethics took on the basic shape it continues to have. This is why the '60s debate was so like the '80s debate, and why both are like the debate on nuclear ethics that we should be having today.

POLICY IMPLICATIONS

From the moral point of view, this conclusion seems pessimistic, even fatalistic. It tells us that there may be nothing we can do to solve the moral quandary in which our technological ingenuity has placed us. Because nuclear weapons cannot be disinvented, the moral paradox of nuclear deterrence cannot be solved. If there is nothing we can do to escape the paradox, there is nothing we should do to escape it. But our situation may be understood in terms of a religious metaphor. In Christian theology, human beings are fallen creatures, having lost their moral innocence with the eating of the apple in the Garden of Eden, with no way to recover that innocence. Likewise, there is a kind of moral innocence we lost with the development of nuclear weapons. From now on, there will be no way for us to conduct our military activities free from the stain of that original sin. We are stuck in the moral paradox.

But in the religious metaphor, our fallen state does not destroy our ability nor preclude our obligation to make moral choices. In fact, awareness of our fallen state is a prerequisite for making effective moral choices. So it is with us in our nuclear fallen state. That we cannot solve the moral paradox does not mean that we cannot make moral improvements in our nuclear world, and understanding the paradox is necessary for the effectiveness of the moral choices we are called upon to make. The possibility of our making moral improvements despite our being mired in the paradox is shown by the distinction between solving the paradox, which is not possible, and temporarily resolving the paradox, which is. The moral direction before us is to work to establish the most enduring temporary resolution of the paradox that we can. To this end, we must be as clear as possible about the nature of the paradox.

So, what are the policy implications? The paradox is temporarily resolved when there is an absence of hostility between states that have nuclear weapons or are capable of building them. So, obviously, we should work to create and sustain an absence of hostility. But, what is the role, if any, of nuclear disarmament in this process? We have seen that nuclear disarmament pursued for its own sake may result in little or no moral improvement. From a moral perspective, we need to understand disarmament not as an end, but as a means to the reduction of hostilities.

Mutual nuclear arms reductions can promote and reinforce warming relations between nuclear powers, both symbolically and substantially. Substantially, they allow each side to convince the other of its nonhostile intentions. Symbolically, they serve as a signal of the warming relationship and provide ceremonial occasions at which the improving relationship can be publicly affirmed. But nuclear arms reductions are not a panacea. They cannot guarantee better relations and in some respects they may have a negative impact. For example, arms reduction may weaken the "nuclear umbrella" of extended deterrence and so increase the likelihood of nuclear proliferation. In addition, when the numbers of weapons decrease below levels necessary to sustain MAD, the kinds of stability problems with complete nuclear disarmament discussed earlier can arise. For example, considering noncrisis stability, the risk of conventional war can be greater when nuclear weapons are below MAD levels or completely eliminated.

But these cautions simply reinforce the point that nuclear disarmament is not to be sought for its own sake. The moral demand that we establish a temporary resolution of the paradox requires that we attempt to do what will bring about such a resolution, which is to lessen hostility. To the extent that reductions in nuclear arms promote this, they should be sought for that reason, and they should be sought in a way that does the most to lessen hostilities. (Part of the value of the reductions is the negotiation process that leads to them.) As hostilities lessen, as relations between formerly hostile nuclear powers move closer to the end of the hostility spectrum currently represented by the relations between the United States and Great Britain, the stability disadvantages of CND discussed earlier become less serious.

The policy implications of the argument could be expressed in this way. We should seek mutual nuclear disarmament, not for the sake of getting to low numbers or zero, but for the sake of reducing hostility to the point where there would be little or no loss of stability in complete elimination of the weapons. When such a state comes to be, the consequentialist objections to nuclear disarmament grow less, and CND can be sought for its own sake, in our efforts to bring our military policy into line with the principle of discrimination. When an end of hostility is combined with the elimination of the weapons, the strongest temporary resolution of the paradox will have been achieved. We should seek nuclear disarmament not for the sake of getting to zero, but for the sake of ending hostility, and thereby creating the conditions under which getting to zero will become a moral demand not in substantial conflict with other moral demands.

The Bush administration proposes that the United States build extensive missile defenses while reducing the number of nuclear weapons. The moral rationale for each of these can be seen in our earlier arguments. Each may be a way of seeking to move beyond MAD, although the proposals are not presented in these terms. According to the administration, we do not need to move beyond MAD with Russia because, since we are no longer military opponents, we are no longer in a MAD relationship. In addition, the stated purpose of the missile defenses is not removing the assured destruction capacity of Russia, but countering a potential missile threat from "rogue states."

Nonetheless, the proposals can be faulted for ignoring the fundamental policy implication of seeking to reduce hostilities with adversarial or potentially adversarial nuclear powers. First, the building of defenses is likely to increase the level of hostility between the United States and Russia, as the initial Russian reaction to the plans indicates. Russia fears that the defenses are the first step in a more elaborate plan that would seek to nullify its capacity for assured destruction. Second, the administration has chosen to pursue its proposals in a way that downplays or undermines the tradition of negotiation between the two nuclear powers. The weapons reductions, according to administration statements, will be enacted unilaterally, and the building of the defenses will require the abrogation of one of the most significant fruits of the past negotiation process, the Anti-Ballistic Missile Treaty. Thus, the administration's proposals would tend to increase hostilities, or at least to squander the opportunity that further negotiations would provide to lessen them.

There is an additional moral concern about the administration's proposals. Under MAD, as mentioned earlier, defenses are morally objectionable because they tend to decrease stability and make nuclear war more likely. The administration would respond that MAD no longer exists and, in any case, that the defenses are directed at the rogue states, with whom the United States is not in a MAD relationship. But, as we argued, the United States may still be in a MAD relationship with Russia, and even if it is not, the MAD relationship will return in a different historical instantiation. If it returns in a situation in which extensive missile defenses have been developed, it will return in a less stable form. This is why there is value to preserving the Anti-Ballistic Missile Treaty, even if it is true that the United States and Russia are not currently in a MAD relationship.

For the future, we can say that if we are lucky, we may be graced with a future free of nuclear war. But such an eventuality, like grace in the religious sense, will come to us only if we work hard at bringing about what moral progress we can in our fallen state of unavoidable and intractable moral paradox.

NOTES

1. My efforts to answer this question in this paper have benefited greatly from comments on an earlier draft by members of the working group on "Ethics and the Future of International Conflict" sponsored by the Carnegie Council on Ethics and International Affairs and the National War College. Especially helpful were a commentary by John Langan and written comments by Martin Cook, Frances Harbour, Thomas Keaney, and Paul Zimmerman. Matt Mattern provided valuable editorial suggestions.

2. The text of this speech, from which my quotations are taken, was found at the Web site of the Department of State <http://www.usinfo.state.gov>.
3. A signal indication of this is the statement issued several years ago by sixty retired high-ranking military officials calling for complete nuclear disarmament. See "Statement on Nuclear Weapons," *Washington Quarterly* 20, no. 3 (summer 1997), pp. 125–130.
4. How one characterizes that debate will, of course, depend on where one stood in the sharp battles of that era. But the following characterization, I believe, captures some basic points shared by a broad cross section of the debate's participants.
5. See Steven Lee, *Morality, Prudence, and Nuclear Weapons* (Cambridge: Cambridge University Press, 1993), Chapter 2.
6. Some of the theorists argued for counterforce capabilities, including missile defenses, not in order to overcome MAD, which they recognized as a permanent feature, but in order to allow for a stronger, more credible form of nuclear deterrence within MAD. But these arguments, in accepting the existence of MAD, involved no prospect of escaping from the moral paradox.
7. For a discussion of the moral issues raised by proliferation, see Steven Lee, "Nuclear Proliferation and Nuclear Entitlement," *Ethics & International Affairs* 9 (1995), pp. 101–131.
8. This is complicated somewhat by the question of whether a newly proliferating state would have an assured destruction capacity. Some theorists, such as Kenneth Waltz, have argued that such a capacity is very easy to obtain, since it requires only a small number of weapons. But even if the state does not immediately have an assured destruction capacity, its early nuclear weapons would almost certainly not be counterforce weapons, due to the greater technological sophistication they involve. Hence, its nuclear threats would be immoral even short of an assured destruction capacity.
9. Some of the material that follows is adapted from Chapter 8 of my *Morality, Prudence, and Nuclear Weapons* (Cambridge: Cambridge University Press, 1996).
10. Jonathan Schell, *The Abolition* (New York: Avon Books, 1986).
11. Schell, *The Abolition*, pp. 181–184.
12. Schell, *The Abolition*, pp. 206, 207.

LIVING WITH CHEMICAL AND BIOLOGICAL WEAPONS

FRANCES V. HARBOUR

George Mason University

As the previous chapter suggested, the United States will have to deal with the political, military, and ethical implications of nuclear weapons for the foreseeable future; nuclear knowledge cannot be eradicated and therefore all of us need to think as rationally as possible about future nuclear policy.[1] Similar conclusions also apply to chemical and biological weapons (CBW). CBW will be with us for the foreseeable future. Indeed, considerations related to ease of manufacture and delivery make their spread even more likely than that of nuclear weapons. Here, too, we need to think through the implications of our own future policy and responding to the threat of use by others. As with nuclear weapons, arms control is an important component of management of present and future threats.

Eschewing chemical and biological weapons is desirable from an ethical perspective, especially the perspective of the Western just war tradition. The most lethal forms of biological weapons, such as those bearing anthrax or botulism, are so destructive of human life that their use is almost certain to fall on the wrong side of any relatively objective analysis of moral costs and benefits. Even the less dangerous forms of biological and chemical weapons, such as Western encephalitis or mustard gas, can easily lead to morally questionable behavior because of their potential effects on noncombatants. And because of the strong cognitive connection we have made between the various forms of chemical and biological weapons, possessing or using even nonlethal CBW offers a serious danger of starting down a slippery slope to ethically unacceptable behavior.

Because chemical and biological weapons will be with us for the foreseeable future, we need to take seriously the question of what to do in the event of an eventual attack on the battlefield or by terrorists, and how to deter such an attack. Because these are real dangers, we need to think clearly in advance about the ethics as well as the strategy of our response. Both as a deterrent and to mitigate any attack that does come we ought certainly to continue to improve defenses and the intelligence capability to track potential terrorism. A further step seems necessary, however. Uncritically accepting every form of chemical and biological weaponry as a full member of a single class hides crucial differences between weapons and among classes of weapons that are both morally and practically significant. Whether we call the category weapons of mass destruction, or nuclear, biological, and chemical (NBC) weapons, or even CBW, differences between and among chemical weapons and biological weapons mean that a "one size fits all" discussion is not appropriate. Forgetting this increases the chances that policymakers may select a highly disproportionate response to the less destructive forms of chemical and biological weapons and strengthens the hands of potential proliferators.

THINKING THROUGH THE ETHICAL IMPLICATIONS OF USING CBW

There is a widely held sense that it is peculiarly wrong to use chemical and biological weapons in war. This emotional reaction is so strong that is has sometimes been called a "taboo."[2] The revulsion may also provide at least part of the explanation for why this relatively simple technology has not been more widely developed and used. It is almost certainly a part of why countries were willing to adopt the Geneva Protocol of 1925, the Chemical Weapons Convention of 1993 (CWC),[3] and the Biological Weapons Convention of 1972 (BWC).[4] In the Geneva Protocol of 1925 parties give up the use in war of either chemical or biological weapons.[5] This promise was extended in content and range through the CWC. In the CWC, 144 countries have promised that they will not manufacture, store, or use any chemical weapons (CW) even in response to a chemical attack by another. The BWC, which has 143 parties, contains similar promises against possession and use of biological weapons (BW).[6] Although vocal critics of CBW arms control remain active—including some in the United States—the vast majority of the countries in the world have thus decided to eschew the legal right to possess and use chemical and biological weapons.

In spite of this widely held view, the more closely one examines chemical and biological weapons, the more complicated evaluating their possession and use becomes. At the simplest level, moral strictures against CW and BW raise questions because keeping enemy military forces from accomplishing their purposes is, after all, central to what war is all about. Once war has begun, and within some limits, killing and wounding combatants by whatever means is available has been regarded as at least potentially acceptable, except by pacifists. It is not obvious that killing by poison, asphyxiation, short circuit of the nervous system, or deliberately implanted disease would be worse, morally or practically, than being torn apart by high explosives. Another source of ethical ambiguity is the multiplicity of weapons we consider members of the category CBW. Indeed, looking closely at chemical and biological weapons makes it clear that there are such great differences among their effects that it is surprising that we have put them in the same category at all.

The methodology for considering the ethics of a particular kind of weapon is not as well developed as that for evaluating the ethics of participating in a war, or even of evaluating tactics and strategy. Indeed, as both the nuclear and land mines debates demonstrate, much of the ethical debate about specific weapons that has occurred simply extend frameworks developed for examining war fighting.

The Western just war tradition provides the ethical framework for this chapter, although it also includes insights drawn from utilitarian traditions. This chapter will draw primarily on the *jus in bello* criteria of proportionality, discrimination, and double effect. This approach suggests that arms whose scale of destruction is too extensive to balance, those that are suitable only or primarily for use on noncombatants, or ones that are almost certain to cause an unacceptable level of collateral harm to noncombatants deserve condemnation. Chemical and biological weapons raise clear ethical problems for policymakers under a just war framework whether we are considering possessing and possibly using them ourselves, or responding to CBW threats by others.

WHAT ARE CHEMICAL AND BIOLOGICAL WEAPONS?

The Geneva Protocol of 1925 forbade the use in war of "chemical and bacteriological weapons" that kill or harm by asphyxiation "or similar" means.[7] Since then the term chemical weapon (CW) usually implies asphyxiating, choking, tear, nerve, and blood agents. This somewhat ambiguous conception was clarified in the Chemical Weapons Convention. The Convention provides explicit lists of regulated or forbidden toxic chemical compounds and their precursors. At present, the term chemical weapon does not include chemical agents such as napalm whose primary effect is burning the objects to which it sticks, or some of the projected products of the chemistry lab for the twenty-first century that have been nicknamed "superglues" or "superlubricants." (These reportedly will have the effect of preventing or slowing mobility by the enemy.) The current lists do include some gases and aerosol suspensions that are not usually directly lethal to humans, such as certain forms of tear gas, disorienting or nauseating agents that are inhaled, and herbicides used for warfare. Biological weapons (BW) are weapons that utilize living organisms (such as viruses, bacteria, algae, fungi, or spores) and toxins (the toxic chemical products of living organisms). Anthrax, smallpox, botulism, and ariatoxin are frequently mentioned as potential biological weapons materials.

In linking chemical and biological weapons, and associating both with nuclear weapons, a central reality of chemical and biological weapons is not accorded enough attention. It is significant in both ethical and strategic terms that the effects of chemical and biological weapons vary widely in terms of scale. Not only are chemical weapons much less lethal than biological (and nuclear) weapons, but different agents within even these narrower rubrics have very different characteristics from each other, only some of which are obviously problematic.

The most destructive biological weapons are the deadly, epidemic-bearing biological agents such as anthrax spores. Unlike conventional arms, CW, or even nuclear weapons, many such disease agents are not self-limiting. Thus they can multiply and spread far beyond the area of exposure. The greatest danger would be a plague that those who unleashed it could not control. So, too, there are persistent reports of governments and other groups working on so-called "designer plagues" to increase the lethality of diseases that occur in nature—and to tailor new organisms to disrupt living systems in unprecedented ways.

Even with existing technology, the high-end biological agents have casualty ranges that overlap with, and may sometimes exceed, nuclear arms. For example, a 1993 Office of Technology Assessment Study suggested that one aircraft delivering 100 kilograms of anthrax spores over Washington, D.C., could kill as many as 3,000,000 people within a few weeks.[8]

But not all biological weapons would be so devastating. Western encephalitis virus, for example, has such a low mortality rate that some experts feel that its intended purpose should be considered incapacitation rather than death.[9] So, too, toxins produced by biological processes have markedly less destructive capacity than the most dangerous live agents, and no ability to spread on their own. This difference is so marked that although toxins produced by biological organisms are legally considered among biological weapons, and the Biological Weapons Convention explicitly covers them, a number of critics argue that this conjunction is a serious conceptual error with important political consequences.[10]

Chemical weapons, too, vary widely in their effects. There are, for example, militarily significant CW agents that are not intended to be lethal to humans at all. Herbicides, special tear gases, and even mind-altering substances can have military uses such as opening up terrain, driving people out of hiding places, and making combatants behave erratically. (The U.S. government resisted calling the nonlethal agents chemical weapons into the 1990s, but most other governments have done so since the 1920s.)

Even with lethal CW there are two important distinctions in terms of scale of effects. The first is the length of time after CW is released until it dissipates. Some CW agents gain their main effect by persisting in an area one wishes to deny to the enemy, while other forms of CW clear away quickly. Obviously, the effects of persistent weapons are multiplied by their longer period of effectiveness. An even more important distinction is between nerve agents and less sophisticated chemical weapons, especially choking and blister agents. Choking and blister agents were developed and widely used during World War I, and because of their ease of manufacture and use are still reportedly in the arsenals of a number of states. Nerve agents are much more lethal and require sophisticated storage capabilities.[11] Stout khaki plus a head mask and hood can defend the wearer against mustard gas, the most effective of the World War I agents. Nerve agents require an air-tight protective suit and headgear or a completely air-filtered environment for protection.[12]

Choking and blister agents do not raise the same specter of large-scale casualties as does nerve gas. The former produce large numbers of deaths and other casualties only against unprotected or badly trained soldiers—and against civilians. The relative simplicity of the defenses against these agents means that death and even long-term incapacity can largely be prevented on the battlefield. For example, U.S. soldiers were far from fully protected against chemical attack when they entered World War I, but official records show that only about 2 percent of all American casualties were attributed to poison gas, and that all but a tiny proportion of CW casualties in the American Expeditionary Force represented incapacity, not death.[13] For those who do receive injury we must certainly add the painful aftereffects. Yet, the ability to almost completely prevent these effects means protected military personnel are far more likely to experience inconvenience and discomfort than permanent harm of any sort. Even nerve agents can, with proper equipment and training, be significantly reduced as a lethal threat. Unprotected people, on the other hand, whether soldiers or civilians, do have a very high casualty rate, as the Iranians and Iraqi Kurds found in the Iran-Iraq War.[14]

There are thus at least three, and, arguably, four distinct levels of destructiveness associated with chemical and biological weapons. Weapon of mass destruction is an appropriate title for the most destructive biological agents, including anthrax, botulism, and designer plagues. Chemical nerve agents, though far less lethal than the high-end biological weapons, also raise issues of scale that might or might not lead them to be categorized as junior members of this most destructive class. But mustard gas, phosgene, and Western encephalitis are only a few of the "CBW" agents that are actually less lethal than conventional weapons, let alone nuclear weapons or designer plagues. And tear gas, herbicides, and mind-altering chemicals are seldom lethal at all, except in very unusual concentrations and for the most vulnerable members of society.

ISSUES OF SCALE

At the high end of the lethality scale, the weapons offer significant ethical problems related to scale. In the middle range, especially the World War I–era chemical weapons, what is most significant in moral terms is the seductive temptation to use them deliberately on noncombatants—and the near certainty of extremely high collateral harm to noncombatants when the weapons are used near a city, town, or village. And at the lowest end of the lethality scale, the real ethical problem lies with their association with the more lethal forms of chemical, biological, and even nuclear weapons. For both the middle- and low-end chemical and biological weapons we have put ourselves in a position where the escalation ladder is unnecessarily short, and dangerously slippery.

In terms of sheer scale of destructiveness, anthrax, botulism, or genetically altered plagues would cause so much harm to military forces and civilians alike that it is extremely difficult to imagine any proportionality—or utility—analysis coming out in their favor, even assuming their use did not escape control entirely. For example, one analyst estimates that a single ballistic missile with a 1-tonne throw weight, armed with a warhead containing anthrax spores could kill 20,000–80,000 people.[15] Both the just war tradition's proportionality and utilitarian's maximum happiness principles require the ethical value of using a weapon be in balance with its moral costs. Because of their scale, any justification for the use of such deadly weapons would have to be in similar terms as strategic nuclear weapons, and would be as controversial.

For just war thinkers, the negative ethical implications of these most-lethal forms of BW are further magnified by the fact that disease-bearing BW would be extremely difficult to use to affect the course of a battle—except to force the other side into CBW-protective gear. Indeed, the need for an incubation period and relatively unpredictable short-term effects were among the factors that led negotiators in the early 1970s to conclude that a Biological Weapons Convention without verification procedures was politically and militarily feasible.[16] Because of the difficulty of protecting against their spread, even strategic uses of BW against the homeland of another country could not be meaningfully directed solely, or even primarily, at military targets.

As noted earlier, lethal chemical weapons fall somewhere in between the biological plagues and nonlethal CBW in terms of scale. Fetter estimates, for example, that the single missile in the earlier example, this time armed with a payload containing the nerve agent sarin, could still kill as many as 3,000 people.[17] Assuming multiple missiles or less conventional modes, the consequences here, too, could be severe enough to raise questions about finding a cause that could balance the huge moral costs.

NONCOMBATANT VULNERABILITY

From the perspective of the just war tradition, except for really massive use of herbicides,[18] for most chemical agents and the less lethal forms of biological weapons the absolute *scale* of harm is not usually the source of ethical problems. For just war thinkers the most serious problem with this group of weapons is CBW's special effectiveness against civilians. The principle of discrimination is, of course, as applicable to chemical and biological weapons as any other kind of military technology. A deliberate chemical or biological attack on noncombatants is thus ethically unacceptable under the just war tradition. Chemical and biological weapons raise unique ethical problems, however, because of the *particular* vulnerability of certain classes of civilians to CBW, combined with our ability to protect members of the armed forces. CW—and to a lesser extent BW—actually possesses a quality of, in effect, picking out noncombatants while leaving combatants relatively safe. In the following paragraphs I focus on the effects of the nerve agent sarin, though the same factors are relevant to other chemical and biological weapons.

Let us start with a statistic. Reportedly, a well-trained, well-protected, young-adult male soldier has only a 1 to 8 percent chance of being killed in an attack using the nerve agent sarin. Civilian deaths, on the other hand, are likely to be 50 to 90 percent of those within range. The higher figure is regarded as more likely, even in a military-oriented attack.[19]

Vulnerability of civilians stems from a number of interrelated causes. First and foremost, they are far less likely than military forces to be provided with even rudimentary protective equipment or to know how to use anything they do receive effectively. Even for the military, substantial training is required in order to utilize the equipment efficiently.[20] Other factors increase the vulnerability of noncombatants. Infants, children, the very old, and women are, on average, biologically more susceptible to injury and death from toxic agents of all kinds than are healthy young-adult males.[21] Moreover, although tightly closed houses and other buildings provide considerable short-term protection from chemical attack, they must be well ventilated as soon as a chemical cloud passes, or within a few hours they will become traps for seeping air-borne chemicals. Once an agent has penetrated a building, it will persist there far longer than out in the open where wind, heat, and rain can dissipate it. Streets and alleyways are similarly better protected from the elements and thus prone to lingering pockets of lethal danger.[22] The particular suitability for killing unprotected women and children and the elderly presents a strong temptation to do so, as the Iraqi campaigns against the Kurds illustrate. This snare may be especially difficult to resist as the military implications of effective protective gear for enemy troops becomes apparent.

This argument is not directly affected by the issue of scale. So even if the numbers killed or harmed with sarin—or even mustard gas—would be far lower than those who would be affected by inflicting anthrax on a population, even the less destructive weapons possess a quality that raises ethical problems, especially for just war thinkers. If used near noncombatants, chemical weapons, in effect, select those noncombatants for harm in a way that is not shared by either nuclear or conventional weapons. This raises the level of collateral harm to noncombatants in a singularly sinister fashion.

The peculiar vulnerability of civilians is somewhat reduced for biological weapons. BW is much more difficult to protect against than CW, even for the military. This reduces the *differential* between the effects on combatants and at least adult male noncombatants. The problem of trapping lethal substances in homes, streets, and alleys, as well as the special biological vulnerability of those we would most like to protect (i.e., children, infants, and the elderly) would, however, remain. So, too, the limited battlefield utility of BW, at least in the short run, could make using it on civilians appear the most efficient use of the weapons in strategic terms.

The special effectiveness for use on civilians is especially troubling since the practical and psychological constraints against the use of CBW more generally may be at their weakest in conflicts already putting civilians in special danger: terrorist attacks or a bloody ethnic war at some distance from one's own home. Living closely together with the enemy would, of course, reduce the practical desirability of CBW in many cases of ethnic conflict, but it is not hard to imagine chemical or biological warfare as part of a campaign of "ethnic cleansing" in a territory one wished to reclaim. Nonlethal forms could provide frightening harassment, and lethal forms a more chilling and final solution.

Dehumanization of the enemy is always a moral danger in war. In terrorism and ethnic warfare, combatants are especially prone to dehumanize their enemies, to view killing and harm to any member of the targeted group as "extermination," not wrongful war against noncombatants. And we know from history that use of chemical weapons has frequently been accompanied by speeches characterizing the enemy as insects, rodents, or as mere pests. As an Iraqi major general put it in 1984 when explaining why gas would be used on Iranian soldiers the next day, the Iranians were "insects who need to be exterminated."[23]

STARTING DOWN THE SLIPPERY SLOPE

One of the dangers of concealing the differences between types of chemical biological weapons is heightening the risks of escalation. If we gloss over morally and practically important differences under the politicized label of "weapons of mass destruction" we are strengthening the psychological and political link between them both in ourselves and in our adversaries. The slippery slope argument is politically strong enough to be responsible for a provision in the CWC forbidding the use of even nonlethal chemical agents in war. It is hard to argue on any other grounds against using a non-persistent, low-casualty, incapacitating agent such as CS or CN tear gas to rescue troops stranded behind enemy lines, for example. Such a tactic not only offers the chance to bring home one's own people with no lasting harm, but might even reduce casualties to the enemy. Analysts who object even to this minimal use of chemical weapons mainly base their arguments on the dangers of taking the first step on a "slippery slope" to all-out use.[24]

How are we to evaluate the slippery slope argument? On the one hand, escalation does not happen by itself. It is not a law of physics or even an iron law of psychology. There is no good evidence, for example, that the United States used lethal chemical weapons in Vietnam even though it did use nonlethal ones. (The 1998 CNN-Time Magazine charges to the contrary evaporated under close scrutiny of independent experts and were rescinded.)

On the other hand, the history of chemical warfare does show progress from small-scale to large-scale use. World War I went from a few clumsy canisters of chlorine gas, to gas hand grenades, to extensive use of phosgene and mustard gas artillery shells. During the Vietnam War, the United States evidently began applying CS and CN tear gas in order to force mixed groups of civilians and combatants out from underground bunkers and caves. The measure allegedly was designed to give Americans an added measure of discrimination, an alternative to simply blowing up the whole bunker. Reportedly, however, this minimal use was soon replaced by a much more extensive and systematic application of force. The tear gas was used to empty the bunkers and then all who emerged were barraged indiscriminately with conventional weapons.[25] And it is clear that the success of the initial mustard gas attacks on Iranian soldiers during the Iran-Iraq war (and the lack of marked international outcry) emboldened Saddam Hussein's forces to expand their attacks to include nerve agents, and later to use the nerve agents on recalcitrant Kurdish civilians in Iraq.

History seems to show that the slippery slope argument has real empirical plausibility. Thus even the least lethal chemical and biological weapons carry with them a clear risk of escalation, especially in a world that has a tendency to treat nuclear, chemical, and biological weapons as a homogeneous category.

There are other important ethical considerations that strongly counsel against using even nonlethal agents. For example, using chemicals to destroy civilian food crops raises issues of discrimination.[26] So, too, the decades-long debate over the long-term effects of Agent Orange, one of the herbicides used in Vietnam, reminds us not only that unintended effects may not be limited to the enemy, but of the difficulty of knowing with any certainty the full range of consequences of applying toxic substances.[27]

It is far too likely that the moral costs of using chemical or biological weapons would end up being very high indeed. If nothing else, the scale of harm that the most deadly biological weapons can inflict and their potential for uncontrollable spread means that these weapons are almost certain to violate an impartial evaluation. The unique vulnerability of noncombatants to deadly chemical weapons and the practical impossibility of vaccinating against all plausible biological threats raises questions even in cases when the number of people killed would lie in the same range as conventional arms. We certainly do not want to encourage the possession of morally seductive weapons that in effect pick out noncombatants while leaving the protected combatant less efficient but basically hale. And when the other parties own more CBW—or nuclear weapons—even nonlethal chemical and biological weapons offer the specter of conflict spiraling out of control.

In other words, the CWC, BWC and other counterproliferation measures can make the possession and use of chemical and biological weapons less likely according to a just war evaluation. These treaties do so by reducing the political legitimacy of CBW, raising the political costs of possession and use, and making it more difficult in practical terms to acquire chemical and biological weapons. Unfortunately, however, critics are correct in arguing that these treaties cannot completely eliminate the strategic or ethical dangers of chemical and biological weapons.

Verification remains a major problem for the CWC, Geneva protocol, and BWC. The elaborate three-tiered verification regime in the Chemical Weapons Convention is the most intrusive ever attempted in an arms control treaty. Perhaps not surprisingly, however, countries have not been willing to pay the considerable financial costs for maintaining this level of vigilance, and many have not fully complied with reporting and inspections provisions found in the treaty.[28] The Geneva Protocol and BWC, by contrast, do not contain verification provisions. In large measure the no-first-use aspect of the Geneva Protocol lends itself at least to the cold comfort of *post hoc* verification. In the case of the BWC, however, longstanding negotiations have finally led to a complex and lengthy Chairman's Text on verification. The Chairman's text was offered in March 2001 to the treaty's Ad Hoc Committee, and has been proposed for consideration at the convention's five-year review conference in 2002. The changes would provide new, formal verification procedures for possession and manufacture of BW and an organization similar to that which monitors the CWC. The Bush administration is not currently supporting the amendments as the U.S. government has indicated that it is concerned that undetected violations could too easily slip through the proposed new net.[29]

Arms control treaties, export controls, and other nonproliferation activities make it harder to acquire materials to make or weaponize lethal chemical or biological agents. Because of funding and other limits on inspection in the CWC and questions about the proposed new verification procedures in the BWC, however, neither treaty can guarantee results, even among signatories. The world's continuing experience with Iraqi efforts to acquire chemical, nuclear, and perhaps biological weapons shows other holes in the nonproliferation regime.[30] This means we need to prepare for the use of chemical or even biological weapons by others. This might take the form of an attack on U.S. forces in the course of a war or humanitarian intervention. It might take the form of a terrorist attack on civilians at home or abroad. Because World War I–era choking and blister agents are considerably simpler to produce, store, and deliver than the more deadly forms CBW, we need to be especially prepared to deal with them. How then should national leaders respond if another country or a terrorist group uses chemical or biological weapons against us? How should we try to deter them from doing so? Here again, the just war tradition can offer counsel.

IMPROVING DEFENSES AND INTELLIGENCE CAPABILITIES

The arguments outlined earlier suggest that, other things being equal, reducing the chances that the most destructive forms of chemical and biological weapons would be used on civilians and even on military personnel would be a good thing in moral as well as practical terms. Since better defenses and more extensive intelligence-gathering capabilities could contribute to this goal, acquiring them would be a moral good. The main issue here would be proportionality. Can the good obtained balance any harm the means may unintentionally cause?

It is difficult to know just how many countries have or are working on the capacity to possess chemical and biological weapons. The United States, France, Russia, India, and Pakistan have acknowledged possession or recent possession of chemical weapons under the provisions of the CWC. U.S. officials reportedly believe that nearly a dozen other countries also have chemical weapons programs. This list includes Ethiopia, Iran, Syria, Israel, Egypt, Libya, Myanmar, Vietnam, China, and North and South Korea.[31] Biological weapons programs are even more secretive than chemical weapons programs, thus estimates of the number of countries with offensive BW programs vary considerably. Reportedly, however, the Central Intelligence Agency tracks at least a dozen countries including Iran, Iraq, Libya, North Korea, and Syria.[32] Some of these countries have grievances against the United States or its allies that might someday lead to a battlefield confrontation. Equally important, some have been suspected of sponsoring terrorism at one time or another.

Although some experts question the need for extensive civil defense programs against CBW terrorism, most continue to emphasize the desirability of building on the ability of military personnel to protect themselves against CBW on the battlefield, and expanding the ability to protect against CBW terrorism at home.[33] The Bush administration is emphasizing this approach in its decision to provide a more centralized decision-making structure through a new Office of National Preparedness within the Federal Emergency Management Agency.[34] Enhancing defense is good practical as well as moral advice since all the well-documented first uses of chemical weapons in the modern era have been against ill-prepared enemies without effective defensive capabilities.

For the military, protective gear, training, state-of-the-art decontamination facilities, and better vaccination against likely BW threats would thus not only be effective for keeping damage to a minimum, but also should help deter battlefield use of CBW. Indeed, CBW defenses at home or abroad are actually stabilizing since they are a plausible deterrent to the kind of small-scale "breakout" from the chemical and biological weapons treaties that would be hardest to detect. Programs that teach and equip national guard and other emergency teams to decontaminate and—hopefully—contain a terrorist CBW attack in American cities should have a similar dual function. Additional funds for less public steps may turn out to be even more important. Detecting and sifting terrorist threats is a labor-intensive activity in intelligence organizations stretched by shrunken budgets.

An ethical objection to CBW defenses along the lines of one of the arguments against nuclear ballistic missile defense would not hold here. (This claim would take the form of a change that an increased defensive capability is really a shield for blunting an adversary's response to an intended first strike.) The answer to this charge is that in the case of chemical and biological weapons the great powers have taken or are taking steps to eliminate their ability to use CBW in a first strike or to demonstrate that they do not have such arsenals. And, in spite of technical difficulties and delay, governments around the world have already begun to destroy their chemical arsenals, and are beginning to open up chemical factories to inspection protocols. Other ways of responding to chemical and biological weapons in the hands of others are more controversial.

RESPONDING TO A CBW ATTACK

As of July 1, 2001, the administration of George W. Bush has not yet made any official pronouncements on its response to use of chemical or biological weapons against Americans by terrorists or on the battlefield. The policy that emerges, however, is likely to be closely related to the Clinton administration's policy, which, in turn, was very similar to the position of George Bush, Senior. The American approach in the past dozen years has been ambiguous, perhaps deliberately so. In the spring of 1997, for example, President Clinton assured the Senate that retaliation for a chemical attack would be "overwhelming and devastating" and that the response would draw on the whole range of weapons in the U.S. inventory."[35] Both of these phrases strongly imply that retaliation could be nuclear, but carefully refrained from saying so explicitly. At the time of the Gulf War George Bush and his team warned Saddam Hussein of an unspecified but devastating response if Iraq used CW on Americans or their allies. Since the CWC was not yet in place, some interpreted the statements to threaten retaliation in kind, that is, a chemical response to a chemical attack. Others, however, assumed that the United States meant nuclear retaliation.[36]

In thinking about what to do in the event of a CBW attack on Americans at home or abroad, the Bush administration ought to take a more nuanced approach than the two earlier administrations. In particular it ought to reconsider the policy of threatening nuclear retaliation for chemical or biological weapons attacks.

UNCERTAINTY AND THE FOG OF WAR

Responding to an act of violence with another act of violence always includes significant negative consequences in addition to whatever positive effects there are. Not least, a forceful response always includes the possibility of transforming a lesser conflict into a greater one through escalation. Projecting consequences, both positive and negative, is an important aspect of the decision of whether to use force under the just war tradition's criteria of proportionality (in the *jus ad bellum* sense) and probability of success. A just war thinker adds evaluations of the rightness of the cause and one's own intentions, as well as the standing of the decision makers to make this decision, and the extent to which other means of settling the dispute have been tried first. For utilitarians, of course, projecting consequences is how one goes about making an ethical decision, although several of the *jus ad bellum* criteria (especially pursuing a just cause) can be subsumed under a broad evaluation of all the future effects.

A key reason that the just war tradition includes the other criteria is the caution with which we must regard our ability to predict the future. Nineteenth-century military strategist Carl von Clausewitz is famous for emphasizing the role of chance and mischance in derailing our plans and strategies for war.[37] Weighing of future consequences always involves estimates and even raw guesses about effects. In the case of responding to CW attack by terrorists on a military base, for example, bombing military targets near a relevant foreign capital might shock the other side into retreat, or it might cause the levels of violence to spin out of control. The actual resolution of the crisis would depend on the capabilities and personalities on the other side. One must engage in clear-eyed speculation because the ethical implications are quite different, depending on which of these is more likely. The just war tradition does not require the ability to predict the future, but the principle of proportionality does require them to make a good faith effort to credibly project the likely effects of their actions. One also needs to consider the costs of actions that may or may not be taken several steps down the path. What will we do? What will the other side do? How much escalation will there be? When contemplating more conflict with a state—or terrorist group—possessing chemical or biological weapons in the middle and high end of the lethality scale, the range of *possible* futures increases dramatically. Uncertainty raises the stakes and directly affects our ability to reliably weigh the ethical as well as prudential considerations.

With chemical and biological weapons another kind of uncertainty must be added to these questions about projected costs. As we have already said, some forms of BW have the potential to cause casualties on a scale similar to, and under some worst-case scenarios, even greater than nuclear ones. Thus if another country used a deadly epidemic-bearing BW agent on the United States it would be breaking the peace on a major scale, but we might not be certain that someone had actually carried out a deliberate attack. An epidemic of an unusual disease might or might not be evidence of the initiation of biological warfare. West Nile Fever, carried by birds and their parasites, had never been found in the Western hemisphere before it started killing New Yorkers in the spring and summer of 1999. What if this exposure had been a deliberate attack? Would we ever have known? Similarly, uncertainty over a possibly naturally occurring toxin is the core of the debate over "Yellow Rain" during the Soviet-Afghan War in the 1980s. Was Yellow Rain the product of bee feces, as critics contend, or was it a biological weapon employed by the Soviets and their clients? And finally, even if one could be fairly sure that an illness was artificially introduced, the source might never be clear.

Chemical weapons, too, can be ambiguous. It could be possible to launch a terrorist attack without giving away the state of origin, even assuming the terrorists were acting with the concurrence of a government. So, too, as with BW, countries producing chemical weapons hide those facilities as well as they are able. Equally to the point, chemical weapons leave fewer clear traces than do conventional arms, especially if the CW agents at issue are not of the persistent varieties. It was years before the outside world was certain Iraq had used chemical weapons in the Iran-Iraq War. Although NATO forces increasingly have equipment to detect chemical attack, the Gulf War seems to have shown that this equipment can yield false positives, especially when the equipment is used by frightened or inexperienced troops. With civilians, however, or even the armed forces of many countries as the target, no detection equipment may even be on the scene. Thus with CBW we may well have to add uncertainty about the attack and the attacker to uncertainty of the effects of our response, especially in the case of terrorism.

This unusual degree of uncertainty adds a real possibility that we may be wrong about the nature of the original attack, about the attacker, about the location of production or storage facilities, about the connection between the attacker and the target. It therefore adds risk of wrongful action to the human costs we know *must* come even if our information and judgment is correct. Action based on a mistake not only puts costs on those who do not deserve them but is less likely to be successful in deterring or preventing future attacks. When weighing proportionality (or utility), uncertainty therefore adds weight to the negative side of the equation. Uncertainty alone does not forbid action, of course, but the greater the uncertainty, the greater a margin for error in our calculations of costs and benefits it should counsel. This latter concern is especially relevant when we talk about using a nuclear response to chemical or biological weapons. Justice-of-war proportionality considerations mean that we must add the very high moral costs of nuclear retaliation and the near certainty of further escalation to the other considerations related to the decision to go to war.

A NUCLEAR RESPONSE?

Countries without nuclear weapons do not have the option of making a nuclear response. But since the United States has implied the probability—or at least the possibility—of a nuclear response to a chemical or biological attack, it is important to decide whether a nuclear response would be reasonable in justice-in-war terms. A danger, both practical and moral, is that an ambiguous declaratory policy can confuse our thinking. This danger is particularly great where the weapons themselves offer complex and often contradictory challenges.

With the most lethal forms of BW, the ethical problems of retaliation and deterrence are very similar to those presented by nuclear attack and nuclear deterrence. Is it permissible to retaliate with massively lethal and potentially uncontrollable weapons as a response to the initial use of massively lethal and potentially uncontrollable weapons? Is it permissible to *threaten* to do so in order to discourage the initial attack? At such a scale of violence does targeting matter? One's conclusions about the permissibility of nuclear retaliation and an implied nuclear threat used for deterrent purposes are likely to be the same for both nuclear and high-end biological attacks.[38]

There are, however, somewhat different issues that arise as soon as we move from agents with the potential to devastate whole countries to the more limited forms of chemical and biological weaponry. From the perspective of the Western just war tradition, *nuclear* retaliation for a CW or lesser BW attack would raise serious problems under the justice-in-war aspects of the principle of proportionality.

In the just war tradition, acts of retaliation are subject to the same justice-in-war proportionality analysis as any other strategy or tactic. On the justice-in-war side, a strategic nuclear response would be disproportionate because, as we have seen earlier, middle- and lower-lethality CBW agents such as mustard gas and Western Encephalitis are nowhere nearly as deadly as strategic nuclear weapons. Even with nerve agents, however, where the casualty rates would be considerably greater than conventional weapons, the effects are still an order of magnitude lower than either nuclear arms or the high-end biological agents. Using nuclear weapons as a response to these lesser agents is starting down the road to Armageddon for a much lesser offense, even if that attack was itself morally wrong. The immediate costs and long-term risks of breaking the nuclear taboo are both well known and potentially catastrophic. Thus, only if one chose counterforce targets and kept collateral harm within extremely firm limits might the targeting as well as the scale and kinds of death and destruction fall within acceptable proportionality limits for a just war thinker.[39] And in such a case it is hard to see why a serious conventional threat would not be just as effective, and considerably less risky.

Some in the just war tradition would go even further. To these thinkers, retaliation in war is not simply "a tooth for a tooth" punishment or an act of vengeance. To be justified, they argue, retaliation must be a future-oriented action designed to prevent the opponent from undertaking *further* morally unacceptable steps, a kind of damage limitation strategy.[40] The way the CBW response policy was described by the previous Bush and Clinton administrations, however, the threat of retaliation, although motivated by a desire to deter, does not sound like damage limitation. As such, the Clinton and earlier Bush policies would not be acceptable to these ethicists.

Closely related to the problem of actual retaliation is the issue of whether one may use the possibility of doing so to try to deter a lesser CBW attack. Here we get into the relationship of intentions and actions in the just war tradition. In the just war tradition, we may not intend what we may not do. A threat is a conditional intention. "I will do X if you do Y." My will is engaged, although not yet my actions.[41] If, as I have argued, an actual nuclear response would be disproportionate, a just war approach would not advocate it. If we cannot morally carry out a nuclear threat, we ought not make it, even obliquely.

We can also apply the principle of proportionality if policymakers adjusted the nuclear threat to otherwise acceptable levels, for example with battlefield nuclear weapons or perhaps a threat to destroy only the facilities that produced or stored the CBW. Reducing the threat does not fully rescue the policy from the perspective of the principle of proportionality, however. Unlike nuclear weapons where the taboo against use has been absolute since August 1945, there is a high probability that some country or terrorist group will actually use chemical or biological weapons at some point in the foreseeable future. If we are threatening a nuclear response in such a case, this makes the long-avoided step into nuclear war considerably more likely than it would be otherwise. A severe conventional threat might not be able to deter a CBW attack either. But the increased likelihood of escalation to nuclear war is much greater with a nuclear threat in place. Here again the principle of proportionality counsels the nonnuclear option.

From a utilitarian perspective, which does not worry about the ethics of conditional intentions, there are some very attractive aspects of a policy that threatens or implies the possibility of a nuclear response to a CBW attack. Not least, if the threat works and adversaries are deterred, then no one on either side has to experience the effects of either the CBW attack or the nuclear response. Furthermore, as the Kosovo campaign showed, there are genuine advantages to not tipping one's hand in advance about self-imposed limits on the use of force. The recent history of the former Yugoslavia might have been very different if NATO leaders had not been so forthcoming about their intention not to deploy ground troops.

But here again, we are brought back to the increased risk of actually having to carry out the nuclear threat. With chemical weapons and the lesser biological agents, we must choose between two futures. Especially when we are talking about choking and blister agents, and the whole range of nonlethal CBW, the choice is stark. Surely we do not want to markedly increase the chances of a future in which we will have to live with the consequences of nuclear war—in response to a threat that is admittedly more likely, but also much less lethal.

CONCLUSION

The analysis in this chapter suggests that we should continue to resist pressures still coming from some circles to give up on our pledges under the Geneva Protocol, Chemical Weapons Convention, and Biological Weapons Convention. Although chemical and biological weapons are different from one another in crucial ways, renouncing them is, on balance, a morally sensible step. Abrogating the treaties would be a mistake in practical and moral terms. The most lethal biological weapons raise undeniable issues of scale. Even the least lethal members of either category risk escalation that runs out of control. And CBW's ability to, in effect, pick out the most vulnerable members of society invites targeting of noncombatants.

A second moral pitfall would be to forget just how incomplete our information is likely to be in cases when an adversary has used chemical and biological weapons. With use of CBW against us, there is likely to be an unusual degree of uncertainty about whether there has been attack at all, uncertainty about its source, and uncertainty about how the adversary will respond to our own retaliation. In any moral analysis carried out under the just war principle of proportionality, all this uncertainty significantly raises the chances of miscalculating and wrongful action. This high degree of risk at minimum counsels strong caution and the search for an extra margin of error in calculations.

The final warning concerns the practice of lumping all chemical and biological weapons into the same category, and then linking them with nuclear weapons under the heading of weapons of mass destruction. The first danger this raises is that our own response to a chemical or biological attack may be badly disproportionate to the offense. Chemical weapons and the lesser biological weapons are simply not on the same scale of destruction as strategic nuclear weapons, and we should not respond as if they are. In particular the implication of a nuclear policy to CBW is a dangerous policy. Linking them in this way also strengthens the hand of potential proliferators who claim to want no more than "the poor man's nuclear weapon." Do we really want to risk eroding the nuclear taboo that has held since the end of World War II by linking nuclear weapons too closely with weapons that are much more likely to be used? These concerns are certainly practical dangers, threats to national security, but their high potential price in lives moves them into the realm of moral concerns as well.

Perhaps not surprisingly, moral objections to particular weapons in history have been highest when a weapon is unconventional or new and taper off or disappear as it becomes part of the usual arsenal of war. Crossbows and submarines both received considerable criticism on ethical grounds at the time they were introduced. Crossbows were criticized as unchivalrous and too easy to use to kill even mounted and fully armored knights. When submarines sank ships, all the victims had to be left to drown, since the undersea boats could not safely surface to rescue them; nor was there space aboard to stow mere passengers, even civilians. As both crossbows and submarines became part of the regular arsenals of their time, criticism disappeared.

Chemical and biological weapons do not fit the usual pattern. A widely shared feeling that there is something wrong about using them has persisted long past the point when they were first introduced in war. Although BW has not played a significant part in any modern wars, forms of biological warfare almost certainly date back as far as the Crusades. And unlike submarines, disapproval of chemical weapons survived widespread use in World War I, technical improvements over four generations, and maintenance in modern arsenals up to the present. This suggests that there is something more to the moral distress we feel in thinking about CBW.

NOTES

1. For a related analysis, see Harvard Nuclear Study Group, Albert Carnesale et al., *Living with Nuclear Weapons* (Cambridge, MA: Harvard University Press, 1983).
2. See Richard Price and Nina Tannenwald, "Norms and Deterrence: The Nuclear and Chemical Weapons Taboo," in *The Culture of National Security: Norms and Identity in World Politics*, ed. Peter J. Katzenstein (New York: Columbia University Press, 1996), pp. 114–152.
3. The treaty is known formally as the "Convention on the Prohibition of the Development, Production, Stockpiling and Use of Chemical Weapons, and on Their Destruction."
4. The treaty is known formally as the "Convention on the Prohibition of the Development, Production, and Stockpiling of Bacteriological (Biological) Weapons and on Their Destruction."
5. So many countries legally reserved the right to respond in kind to a chemical or biological attack that this treaty might more accurately be known as a "no first use" pact. Explicit language in the CWC reminds us that the CWC is not intended to replace existing national obligations under the Geneva Protocol. See Frances V. Harbour, *Thinking About International Ethics: Moral Theory and Cases from American Foreign Policy* (Boulder, CO: Westview Press, 1999), pp. 42–59, for an extended discussion of the politics and ethics of ratifying the Geneva Protocol and CWC.
6. Ratification totals as of June 28, 2001: Stockholm International Peace Research Institute, "CWC Ratification," on-line: <http://projects.sipri.org/cbw/docs/cw-cwc-rat.html> and "BWC Ratification," <http://projects.sipri.org/cbw/docs/cw-cwc-rat.html>.
7. So many countries legally exempted responding in kind from their promises under the Geneva Protocol that many observers consider it a "no-first-use" pact.
8. U.S. Congress, Office of Technology Assessment, *Proliferation of Weapons of Mass Destruction: Assessing the Risks* (Washington, D.C.: U.S. Government Printing Office, 1993), p. 54.
9. Erhard Geissler, ed., *Biological and Toxin Weapons Today*, Stockholm International Peace Research Institute (Oxford, UK: Oxford University Press, 1986), p. 24.
10. Ibid., p. 5.
11. Specific vaccination would, however, be required against viruses. Moreover, fighting a war in a protective suit is far from ideal. In the 1980s NATO estimated that wearing full protective suits significantly reduces the military effectiveness of soldiers by 30 percent or more. In addition, suits can only be worn for a matter of hours without beginning to cause heat prostration—and proper decontamination of the protective gear is very difficult under battlefield conditions. Indeed, during the Cold War, advocates of maintaining a chemical weapons capability often cited the ability to force the Warsaw Pact armies into their rubber-skinned protective garments as the most important military effect of the weapons. See, for example, T. J. Gander, *Nuclear, Biological, and Chemical Warfare* (London: Ian Alan, 1987), pp. 77, 81; R. S. Wagner and T. S. Gold, "Why We Can't Avoid Developing Chemical Weapons," *Defense* 82 (July 1982), p. 4.
12. L. F. Haber, *The Poisonous Cloud: Chemical Warfare in the First World War* (Oxford, UK: Oxford University Press, 1986), pp. 46–47; Gander, pp. 76–91.
13. Haber, p. 243.
14. See, for example Thomas L. McNaugher, "Ballistic Missiles and Chemical Weapons: The Legacy of the Iran-Iraq War," *International Security* 15, no. 2 (fall 1990), p. 21; Gary Sick, "Moral Choice and the Iran-Iraq War," *Ethics & International Affairs* 3 (1989), p. 130.

15. Steve Fetter, "Ballistic Missiles and Weapons of Mass Destruction: What is the Threat? What Should Be Done?" *International Security* 16, no. 1 (summer 1991), p. 27. (N.B. These are deaths not over-all casualties.)

16. Matthew Meselson, "Behind the Nixon Policy for Chemical and Biological Warfare," *Bulletin of Atomic Scientists* (January 1970), p. 26.

17. Fetter, pp. 23–27.

18. John Llewallen, in *Ecology of Devastation: Indochina* (Baltimore: Penguin Books, 1971), called such a policy "ecocide."

19. Valerie Adams, *Chemical Warfare, Chemical Disarmament* (Bloomington: University of Indiana Press, 1990), p. 204.

20. United Nations, Department of Political and Security Council Affairs, *Chemical and Bacteriological Weapons and the Effects of their Possible Use: Report of the Secretary General* (New York: United Nations, 1969), p. 28; Edward M. Spiers, *Chemical Weaponry: A Continuing Challenge* (New York: St. Martin's Press, 1989), pp. 147, 151–152.

21. John Cookson and Judith Nottingham, *A Survey of Chemical and Biological Warfare* (New York: Monthly Review Press, 1969), p. 178.

22. Edward Spiers, *Chemical Warfare* (Chicago: Chicago Press, 1986), p. 9.

23. "Renewing Concern," *Sidney Morning Herald*, 31 March 1984, reprinted in *World Press Review*, June 1984, p. 40.

24. See, for example, Richard A. Finberg, "No More Chemical/Biological War," *The New Republic* 167, no. 21, pp. 17–19.

25. Edward M. Spiers, *Chemical Weaponry, A Continuing Challenge* (New York: St. Martin's Press, 1985), p. 105.

26. See, for example, Richard McCarthy, *The Ultimate Folly: War by Pestilence, Asphyxiation, and Defoliation* (New York: Vintage Books, 1969), p. 47.

27. See Frances V. Harbour, "Just War Tradition and the Use of Nonlethal Chemical Weapons during the Vietnam War," *Ethics in International Affairs: Theories and Cases*, ed. Andrew Valls (Totowa, NJ: Rowman and Littlefield, 2001) for a discussion of these issues.

28. The U.S. implementation of legislation for the CWC departs from the inspection provisions on several important dimensions. So, too, the United States is behind in its dues to the organization that monitors the treaty and conducts inspections. Judith Miller, "Chemical Weapons Ban May Suffer for Lack of Dues From Treaty's Parties," *New York Times*, 27 April 2001, p. A-7.

29. See, for example, James F. Leonard, "An Essential First Step," *Arms Control Today* (May 2001), on-line: <http://www.armscontrol.org/ACT/May2001/leonard.html> (accessed May 30, 2001).

30. Associated Press, "Russia Rejects Iraq Sanctions Plan," *New York Times*, 27 June 2001, on-line: <http://www.nytimes.com/aponline/world/AP-UN-Iraq.html?searchpv=aponline> (accessed June 28, 2001).

31. Associated Press, America Online News, "Countries Acknowledge Chemical Arms," 16 August 1997.

32. John Diamond, "CIA: Bio Weapons Threat Increasing," Associated Press, America Online News, 31 March 1999.

33. See, for example, U.S. Department of State, *Defense Department Report on Defense Transformation Study*, 12 June 2001, on-line: <http://www.usinfo.state.gov/topical/pol/arms/stories/01061201.htm> (accessed June 28, 2001).

34. *Newsday* "Better Way to Respond to Terror Attacks," 31 May 2001, p. B-9.

35. Associated Press, America Online News, "Clinton Offers Treaty Pledge," 14 February 1997, 23:51:30 EST.

36. Contemporary intelligence sources indicated that a key reason Iraq did not use CW in the Gulf War was that Saddam Hussein assumed the United States intended nuclear retaliation. (See, for example, W. Andrew Terrill, "Chemical Warfare and Desert Storm: The Disaster that Never Came," presented at International Studies Association Annual Conference, 1992.) There were chemical weapons in positions near the battlefield. For example, the Pentagon has acknowledged that Americans blew up a bunker containing sarin, thereby accidentally exposing thousands of allied troops to minute amounts of the chemical. Since the war there have been persistent reports of isolated incidents that may or may not have involved use of chemical weapons by the Iraqis, although this is denied by U.S. military sources. (See, for example, Susanne M. Schaffer, "No Chemical Weapons Evidence Found," Associated Press, America Online News, 14 August 1998). Whether any of these is true is impossible to know from the unclassified literature. Even if one or more accounts turns out to be correct, however, the incidents are so small and hard to trace that it seems unlikely that they could have been part of a decision from the top to unleash chemical warfare. Allegations that at least some elements of the

so-called Gulf War syndrome could be the result of chemical or biological attack are even harder to evaluate. A number of other explanations have been suggested for the various aspects of the complex of medical problems soldiers have experienced (including reactions to the still-experimental anthrax vaccination and to pyridostygmine bromide, a drug given as part of a defense against two nerve agents). More recent charges suggest that Gulf War syndrome may be traceable, at least in part, to the use by the allies of armor-piercing depleted uranium shells against Iraqi tanks. We can only say for certain, however, that Saddam Hussein has not claimed credit for the array of illnesses, and that the wide variety of symptoms do not correspond to the known symptoms of existing chemical or biological agents.

37. See Chapter 1, Albert C. Pierce, "War, Strategy, and Ethics" for an ethical analysis that draws on Clausewitz.

38. See Chapter 6, Steven Lee, "What's Living and What's Dead in Nuclear Ethics?" for elaboration on this point.

39. A liar on the other side might well suspect the United States of failing to tell the truth about targeting under such circumstances, but that would be a happy if unintended side effect of the claim to limit targeting.

40. John Finnis, Joseph Boyle, and Germain Grisez, *Nuclear Deterrence, Morality, and Realism* (Oxford: Clarendon Press, 1987), pp. 147–148.

41. Finis, Boyle, and Grisez offer a particularly cogent discussion of this idea; ibid., pp. 82–83.

TECHNOLOGY AND WAR

MORAL DILEMMAS ON THE BATTLEFIELD

CHARLES J. DUNLAP, JR.
Air War College

So by the benefit of this light of reason, they have found out Artillery, by which war-res come to a quicker ends than heretofore, and the great expence of bloud is avoyed; for the numbers slain now, since the invention of Artillery, are much lesse than be-fore, when the sword was the executioner.

John Donne, 1621

To a French Foreign Legionnaire reeling under murderous Viet Minh bombard-ments at the siege of Dien Bien Phu, the notion that the advent of artillery would diminish the carnage of war would seem to be the cruelest and most preposterous of ironies.[1] Yet often the introduction of new military technology is accompanied by enthusiastic predictions that the savagery of war will somehow be mitigated. All too often, however, these promises remain unfulfilled. Consider, for example, the widely held seventeenth-century belief that the invention of gunpowder made war "less horrible."[2]

Such is the faith in scientific progress. In truth, technological advances bear great responsibility for the exponential growth in the sheer destructiveness of war.[3] Fur-thermore, as the grim statistics of modern conflicts amply demonstrate,[4] much of that destructiveness falls not just upon belligerent armies and their weaponry, but in-creasingly upon noncombatants and their property.

Today we are once again seeing renewed optimism that technology might yet pro-vide relief from the nightmare of war. Recent scientific developments raise hopes that twenty-first century warfare—if not avoided altogether—might nevertheless be

The views expressed in this article are those of the author and do not necessarily represent those of the U.S. government or any of its component parts. The author would like to thank Tony Lang for his consider-able assistance with this project.

waged in a more humane manner. Much of this optimism is traceable to the Gulf War where the application of high technology seemed to minimize allied and Iraqi casualties alike. Key to this new perception of war were the widely televised images of precision-guided munitions (PGMs).[5] As one recent analysis notes[6]:

> The accuracy of PGM[s] *promises to give us a very different age; perhaps a more humane one.* It is odd to speak favorably about the *moral character of a weapon,* but the image of a Tomahawk missile slamming precisely into its target when contrasted with the strategic bombardments of World War II does in fact contain a deep moral message and meaning. War may well be a ubiquitous part of the human condition, but war's permanence does not necessarily mean that the slaughters of the twentieth century are permanent.[7]

To many, PGMs are not the only means of fulfilling the dream of more humane war. The advocates of "information operations"[8] and cyberwar[9] contend that twenty-first century conflicts can be fought virtually bloodlessly in cyberspace. In a cyberwar scenario depicted in a 1995 *Time* magazine article, a U.S. Army officer conjured up a future crisis where a technician ensconced at a computer terminal in the United States could derail a distant aggressor "without firing a shot" simply by manipulating computer and communications systems.[10] Likewise, the proponents of a growing plethora of "nonlethal"[11] technologies argue that a range of adversaries can be engaged without deadly effect.

Collectively, most experts believe these innovations reflect an ongoing "Revolution in Military Affairs" (RMA). The RMA seeks to produce radically more effective—and, as the Friedmans indicate, more humane—militaries by profoundly altering their doctrine, organization, and weaponry through the widespread application of emerging microchip-based technologies, especially advanced computer and communications' systems.[12] Many observers believe that the RMA will give the United States a virtually insurmountable military advantage for the foreseeable future.[13]

The impetus to seek technological solutions to virtually every human dilemma—even the costly viciousness of war—is quintessentially American.[14] "Yankee ingenuity" has long sought to substitute machines for manpower.[15] Unsurprisingly, therefore, the United States has enthusiastically embraced the RMA; technology has rapidly become the cornerstone of America's military planning. The U.S. military's *Joint Vision (JV) 2010*[16] furnishes "an operationally based template"[17] as to "how America's armed forces will channel the vitality and innovation of our people and *leverage technological opportunities to achieve new levels of effectiveness* in joint war fighting."[18]

All of this would seem to bode well for those concerned with the ethical conduct of war. But are new technologies unqualified virtues? In *Why Things Bite Back: Technology and the Revenge of Unintended Consequences* author Edward Tenner reminds us that technological "advances" have the nasty habit of surprising us with unexpected adverse qualities once their full import is experienced.[19] Well-intentioned efforts can paradoxically create problems worse than the ones a specific invention was meant to solve. Even generally favorable scientific developments frequently manifest "revenge effects" which at best "recomplicate" a particular task or situation.

This chapter examines the moral conundrums that arose during the 1990s. In order to focus the analysis, five interrelated issues will be examined: precision-guided missiles (PGMs), the status of noncombatants, information operations, outer space, and the threshold of conflict. These five themes all reveal the morally challenging dimensions of technology and warfare. Understanding how they have changed the battlefield will help identify those areas where more sustained normative analysis is necessary.

PRECISION-GUIDED MUNITIONS

As already indicated, PGMs[20] are considered by many as a key to more humane warfare. *JV 2010* touts "precision engagement" as a means to "lessen risk to [U.S.] forces, and [to] minimize collateral damage."[21] PGMs aim to diminish the horror of war not only because they reduce collateral damage, but also because their accuracy decreases the number of attackers required to go in harm's way to strike a given target.[22] PGMs fulfill many traditional legal and moral norms by providing a greatly enhanced capability to limit the application of force to belligerent militaries and those implements of war whose destruction is mandated by military necessity.[23] In short, unlike other high-tech armaments (e.g., nuclear weapons) that provide military advantages but political liabilities, PGMs seem to offer both military efficiency and an unparalleled opportunity to seize the moral high ground so conducive to maintaining the necessary public support for military operations.

What then might be the recomplicating effects of their use? One of these is the unpredictability of the enemy response. Among other things, we cannot expect future adversaries to be "grateful" that the United States used "humane" PGMs against them. The February 1997 issue of *Air Force Magazine* reports a startling illustration of how one potential opponent might react:

> Many Russian military theorists believe nuclear weapons provide the best answer to the challenge posed by conventionally armed precision guided munitions, which have become such an important part of Western military strategies. Russian generals fear that, in a general war, Western nations could employ such "smart munitions" to degrade Russian strategic forces, without ever having to go nuclear themselves. Consequently, said General Volkov, Russia "should enjoy the right to consider the first [enemy] use of precision weapons as the beginning of unrestricted nuclear war against it."[24]

While the risk of nuclear holocaust might be an extreme example of an unintended consequence of PGM use, there are plenty of more conventional results of great concern. For example, it has been received wisdom since the Gulf War that Iraq's firing of Kuwaiti oil fields was a monstrous environmental crime.[25] Yet the fact remains, Michael Schmitt acknowledges, that "[I]t could be argued that the fires were intended to take advantage of "weaknesses" in high-tech Coalition weapons. . . . [S]moke can foil guided munitions. Consider the difficulty, for example, of using an electro-optical guided weapon on a smoke-covered target."[26] As a matter of fact, the fires' smoke *did* degrade the effectiveness of PGMs as well as coalition intelligence-gathering satellites.[27] Michael R. Gordon and Bernard E. Trainor argue that the Iraqis torched the Kuwaiti oil fields to "erase the American's high-tech advantage."[28] Indeed, the Iraqis were able to launch one of their few offensive actions when an armored formation emerged from the smoke of the burning Burqan oil fields and struck U.S. Marines early in the ground war.[29]

As the Iraqi actions suggest, the use of PGMs might well drive adversaries—especially in less-developed nations—to employ pernicious methodologies to counteract them. It is possible, therefore, that PGM use in certain instances may render the war more, not less, destructive. If a belligerent is attacked with high-tech systems against which it lacks the ability to resist or respond in kind, does it not have the right to respond with whatever resources it has available?[30] Just because a country has the resources to develop and deploy high-tech weaponry does not *ipso facto* endow it with moral superiority over economically inferior opponents. Moreover, sheer destructiveness does not make a specific method of warfare necessarily illegal so long as the requisites of the law of armed conflict are observed.

But it is also evident that when accepted methods of defense against bombardment (e.g., hardening and battlefield dispersal) are circumvented relatively easily by the deadly accuracy of virtually unstoppable PGMs, frustrated defenders may resort to conduct clearly in violation of international norms. One such behavior may have been inspired by an unintended consequence of the Gulf War use of PGMs to destroy the Al Firdos bunker in Baghdad. Unbeknownst to coalition targeteers, that command and control facility was also being used as a shelter by the families of high Iraqi officials. The broadcast of pictures of bodies being pulled from the wreckage caused U.S. leaders—concerned about adverse public reaction to the noncombatant deaths—to virtually end further attacks on the Iraqi capital.[31] Though the decision to forego strikes on Baghdad had little effect on the outcome of the war, the *precedent* is important in the context of Tenner's "recomplicating" effect thesis. The U.S. response to the unexpected results of the Al Firdos bombing could suggest to some opponents a reliable (albeit unconscionable) method of defending against PGM attacks: Cover the target with noncombatants.[32]

Such brute behavior creates complications for combatants seeking to respect a battlefield ethic. Seeking to respect those norms makes soldiers vulnerable to tactics that aim to manipulate their innate respect for human life. For example, using human shield tactics enabled the Serbs to discourage PGM strikes by U.S. and other NATO planes by the simple expedient of chaining captured UN troops to potential targets.[33] Other nations can be similarly affected by the exploitation of noncombatants. During the war in Chechnya, for example, insurgents offset their technological inferiority by threatening civilian hostages to force the Russians to meet various demands.[34]

Several potential U.S. adversaries appear prepared to use noncombatants to blunt the power of high-tech weaponry. Libya threatened to surround the reported site of an underground chemical plant with "millions of Muslims" in order to ward off attacks.[35] When Western military action seemed imminent, Saddam Hussein inundated his palaces and other buildings with noncombatant civilians (some of whom may have genuinely volunteered) in order to discourage PGM attacks by Western forces sensitive to the effect on their publics of civilian deaths, regardless of the circumstances.[36]

All of this suggests that PGMs are no panacea. The expectations of decision makers that their employment will reduce the dangers to noncombatants may be frustrated; indeed, noncombatants could—paradoxically—be placed at *greater* risk by PGM use in some instances. In truth, the inclination of unscrupulous foes who are determined to counter technologically superior U.S. forces to revive the age-old strategy of human shields may herald a new era of barbarism in warfare. In commenting on the actions of Somali warlords who used human shields, James F. Dunnigan ominously warns that "[i]f the opponents are bloody-minded enough, they will always exploit the humanitarian attitudes of their adversaries."[37]

One argument for PGMs is that they help control costs. But cost is a two-edged sword in the context of the RMA. While computers and other information technologies often produce economies, the price of many new weapons is still quite high. PGMs are significantly more expensive than unguided "dumb" bombs.[38] This fact produces a new question for statesmen and soldiers: To what extent must a nation's people sacrifice in order to acquire systems to protect *enemy* civilians? If a relatively inexpensive artillery barrage can neutralize an enemy force notwithstanding a few noncombatant casualties, is the commander obliged to employ a costly bevy of PGMs to reduce that number to zero? It could be argued that simply having PGMs mandates their use under the theory that the commander has an available alternative that can save noncombatant lives. The accepted view, however, holds that there is no *per se* obligation to use PGMs so long as the tenets of the law of armed conflict are observed.[39] The commander can properly consider the price of the weapons as a factor in deciding the means of attack.[40]

For statesmen and soldiers, however, there is the further question of expectations raised by Gulf War videos of PGMs.[41] Undoubtedly, the perception that PGM use avoids virtually all collateral losses is something that could create a new precept in the court of world opinion. A paradigm might arise that assumes that if the United States wishes to do so, it can employ force via PGMs in any circumstance with few or no noncombatant casualties.[42]

It is the converse that statesmen and soldiers may find most vexing, that is, the perception that the *failure* to use PGMs represents a considered American decision to *cause* noncombatant deaths. If this perception comes to represent the consensus of world opinion, it is not inconceivable that international law may someday *require* PGM use (as well as other high-tech instrumentalities) by those nations with the resources to produce or acquire them.[43] At first blush such a development would appear to be morally and ethically attractive, but consider that even for wealthy nations like the United States, national budgets are zero-sum games. For each dollar spent to acquire an expensive PGM, one less dollar is available for other desirable social purposes. President Dwight Eisenhower captured this dilemma in a 1953 speech when he pointed out that:

> Every gun that is made, every warship launched, every rocket fired, signifies in the final sense a theft from those who hunger and are not fed, those who are cold and are not clothed. The world in arms is not spending money alone. It is spending the sweat of its laborers, the genius of its scientists and the hopes of its children.[44]

This raises an intriguing question: To what extent is the civilian populace of an *aggressive* belligerent entitled to the treasure of a *rightful* defender?[45] How many of the rightful defender's own people should be denied, for example, prenatal care to make resources available to procure PGMs so that if it must defend itself the danger of collateral civilian casualties in the *aggressor* state is minimized? In analyzing this question one may wish to ponder historian Daniel Boorstin's contention that Americans suffer from the "Myth of Popular Innocence," that is, the tendency to demonize enemy leaders but absolve adversary populations of responsibility in war.[46] Americans often assume that enemy societies are helpless victims of powerful tyrants—despite evidence, Boorstin contends, that "[r]ecent history proves that ruthless rulers can be removed by popular will."[47]

PGMs clearly raise a host of moral complications. While many have argued that these weapons will humanize warfare, the possible reactions of adversaries and use of noncombatants as human shields force political leaders, military planners, and analysts to think carefully about the moral implications of these weapons.

CIVILIAN COMBATANTS

Dispersing combatants and military objects into the civilian community is offensive to international law because it violates the principle that defenders have an obligation to separate military targets from civilians and their property.[48] Iraq was rightly criticized for purposely ignoring this tenet during the Gulf War.[49] But as societies become increasingly technologically integrated and, more importantly, *dependent* upon technology, separating military and civilian facilities becomes immensely more complicated, even for morally conscious statesmen and soldiers.

Largely due to budgetary pressures, the United States itself can no longer afford to maintain very many high-tech capabilities separate from those found in the civilian sector (where the cutting-edge technology often first appears[50]). Dan Kuehl worries that this "growing intermingling in the integrated information society of systems used and needed by both the military and civil sides of society . . . is making our national information infrastructure a viable, legal and ethical target in the case of conflict."[51] Nowhere is this use more extensive than in the communications' area.[52] The U.S. armed forces—like other modern militaries—relies heavily upon the civilian communications infrastructure; more than 90 percent of its messages flow through commercial channels.[53] If that system is attacked by a belligerent intent upon cutting that flow, what does its loss mean to noncombatants in today's society?

One of the most important effects of increased technology in the use of military force is the problematic commingling of military and civilian high-tech facilities is the infusion of civilians into formerly military jobs. In the past few years there has been a determined effort to convert as many military billets as possible to less expensive civilian positions.[54] For much the same reason, other efforts have attempted to privatize and outsource many functions traditionally performed by uniformed personnel. These initiatives have resulted in thousands of civilians filling what were once military assignments at stateside bases and, increasingly, on foreign deployments.[55]

While these actions are principally motivated by a desire to save scarce defense dollars, they are also a tacit recognition that the growing sophistication of the technologies of war require the military to ever more frequently tap civilian expertise. *Armed Forces Journal* reports, for example, that in fiscal year 1997, 70 percent of the Department of Defense's information technology transactions were outsourced to private vendors.[56]

This trend exacerbates the long-held fear that new technology requiring ever-greater civilian involvement will cloud a principle vital to the law of armed conflict:[57] the requirement to distinguish between combatants who could be legitimately attacked, and noncombatants who could not. As with civilian *objects*, current international law requires belligerents to exercise "care to separate individual civilians and the civilian population as such from the vicinity of military objectives."[58]

International law does, however, recognize that civilian technicians and contractors are necessary for modern militaries. It holds that they are subject to attack only when actually performing tasks in support of the armed forces. Unlike uniformed personnel, they would not ordinarily be targeted when they are away from their jobs. If captured, they are entitled to treatment as prisoners of war.[59] Nonetheless, the law has always held that noncombatants' "immunity from damage and harm was predicated upon their obligation to abstain from hostile acts. If they took action against a party's armed forces, they automatically lost immunity."[60]

Unfortunately, that appears to be exactly the direction we are heading. *Defense News* characterized the large numbers of civilian technicians required for the Army's digitized battlefield as "surrogate warriors."[61] Indeed, the operation of high-technology systems is moving civilian technicians and contractors from traditional support functions to what are arguably "hostile" activities. For example, a civilian technician who helps *execute* a computerized offensive information *attack* against an enemy system may well have gone beyond mere "support."

Likewise, the Air Force, probably unaware of the implications of its statement, has openly announced its intention to use civilians *operationally*. In *Global Engagement: A Vision for the 21st Century Air Force*, the service states that "combat operations in the 21st century" will broaden "the definition of the future operator."[62] It goes on to state: "In the future, any military *or civilian* member who is experienced in the employment and doctrine of air and space power will be considered an *operator*."[63]

Once civilian technicians or contractors become involved as "operators" in "combat operations," they risk being characterized as "unlawful combatants" under international law.[64] This has a number of consequences, including the possibility that if captured they can be tried and punished for their hostile acts, to include the same things for which a uniformed combatant would be immune.[65] It is very doubtful that many of these "surrogate warriors" are cognizant of their new status or comprehend the ramifications of it.

Since it is unlikely that military dependence on civilian expertise will diminish any time soon, several writers suggest establishing a new type of part-time military.[66] It would be composed of engineers, information specialists, and other technical experts who could be called into military service when necessary. Endowing civilians with military status would support recognition as lawful combatants under international law, and would also be a step toward solving another problem with civilianizing military functions: the fact that civilians cannot be compelled to stay on the job in times of crisis.[67] Only those subject to military discipline have a legal or moral responsibility to remain at their posts.

While this approach would solve one technology-driven problem, it creates a new recomplication for statesmen and soldiers. Specifically, these proposals differ from ordinary Guard and reserve membership in that the military affiliation contemplated would not require the technical experts to undergo all the rigors of military training.[68] In describing such an organization composed of information specialists, Bruce M. Lawlor argues that the well-paid "innovators, intellectuals, and highly-skilled technicians" most needed would "not likely be impressed by the opportunity to wear hair 'high and tight' or do pushups and two-mile runs."[69] Accordingly, he recommends that "much of the military regimen" be discarded.[70]

Soldiers and statesmen need to be cautious, however, about abandoning "much of the military regimen" simply to indulge the predilections of civilian technical experts. Military personnel are not just people in uniforms. There are instead, as Stephen Crane, the author of *The Red Badge of Courage*, put it, "a mysterious fraternity born out of smoke and the danger of death."[71] In his book, *Acts of War: The Behavior of Men in Battle*, Richard Holmes explains:

> However much sociologists might argue that we live in an age of "narrowing skill differentials," where many of the soldier's tasks are growing ever closer to those of his civilian contemporaries, it is an inescapable fact that the soldier's primary function, the use—or threatened use—of force, sets him apart from civilians. . . . [T]he fact remains that someone who joins an army, is both crossing a well-defined border within the fabric of society, and becoming a member of an organization which, in the last analysis, may require him to kill or be killed.[72]

Importantly, Holmes argues that much of the military's regimen (even including such things as haircuts) has psychological importance beyond its obvious practical value. Many military requirements and rituals serve to acculturate an individual to the armed forces and to build the kind of unit cohesion and *esprit de corps* necessary to endure the enormous pressures of combat. Importantly, for statesmen and soldiers concerned about the ethical conduct of war, such a transformation also helps to create a selfless, morally conscious combatant.

The uncertainties and unpredictable dynamics of twenty-first-century battlefields make it unwise to assume that technical experts will always be in situations that render unnecessary the kind of bonding and mental preparation that has sustained winning military organizations for centuries. Notwithstanding the need to secure sufficient numbers of technical experts for twenty-first-century conflicts, statesmen and soldiers must be especially wary of any actions that might erode the altruistic warrior ethos that underpins instinctively proper behavior in the crucible of war.

INFORMATION OPERATIONS

Fighting democracies provides its own set of ethical dilemmas. Some of these dilemmas are directly related to technology and its role in democratic societies. Powerful information and cyberwar technologies are becoming available that can radically affect an electorate's perceptions of its leaders. Thomas Czerwinski indicates how such technologies might be used when he asks: "What would happen if you took Saddam Hussein's image, altered it, and projected it back to Iraq showing him voicing doubts about his own Baath Party?"[73] Quite obviously, the technology implicit in Czerwinski's proposition could just as easily be applied against a democratically elected leader.

Moreover, the capability is hardly science fiction. As anyone who has seen the film *Forrest Gump* can attest, technology now permits the creation of extraordinarily convincing but false images.[74] Of course, propaganda aimed at enemy populations has long been considered a legitimate method of warfare. But this norm may need reexamination when the government affected is a democratic one. It needs to be reconciled with a key component of U.S. national security policy: the promotion of democracy.[75] While no one would dispute that the improper *actions* of the leaders of any enemy state—including those of democracies—must be stemmed, it is something altogether different to hold that it is an appropriate strategy to attempt to change democratically elected leadership via the dissemination of manipulated information.[76]

Furthermore, Michael Walzer asserts that "war aims legitimately reach to the destruction or defeat, demobilization, and (partial) disarming of the aggressor's armed forces. Except in extreme cases, like that of Nazi Germany, *they don't legitimately reach to the transformation of the internal politics of the aggressor state or the replacement of its regime.*"[77] Surely, a democratic government is not the kind of extreme case that Walzer exempts. Thus, statesmen and soldiers may wish to develop policies that restrain information warriors from engaging in tactics that damage the democratic process. Democracy has an intrinsic human value even when it produces governments whose actions lead to war.

The interplay of democratic values and modern technology presents other recomplications for statesmen and soldiers. Specifically, *JV 2010* insists that the U.S. military must have "information superiority" in future conflicts. To do so requires not simply controlling the adversary's information sources, but also the avalanche of data available from third parties, including the global media. This latter source would be extremely difficult to dominate.[78] With the latest technology freeing the press from reliance on—and control by—belligerent governments,[79] it is unlikely that any major aspect of future military operations will escape near-instantaneous reporting by international news agencies. In a very real sense, global news sources could become the "poor man's intelligence service."

In addition, information about current operations will be obtainable from other sources for a modest investment. Already commercial satellites are providing high-resolution images heretofore the exclusive province of the intelligence agencies of the developed nations.[80] Another information source, the Internet, is now being described as a "simple, low-cost, non-threatening and relatively risk-free" way of collecting data valuable to intelligence agencies.[81] All of this makes a strategy of information superiority questionable.

One further element of information operations is the use of modeling to analyze and predict military operations. Military commanders need a firm grasp of the long-term, *indirect* impact upon noncombatants *prior* to the authorization of an attack. Clearly, an enhanced intelligence architecture is necessary to provide the right kind of data to conduct the more probing proportionality calculation these new technologies require.[82]

One way of analyzing the data that an enhanced intelligence system might provide would be to employ the new modeling and simulation techniques now becoming available. For example, using data drawn from the Joint Resource Assessment Data Base, U.S. Strategic Command's Strategic War Planning System (SWPS), can project the expected numbers of killed and injured when a given nuclear weapon is delivered by a designated platform in a certain fashion on the selected target.[83] Similar systems could be developed to analyze the effects of conventional attacks on high-tech networks.

However, modeling and simulation themselves present significant recomplications for statesmen and soldiers. Specifically, are leaders legally or morally *obliged* to follow the model? Suppose, for example, that a decision maker chooses a course of action that the model shows will result in greater noncombatant casualties than another available option. Since the legal and moral duty is to "take all feasible precautions" to avoid noncombatant casualties,[84] if a computer calculates that a certain method of attack among several options most minimizes noncombatant losses, does that automatically preclude consideration of the other options? If a commander selects another option, has he failed to do everything "feasible" to avoid noncombatant losses? How will a commander justify a decision that seems to fly in the face of dispassionate computer logic? Consider that casualty estimates from whatever source can create very real quandaries for commanders at a later time. In the recent controversy over the decision to use the atomic bomb on Japan to end World War II, the relatively crude casualty estimates of nearly fifty years ago were relied upon by some to assert that an invasion would have cost fewer lives than the atomic attack.[85]

As technology progresses one might fairly expect the fidelity of the models to improve,[86] but it is not yet clear that they can *ever* substitute for the judgment of the commander in the performance of the war-fighting *art*. The linear, mathematical nature of computer processes may never be able to replicate the nonlinear and often nonquantifiable logic of war.[87] The history of human conflict is littered with examples of how military forces achieved results that no algorithm would have predicted.[88] Still, in a world that increasingly considers reports provided by an electronic brain innately more authoritative than human-derived analyses, it may well behoove decision makers in future conflicts to somehow capture the essence of their rationale when they select a computer-produced option that on its face seems to be more casualty-intensive than another course of action assessed by the same source.

Thus, the capabilities of new technology present statesmen and soldiers with several unattractive options. If "information superiority" is truly imperative, achieving it may require aggressive, draconian measures against international information sources that are not parties to the conflict. Such measures are of doubtful legal and moral validity, and they could have the unintended consequence of antagonizing allies and even bringing the United States into conflict with third parties.[89] Another approach might be to develop means that discretely deny the transmission of internationally produced information to an adversary. Given the number and variety of sources, however, it would not seem practical or even possible to do so. Finally, we could change our approach, that is, develop doctrine and strategies for conducting military operations in an environment of information *transparency* or information *parity*. It seems that this last alternative, which obviates the need to interfere with information produced by entities not otherwise involved in the particular conflict, would most readily mesh with our legal and moral norms.

OUTER SPACE

As already implied, any discussion of information operations necessarily brings up the issue of space. Satellites provide critical surveillance and communication support for U.S. forces, as well as those of potential adversaries. According to Charles A. Horner, space systems are "fundamental to modern warfare."[90] For example, PGMs, the weapons that so many hope will produce more humane warfare, very often require satellite-derived information for guidance.[91] Because of the importance of space to high-tech operations, American military leaders believe that war in space is inevitable.[92] Accordingly, several preparatory steps have been taken, including testing laser weapons against satellites.[93]

However, space warfare presents significant moral recomplications for statesmen and soldiers. Most fundamentally, there is the question as to whether combat operations ought to be conducted there at all. In fact, the nature of space systems creates legal and ethical reasons that weigh against doing so. As previously discussed, a basic LOAC principle is the obligation of belligerents to separate military targets from civilian objects.[94] Since the very beginning of space exploration, however, military and civilian developments commingled to a such a degree that "the separation of military from civilian . . . space technology [is] meaningless."[95] While there are some purely military systems today,[96] the United States itself relies heavily on civilian satellites, many of which are owned by international consortiums.[97]

Future opponents will likewise depend upon commercial communication and surveillance systems.[98] As a result, space presents the classic legal and moral conundrum of multiuser systems: How do you attack them without causing disproportionate injury to noncombatants and their property, especially when the same system is used by nations not involved in the conflict? As a practical matter, it is difficult to foresee many scenarios where a proportionality analysis[99] would justify attacks on *multi*user systems. This is especially true as noncombatants in a growing number of countries become ever more reliant on space-based technologies for a whole range of essential communications and other services.

Nonetheless, U.S. Space Command is seeking to have "space" declared its area of operations so as to facilitate planning for conflict there.[100] Little international appetite exists for the notion of militarizing space, however. Virtually every treaty related to space asserts that it is to be used only for "peaceful purposes."[101] (The United States interprets these provisions to prohibit only aggressive military actions.[102]) Is it wise, therefore, for the United States to take actions—such as declaring space as an area of operations for one of its combatant commands—that suggest that space is simply another field of battle?[103] Should statesmen and soldiers advocate a course of action that might stimulate a space arms race, akin to the nuclear arms race, as many fear?[104]

It may be shrewder to pursue a legal regime that declares space a "sanctuary" similar to that afforded communications facilities located in neutral territory.[105] This would permit any nation to use space for communications, surveillance, and comparable activities—even during armed conflicts—with the systems not being subject to attack. Arguably, this strategy would renew the original U.S. policy toward space. President Eisenhower established a "self-imposed space sanctuary policy . . . [in order to] establish the principle of freedom of space, to protect U.S. satellites from interference, *and to avoid an arms race in space. . . .*"[106] "Neutralizing" space would not appear to degrade America's war-fighting capability if U.S. space systems were therefore protected and, in any event, existing legal and policy norms already limit or preclude attack on the multiuser international systems that adversaries will rely upon during war.

This proposal would not preclude subspace means that selectively deny adversaries' military forces the use of signals from space platforms. However, the development of lasers and other space weapons would be prohibited, although passive defensive measures (hardening, stealth, etc.) would be allowed. Accordingly, the proposal would not be inconsistent with current U.S. space policy, which advocates diplomatic and legal "measures to preclude an adversary's hostile use of space systems and services."[107] Some may argue that the movement of weaponry into space is inevitable and cannot be effectively banned.[108] But the remarkable history of nuclear arms control (during which many of the same arguments were made) leaves room for optimism—especially if action is taken soon.

LOWERING THE THRESHOLD OF CONFLICT

Another recomplicating effect of the new technologies is the danger that they may inadvertently lead to a lowering of the threshold of violent conflict. Peacetime information operations are one example of how this might occur. Consider, for instance, that there is no clearly accepted definition of what kind of data manipulation constitutes "aggression" contrary to international law and condemned by the U.N. Charter.[109] Current interpretations of "aggression" were largely built upon notions of "armed attack" committed by aggressors employing traditional kinetic-effect weapons.[110] While legal definitions of "armed attack" may seem to allow peacetime data manipulations so long as bombs or bullets are not used,[111] the recipient country may not share such a pacific interpretation and react violently, starting a cycle of escalation unintended by the initiating info-warriors.

The growing proliferation of the popular new "nonlethal" technologies presents similar recomplications.[112] Part of the recomplication results from misunderstanding the terminology. The characterization of these capabilities as "nonlethal," for example, is a source of real confusion—virtually all of them are potentially deadly to some persons.[113] Moreover, certain of them also clash with existing treaties such as those that limit or prohibit the use of chemical and biological agents.[114] Consequently, while items like rubber bullets, sticky foam, and so forth do have the potential to lower the risk of casualties in particular situations, there is the danger that decision makers will be seduced by the same misconception discussed previously in this chapter, that is, the flawed notion that military operations can be conducted without risk to soldiers or civilians.[115]

All of this is especially worrisome because of the unpredictability of the reaction of those against whom supposedly nonlethal means are used. To reiterate a central theme of this chapter: What was intended as a "bloodless" means of coercion may well generate a lethal response. It would seem prudent then for statesmen and soldiers to view information operations and "nonlethal" technologies principally as means to minimize noncombatant casualties under circumstances where the use of force is otherwise necessary and appropriate. If this is clearly understood, miscalculation is averted, and the unintended involvement in unexpectedly hostile situations is precluded.[116]

It is worth noting that a similar issue exists with regard to other high-tech systems. Indeed, the post–Gulf War uses of PGMs against Iraq raise the issue. Quite often the declared purpose is to "send a message" to that government, a function traditionally the role of a diplomatic bag. Analysts A. J. Bacevich and Lawrence F. Kaplan ask, "Given the precision weapons that the United States advertises as central to the new American military doctrine, how many people is it permissible to kill merely to send a message?"[117]

It is true that affecting the psychology of an adversary could constitute a legitimate military objective.[118] The difficulty, as Geoffrey Best notes, is quantifying the often very subjective estimates of psychological effects into something rational enough to support a meaningful finding of the "definite military advantage" that the law requires to warrant the use of force.[119] How does one definitively assess, for example, the psychological effect of an incremental use of force on persons of another culture?[120] Absent the supporting data, the use of force for psychological purposes may be difficult to justify. The real issue for statesmen and soldiers is ensuring that the casualty-minimizing features of high-tech weaponry do not induce decision makers to inappropriately lower the threshold for the use force. Bacevich and Kaplan warn:

> Ultimately, a doctrine that relies on antiseptic methods of warfare may prove dangerously seductive. Seemingly tailor-made for an era of post-modern politics, precision weapons also have the potential to increase the propensity of political leaders to resort to violent means. The ready availability of [PGMs] may tempt them to conclude that force need no longer remain the option of last resort, and induce them to employ their arsenal without due reflection.[121]

ORGANIZATIONAL CULTURE

High technology also carries potential unexpected consequences for the organizational cultures of militaries on twenty-first-century battlefields. Communications advances will be the most important agent of organizational change. As *JV 2010*[122] indicates, technology is already becoming available that will provide individual soldiers with unprecedented access to all kinds of information.[123] Such technology will allow the elimination of various levels of command and supervision resulting in a "flattening" of traditionally hierarchical military organizations. Other technology fathered changes will directly affect battlefield organization. The Marine Corps, for example, is experimenting with a new concept called "infestation tactics" which capitalizes on the new technologies.[124] The technique relies on advanced communications systems to coordinate large numbers of small infantry teams assaulting the same objective.

While increased combat effectiveness should result from these and other technology-driven organizational changes, there are, nevertheless, potential "revenge effects" of concern to statesmen and soldiers. In his book, *The Unintended Consequences of Information Age Technologies*, David S. Alberts warns that when subordinates are provided with the "larger picture" that new data transfer capabilities allow, they are "likely to second-guess decisions made at higher levels and . . . have the information required to undertake initiatives their superiors may find inappropriate."[125]

It seems therefore that, ironically, *controlling* the actions of lower echelon troops may not necessarily be enhanced by better communications technologies. Regrettably, it is at those very levels that the risk of indiscipline is the greatest—the My Lai massacre during the Vietnam War being just one example.[126] Sadly, atrocities seem to be an enduring feature of war. Stephen Ambrose notes that:

> When you put young people, eighteen, nineteen, or twenty years old, in a foreign country with weapons in their hands, sometimes terrible things happen that you wish never happened. This is a reality that stretches across time and across continents. It is a universal aspect of war, from the time of the ancient Greeks up to the present.[127]

What is worrisome about twenty-first-century battlefield technology is that it will put ready access to vastly more potent firepower into the hands of the young troops that Ambrose describes. The new battlefield organization produced by infestation tactics is illustrative. Analysts assert that the "most revolutionary aspect" of the new concept is that the infantryman does not rely on his personal weapon to engage the enemy, but will instead call in external fire support.[128] In short, the experts say, "[r]ather than a 'shooter,' the infantryman becomes a 'spotter.'"[129] They further observe that:

> This change of identity for the infantryman stems from technological advances. With enhanced digital communications, more accurate smart munitions, and man-portable guidance systems, fire support . . . is the king of the battlefield. In addition to traditional tube artillery, the individual team can call for and direct close air support, rocket fires, naval gunfire, and missile attacks.[130]

Quite obviously, whatever havoc troops were able to wreak with their personal weapons at places like My Lai, that terrible potential will be markedly greater in future conflicts because of the new technologies of war, particularly since the command and supervisory structure that might intervene is, by design, less robust.

By empowering junior personnel, the new technologies of war create other recomplications as well. *Aviation Week & Space Technology* reports that senior American officials are concerned about the effect of the absence of clear rules concerning information operations.[131] They believe that "[o]nce soldiers and airmen start dying in a war, the young computer-literate officers and enlisted men are going to start making their own efforts to crack enemy computer systems."[132] Freelance efforts of this sort can create serious problems. For example, a computer virus loosed on an enemy might have "unintended consequences and come back and cripple friendly computers."[133] The adverse "reverberating effects" of such actions on noncombatants may be quite significant.

Still, the solution is not to deny lower echelons the benefits of the technology. Rather, when technology dramatically empowers junior personnel, steps must be taken to ensure that they are fully prepared, both technically and psychologically, to handle the greater legal and moral responsibilities that the enhanced capabilities impose upon them. Unquestionably, maintaining discipline and professionalism under the new combat conditions is more essential than ever—yet ever more difficult to guarantee.

Another recomplicating effect is caused by the proliferating numbers of e-mail-equipped laptop computers, fax machines, and similar technologies that troops themselves own and carry with them into war zones.[134] What is more is that according to former Speaker of the House Newt Gingrich, "virtually every soldier in combat in 2010 will have somewhere on their body a personal telephone linked by satellite to a world telephone network."[135] Such devices raise a number of complications, not the least of which is that they are extremely vulnerable to monitoring by hostile forces.[136]

Equally important is that these devices hasten the day when the authority of the military commander could be questioned on the battlefield—a development with potentially disastrous consequences. Instant communications by soldiers from future battlefields causes Nicholas Wade to question, "Would any commander want his soldiers to receive parental advice in the midst of a firefight? What if Dad disagrees with the officer in the scene? As Napoleon said, one bad general is better than two good ones."[137] Similarly, *Newsweek* asked, "[I]f soldiers can phone mom or the local newspaper from the middle of the battlefield, what are the implications for maintaining military discipline or secrecy?"[138]

To answer such concerns some commanders will attempt to restrict the use of these communications devices. But is this realistic? Can a democracy reliant on an all-volunteer force expect to isolate forward-deployed troops from contact with their friends and families, especially when they may have grown up in an environment of instant communications gratification? It may be more practical, as suggested previously, to abandon the goal of information security and plan accordingly.[139]

Finally, the inculcation of the revolutionary technologies into the armed services might create a generation of "console warriors" who wage war without ever confronting the deadly consequences of their actions. Statesmen and soldiers should not assume that such combatants will automatically share the military's traditional values that restrain illegal and immoral conduct in war. Up until now, much of the military's ethos was drawn from concepts of honor and chivalry sourced in the physical reality of direct combat. Although the extent to which the proliferation of long-distance, push-button war serves to replace that ethos with a new ethic is as yet uncertain, it is imperative that whatever emerges instills in tomorrow's soldiers those moral underpinnings which will further develop the application of ethical and legal norms in future conflicts.

SUMMARY AND CONCLUSIONS

At this point the reader may agree that the promise of the introduction of this chapter has been fulfilled: Far more questions have been raised than solutions offered. Hopefully, it is now clear that despite their many beneficial aspects, the emerging RMA technologies have great capacity for unintended consequences and revenge effects. Our examination reveals several broad themes that statesmen and soldiers may wish to address:

1. *The unpredictability of an adversary's response to high-tech attack.* While U.S. intent in using PGMs or other high-tech means in a particular conflict might be to minimize casualties on both sides, their use may, nevertheless, drive an enemy incapable of responding in kind to resort to measures that could make war, paradoxically, *more* destructive or inhumane than if the high-tech weapons had not been used at all.

2. *The increasing commingling of military and civilian high-tech systems.* Although this dual- and multiuse trend is unlikely to change in the future, greater consideration should be given to the moral and legal implications of

making legitimate targets out of systems upon which technology-dependent societies rely. Where possible, steps should be taken to ensure that essential services are preserved in the event of war. At a minimum, decision-support systems need to be developed not only to analyze the vulnerability of friendly populations but also to assess high-tech targets in hostile countries in order to assist military commanders in making an informed proportionality judgment. Such systems need to be able to evaluate secondary, reverberating effects on civilian populations.

3. *The blurring of the distinction between noncombatant civilians and combatant military personnel.* Technologies, along with budget-driven decisions to outsource and privatize and otherwise civilianize military functions, carry moral and legal implications. Care must be taken to ensure that a whole class of unlawful combatants is not inadvertently created. There may be utility in devising new kinds of reserve organizations for technologically skilled personnel which do not require members to conform to all the rigors of a professional military. However, such efforts must not compromise those aspects of the military regimen that develop military's altruistic, warrior ethos which underpins moral conduct in war.

4. *Information operations.* Information operations (IO) and cyberwar can complicate the moral life for statesmen and soldiers in many ways, but of particular concern are the new techniques that can interfere with democratic societies. IO and cyberwar techniques are properly applied to control the aggressive behavior of nations, but they should not be permitted to destroy democratic values in the process. Moreover, the proliferation of third-party communications sources renders suspect military strategies aimed at achieving information superiority.

5. *The militarization of space.* Satellites and space vehicles are irrevocably integrated into modern warfare. However, this does not mean that space should become another battlefield. Rather, the United States should use its prestige as the preeminent space power to forge an international consensus that designates space a neutral area and, therefore, possibly avoid a space weapons race.

6. *The lowering of the threshold of conflict.* Advanced technology provides the capability to employ coercion via non- or low-lethal means in a way that greatly minimizes the immediate noncombatant losses. Because of the unpredictability of the response of those targeted, however, care must be taken to ensure that misapprehensions of the nature and implications of military means do not delude decision makers with visions of "bloodlessly" compelling opponents short of violent conflict. Absent such caution we risk taking actions with the dangerous potential to spin out of control into full-scale war.

7. *Organizational Culture.* Vastly enhanced communications capabilities that shift more and more battlefield responsibilities to lower levels of command must be accompanied by appropriate training to ensure that legal and moral norms of the law of war are observed by technology-empowered junior personnel.

These are by no means all the high technology issues with potential to recomplicate moral life for twenty-first-century statesmen and soldiers. Of course, it would be a mistake to conclude that the problems just discussed somehow warrant a retreat from infusing RMA technology into defense planning. After all, high-tech weapons ordinarily *do* have their *intended* effect—and sometimes *that* is the unexpected consequence. For example, military historian Martin Van Creveld observes that, ironically, "in *every* region where [nuclear weapons] have been introduced, large-scale, interstate war has as good as disappeared."[140] In short, however horrific their potential, nuclear weapons have successfully performed the deterrent function that creators hoped they would, to the surprise of a myriad of naysayers. To many it is, perhaps, the ultimate unexpected—though not unintended—consequence that the advent of the nuclear age has coincided with the absence of the kind of savage global war that twice visited the world this century.

While technology can obviously deter war, it is still true that "technology and warfare have never been far apart."[141] Clearly, statesmen and soldiers need to be concerned about procuring the technology necessary for U.S. forces to prevail in any conflict. Analysts Ronald Haycock and Keith Neilson ominously warn that "technology has permitted the division of mankind into ruler and ruled."[142] In that regard, even America's vaunted free-enterprise system, the engine that fuels its technological might, has its own recomplications.

Consider that American values—in this instance the commitment to full and fair competition within a capitalistic economy—might deny U.S. troops the best technology on twenty-first-century battlefields. Author David Shukman explains: "While the Western military struggle for a decade on average to acquire new weapons, a country with commercially available computer equipment and *less rigorous democratic and accounting* processes could field new systems within a few years. It is the stuff of military nightmares."[143] Although high-tech systems are touted as a means to get inside an adversary's "decision loop,"[144] the reality is that nations unencumbered by Western-style procurement regulations, may well be able to get inside our "acquisition loop" and field newer weaponry even before the United States finishes buying already obsolete equipment.

Just as the speed of technological change creates difficulties for the procurement process, so it does for those concerned with law, ethics, and policy. President Harry Truman once remarked that he feared that "machines were ahead of morals by some centuries." That certainly is the case in today's RMA environment.[145] Consequently, statesmen and soldiers must accelerate their efforts to develop norms of law, ethics, and policy that honor this nation's finest ideals while at the same time appreciating that "technology is America's manifest destiny."[146]

This is not an easy task. Nor is the problem without historical precedent. Russell F. Weigley notes in his 1977 classic, *The American Way of War* that: "To seek refuge in technology from hard questions of strategy and policy [is] another dangerous American tendency, fostered by the pragmatic qualities of the American character and by the complexities of nuclear-age technology." Quite obviously statesmen and soldiers must recognize technology's potential, but they must do so with the clear understanding that it will never substitute for answering the kind of "hard questions" of law, ethics, and policy that will continue to recomplicate moral life on twenty-first-century battlefields.

NOTES

1. Viet Minh artillerymen fired more than 130,000 rounds from over 200 heavy cannons and mortars during the siege. See J. D. Morelock, *The Army Times Book of Great Land Battles* (New York: Borkley Books, 1994), p. 262.
2. Bernard and Fawn Brodie, *From Crossbow to H-Bomb* (Bloomington: Indiana University Press, 1973), p. 70.
3. See Nathan Perry, "Revolution in Military Affairs," *National Guard Review* (summer 1997), pp. 23, 51.
4. This is not to say that wars of previous eras were not destructive. Consider that the Thirty Years' War may have caused a population decline in Europe of as much as a third. See Curt Johnson, "Thirty Years' War," in *Brassey's Encyclopedia of Military History and Biography*, ed. Franklin D. Margiotta (Washington, D.C.: Brassey's, 1994).
5. See Jeffrey A. Harley, "Information, Technology, and Center of Gravity," *Naval War College Review* (winter 1997), pp. 65, 80.
6. George and Meredith Friedman, *The Future of War* (New York: Crown Publishers, 1996).
7. Ibid., p. xi.
8. There are many possible definitions of information operations but a common official definition is that used by the Air Force, which is, "actions taken to gain, exploit, defend, or attack information and information systems." Air Force Doctrine Document 1, *Air Force Basic Doctrine* (September 1997), p. 44 (hereinafter AFDD-1). This definition is almost identical to that once used by the Air Force to describe information *warfare*. See Captain Robert G. Hanseman, USAF, "The Realities and Legalities of Information Warfare," *A.F.L. Rev.* 42 (1997), pp. 73, 176, citing USAF Fact Sheet 95-20 (November 1995).
9. Cyberwar suggests a form of warfare more holistic, strategic, and manipulative of information in its concept than the "information operations" definition set forth in note 251 *supra*. AFDD-1 notes the following:

   > In describing information operations, it is important to differentiate between "information in war" and "information warfare." The second element, information warfare, involves such diverse activities as psychological warfare, military deception, electronic combat, and both physical and cyberattack. (AFDD-1, ibid.)

   For an excellent cyberwar scenario, see John Arquilla, "The Great Cyberwar of 2002," *Wired*, February 1998, p. 122.
10. See Douglas Waller, "Onward Cyber Soldiers" *Time*, 21 August 1995, p. 38.
11. The Department of Defense defines these weapons as follows:

    > Weapons that are explicitly designed and primarily employed so as to incapacitate personnel or material, while minimizing fatalities, permanent injury to personnel, and undesired damage to property and the environment. Unlike conventional lethal weapons that destroy their targets principally through blast, penetration and fragmentation, nonlethal weapons employ means other than gross physical destruction to prevent the target from functioning. Non-lethal weapons are intended to have one, or both, of the following characteristics: a. they have relatively reversible effects on personnel or material, b. they affect objects differently within their area of influence.

    Nonlethal Weapons: Terms and References, USAF Institute for National Security Studies, Colorado Springs, CO, ed. Robert J. Bunker (July 1997), p. ix, citing Department of Defense Directive 3000.3, *Policy for Non-Lethal Weapons*, 9 July 1996.
12. For discussions of "the revolution in military affairs" in the information age, see "Select Enemy, Delete," *Economist*, 8 March 1997, p. 21; Eliot A. Cohen, "A Revolution in Warfare," *Foreign Affairs* (March/April 1996), pp. 37; Andrew F. Krepinevich, "Cavalry to Computers: The Pattern of Military Revolutions," *National Interest*. (fall 1994), p. 30; and James R. Fitzsimonds and Jan M. Van Tol, "Revolutions in Military Affairs," *Joint Force Quarterly* (spring 1994), p. 24.
13. "The Future of Warfare," *Economist*, 8 March 1997, p. 15.
14. See Robert N. Ellithorpe, "Warfare in Transition? American Military Culture Prepares for the Information Age" (a presentation for the Biennial International Conference of the Inter-University Seminar on Armed Forces and Society, Baltimore, MD, October 24–26, 1997), p. 18; "American military culture historically emphasized scientific approaches to warfare to the point of holding an

almost mystical belief in the power of technology to solve the challenges of war" (unpublished paper on file with author).

15. See Colin S. Gray, "U.S. Strategic Culture: Implications for Defense Technology," in *Defense Technology*, ed. Asa A. Clark IV and John F. Lilley (New York: Preager, 1989), p. 31. Gray quotes George S. Patton, Jr:

> The Americans, as a race, are the foremost mechanics of the world. America, as a nation, has the greatest ability for the mass production of machines. It therefore behooves us to devise methods of war which exploit our inherent superiority. We must fight the war by machines on the ground, and in the air, to the maximum of our ability. . . .

> George S. Patton, Jr., *War as I Knew It* (New York: Bantam Publishers, 1947; Bantam reprint 1980), p. 345.

16. Chairman of the Joint Chiefs of Staff, *Joint Vision 2010* (1996) [hereinafter referred to as *JV 2010*].
17. General John M. Shalikashvili, ibid., p. ii.
18. Ibid., p. 1.
19. Edward Tenner, *Why Things Bite Back: Technology and the Revenge of Unintended Consequences* (New York: Knopf Publishers, 1996).
20. There are at least six categories of PGMs: (1) "man-in-the-loop" weapons such as laser-guided bombs that require an operator to "illuminate" the target or weapons that have on-board sensors that allow an operator to guide the weapon to the target; (2) autonomous weapons relying only on inertial navigation systems (INS) and autonomous weapons updated by Global Positioning Satellites (GPS) for guidance to the target; (3) autonomous weapons with terrain-aided INS/GPS systems; (4) autonomous weapons with INS/GPS systems and template matching algorithms for guidance; (5) anti-emitter PGMs that rely on onboard systems to home on emitting targets such as enemy radars; and (6) PGMs with "smart" submunitions that use various sensors to guide themselves to targets. See John Birkler et al., *A Framework for Precision Conventional Strike in Post-Cold War Military Strategy* (Rand Corporation, 1996), pp. 6–11.
21. *JV 2010, supra* note 259, p. 21.
22. See Benjamin S. Lambeth, "Technology and Air War," *Air Force Magazine*, November 1996, pp. 50, 53. See also Lt. Col. Edward Mann, "One Target, One Bomb," *Military Review*, September 1993, p. 33; contra, see, e.g., Sean D. Naylor, "Technology Is No Substitute for Troops," *Air Force Times*, 3 March 1997, p. 26 (citing remarks by General John Sheehan, USMC, then Commander-in-Chief of U.S. Atlantic Command).
23. Military necessity may be defined as follows:

> Military necessity is the principle which justifies measures of regulated force not forbidden by international law which are indispensable for securing the prompt submission of the enemy, with the least possible expenditure of economic and human resources. . . . The principle of military necessity is not the 19th Century German doctrine, *Kriegsraison*, asserting that military necessity could justify any measures—even violations of the laws of war—when the necessities of the situation purportedly justified it.

> Department of the Air Force Pamphlet 110-31, *International Law—The Conduct of Armed Conflict and Air Operations* (19 November 1976) at paragraph 1-3a(1) [Hereinafter referred to as AFP 110-31].

24. David R. Markow, "The Russians and Their Nukes," *Air Force Magazine*, February 1997, p. 41.
25. Colonel James P. Terry, USMC, "Operation Desert Storm: Stark Contrasts in Compliance with the Rule of Law," *Naval L. Rev* 41 (1993), pp. 83, 92–94 (more than 600 wells were fired).
26. Michael N. Schmitt, "Green War: An Assessment of the Environmental Law of International Armed Conflict," *Yale J. of Int'l L.* 22 (1997), pp. 1, 21. Schmitt concludes that, in any event, "the damage inflicted so outweighed possible gains the acts were wrongful under international law."
27. See also Adam Roberts, "Environmental Issues in International Armed Conflict: The Experience of the 1991 Gulf War," *International Law Studies 1996: Protection of the Environment during Armed Conflict* (1996), pp. 222, 248.
28. See Michael Gordon and Bernard E. Trainor, *The Generals' War: The Inside Story of the Conflict in The Gulf* (Boston: Little Brown, 1995), p. 364.
29. Ibid., pp. 363–371.
30. However, the Hague Convention IV (1907) provides that "the right of belligerents to adopt means of injuring the enemy is not unlimited."
31. See Gordon and Trainor, *supra* note 271, pp. 324–326.

32. AFP 110-31, *supra* note 266 provides as follows:

The term noncombatant includes a wide variety of disparate persons . . . civilians (who are not otherwise lawful or unlawful combatants, combatants who are *hors de combat* (PWs and wounded and sick), members of the armed forces enjoying special status (chaplains and medics), and civilians accompanying the armed forces. (paragraphs 3–4)

33. See Lt. Col. Thomas X. Hammes, "Don't Look Back, They're Not Behind You," *Marine Corps Gazette*, May 1996, pp. 72, 73 (discussing the military implications of chaining hostages to targets). Hostage-taking was not clearly prohibited until after World War II. See H. Wayne Elliot, Lt. Col., U.S. (Ret.), "Hostages or Prisoners of War: War Crimes at Dinner," 149 *Mil. L. Rev.* (summer 1995), p. 241.

34. See Stephen Erlanger, "Russia Allows Rebels to Leave with Hostages," *New York Times*, 20 June 1995.

35. See "Libyans to Form Shield at Suspected Arms Plant," *Baltimore Sun*, 17 May 1996, p. 14.

36. See Barbara Slavin, "Iraq Leaves U.S. Few Options," *USA Today*, 14 November 1997, p. 13-A.

37. James F. Dunnigan, *Digital Soldiers: The Evolution of High-Tech Weaponry and Tomorrow's Brave New Battlefield* (New York: St. Martin's Press, 1996), p. 219.

38. A PGM is, on the average, fifteen times more expensive than an unguided bomb. See Dunnigan, *supra* note 280, p. 135.

39. See Infield, *supra* note 292, pp. 140–141.

40. Ibid., p. 131.

41. See note 248, *supra*.

42. Iraq enjoyed some success in characterizing itself as a victim using similar logic. See William M. Arkin, "Baghdad: The Urban Sanctuary in Desert Storm?" *Airpower Journal* (spring 1997), pp. 4, 17.

43. Existing international agreements contain a *de Martens Clause* which addresses new methods and means of warfare. It states:

[I]n cases not included in the regulations adopted by them, the inhabitants and the belligerents remain under the protection and rule of the principles of the law of nations, as they result from the usages established among civilized peoples, from the laws of humanity, and dictates of the public conscience.

Preamble, 1907 Hague Convention (IV) Respecting the Laws and Customs of War on Land. Accord, Common Article 63/62/142/158 of the Geneva Conventions of 12 August 1949; Article 1 (2) of the Protocol I Additional to the Geneva Convention of 12 August 1949; and, the Preamble to the Convention on Prohibitions or Restrictions on the Use of Certain Conventional Weapons which may be deemed to be Excessively Injurious or to have Indiscriminate Effects.

44. As quoted in David Shukman, *Tomorrow's War: The Threat of High-Technology Weapons* (San Diego: Harcourt, Brace, Jovanovich, 1996), p. 233.

45. However, it must be recognized that generally LOAC does not attempt to apportion responsibility in the context of *jus in bello*.

46. Daniel J. Boorstin, "Myths of Popular Innocence," *U.S. News & World Report* 4 March 1991, p. 41.

47. Boorstin cites as examples the downfall of the Shah of Iran and the liberation of Eastern Europe from Soviet rule. Ibid.

48. W. Hays Parks, "Air War and the Law of War," *A. F. L. Rev.* 32 (1990), pp. 1, 168.

49. See Danielle L. Infield, "Precision-Guided Munitions Demonstrated Their Pinpoint Accuracy in Desert Storm, but Is a Country Obligated to Use Precision Technology to Minimize Collateral Civilian Injury and Damage?" *Geo. Wash. J. Int'l L. & Econ* 26 (1992), pp. 109, 110–111.

50. See Lev S. Voronkov, John Grin, and Wim A. Smit, "Some Conclusions on Future Studies and Policies," in *Military Technological Innovation and Stability in a Changing World*, ed. Lev S. Voronkov, John Grin, and Wim A. Smit (Amsterdam: Vu University Press, 1992), p. 287.

51. Daniel Kuehl, "The Ethics of Information Warfare and Statecraft" (paper presented at InfoWARcon 96, Washington, D.C., September 1996).

52. However, the dual-use of facilities does occur in other areas. See Matthew L. Wald, "U.S. to Put Civilian Reactor to Military Use," *New York Times*, 11 August 1997, p. 20.

53. John T. Correll, "Warfare in the Information Age," *Air Force Magazine*, December 1996, p. 3.

54. The GAO found that 45 percent of military personnel performed support functions that could be done by civilians for an average of $15,000 less. See Tom Bowman, "Drift Military Support Jobs to Civilians, Close Inefficient Facilities, GAO Urges," *Baltimore Sun*, 5 April 1997, p. 4.

55. Katherine M. Peters, "Civilians at War," *Government Executive*, July 1996, p. 23.

56. David Silverberg, "Crossing Computing's Cultural Chasm," *Armed Forces Journal International* (February 1997), pp. 38, 39.
57. AFP 110-31, *supra* note 266, at paragraphs 3–5.
58. Parks, *supra* note 291.
59. Ibid., p. 3.
60. Paul Kennedy and George J. Andreopoulos, "The Laws of War: Some Concluding Reflections," in *The Laws of War: Constraints on Warfare in the Western World*, ed. Michael Howard, George J. Andreopoulos, and Mark L. Shulman (New Haven: Yale University Press, 1994), p. 215.
61. See Bryan Bender, "Defense Contractors Quickly Becoming Surrogate Warriors," *Defense Daily*, 28 March 1997, p. 490.
62. U.S. Air Force, *Global Engagement: A Vision for the 21st Century Air Force* (1997), p. 7.
63. Ibid., p. 19.
64. AFP 110-31, *supra* note 266, paragraph 3–3 provides:

> An unlawful combatant is an individual who is not authorized to take a direct part in hostilities but does. The term is frequently used also to refer to otherwise privileged combatants who do not comply with requirements of mode of dress, or noncombatants in the armed forces who improperly use their protected status as a shield to engage in hostilities. . . . Unlawful combatants are a proper object of attack while engaging as combatants. . . . If captured, they may be tried and punished.

See also Lt. Col. Robert W. Gehring, "Loss of Civilian Protections under the Fourth Geneva Convention and Protocol I," *Mil. L. Rev.* 90 (1980), p. 49.
65. "Unlawful combatants" are not ordinarily considered "war criminals." Rather, they would be subject to prosecution under the domestic law of capturing belligerents much as out-of-uniform saboteurs would be. During World War II, for example, the United States captured eight German saboteurs and executed six. See C. Sulzberger, *American Heritage New History of World War II*, Rev. and updated by Stephen E. Ambrose (New York: Viking Press, 1997).
66. See Stephen Bryen, "New Era of Warfare Demands Technology Reserve Force," *Defense News*, 17–23 March 1997, p. 27 and Brig. Gen. Bruce M. Lawlor, ARNG, "Information Corps," *Armed Forces Journal International* (January 1998), pp. 26, 28.
67. Lou Marano, "Perils of Privatization," *Washington Post*, 27 May 1997, p. 15.
68. Ibid.
69. Lawlor, *supra* note 309.
70. Ibid.
71. As quoted in Richard Holmes, *Acts of War: The Behavior of Men in Battle* (New York: The Free Press, 1985), p. 31.
72. Ibid.
73. As quoted by Peter Grier, "Information Warfare," *Air Force Magazine*, March 1995, p. 35.
74. See Dennis Brack, "Do Photos Lie?" *Proceedings* (August 1996), p. 47.
75. The White House, *A National Security Strategy for a New Century* (May 1997), p. 19.
76. See Sidney Axinn, *A Moral Military* (Philadelphia: Temple University Press, 1989), pp. 159–160.
77. Michael Walzer, *Just and Unjust Wars*, 2nd ed. (New York: Basic Books, 1992), p. xvii.
78. See Eviathar H. Ben-Zedeff, "Achilles' Heel: Feasibility of Military Censorship of the News Media in the 'Third Wave' Era of Technology" (a presentation for the Biennial International Conference of the Inter-University Seminar on Armed Forces and Society, Baltimore, MD, October 24–26, 1997). (Unpublished paper on file with author.)
79. Douglas Waller, a *Time* magazine correspondent, observes:

> The same technology that is revolutionizing the way the Pentagon fights wars is also changing the way the media cover them. The media can now provide viewers, listeners and even readers almost instant access to a battlefield. With lighter video cameras, smaller portable computers, cellular phones, their own aircraft, and worldwide electronic linkups, the media can report on any battlefield no matter how remote and no matter how many restrictions the Defense Department tries to place on coverage.

Douglas Waller, "Public Affairs, the Media, and War in the Information Age" (a presentation for the War in the Information Age Conference, Tufts University, November 15–16, 1995). (Unpublished paper on file with author.)
80. See William J. Broad, "Private Ventures Hope for Profits on Spy Satellites," *New York Times*, 10 February 1997, p. 1.

81. Compare Bill Gertz, "Spies Use Internet to Build Files on U.S., *Washington Times*, 3 January 1997, p. 5.

82. Essentially, the concept of proportionality requires commanders to refrain from attacks when it "may be expected to cause incidental loss of civilian life, injury to civilians, damage to civilian objects or combination thereof, which would be excessive in relation to the direct and concrete military advantage anticipated." See AFP 110–131, *supra* note 266 at paragraph 5-3c(1)(b)(I)(c).

83. The system uses terms that have specific definitions and this affects the evaluation. For example, "casualties" are defined as the "estimated number of people who die or receive injuries that require medical treatment due to short term effects (6 months) of nuclear detonations." "Population at Risk" is defined as the "total civilian population in danger of dying, independent of shelter, from short term (6 months) effects of nuclear detonations." See Memorandum, *Acronyms/Definitions Used in SIOP Analysis* (U), USSTRATCOM Plans and Policy Directorate, Force Assessment Branch (April 1997) (on file with author).

84. See AFP 110–131, *supra* note 266, at paragraph 5-3c(1)(b)(I)(c).

85. See D. M. Giangreco, "Casualty Projections for the U.S. Invasions of Japan, 1945–1946: Planning and Policy Implications," *Journal of Military History* (July 1997), p. 521 and Ralph Capio, "FDR and Truman: Continuity and Context in the A-Bomb Decision," *Airpower Journal* (fall 1995), p. 56.

86. See Paul R. Camacho, "Further Development in the Construction of Political Action Expert Systems Software: Fuzzy Logic Techniques on Social Science Variables" (a presentation for the Biennial International Conference of the Inter-University Seminar on Armed Forces and Society, Baltimore, MD, October 24–26, 1997). (Unpublished paper on file with author.)

87. "War is typically nonlinear, meaning the smallest effects can have unpredicted, disproportionate consequences." See Jeffrey McKitrick, James Blackwell, Fred Littlepage, George Kraus, Richard Blanchfield, and Dale Hill, "Revolution in Military Affairs," in *Battlefield of the Future* (Air University, 1995). See also Glenn E. James, *Chaos Theory: The Essentials for Military Applications* (Newport Paper No. 10, Naval War College, 1996), pp. 57–95 (discussing the limitations of computer modeling).

88. Ellithorpe, *supra* note 257, p. 4, "History has demonstrated the fatal error of military decisions based on the use of scientific and technical analysis at the expense of understanding the warfighting art."

89. Compare Eliot Cohen, "What to Do about National Defense," *Commentary* (November 1994), pp. 21, 31, "Far more worrisome, however, is the possibility that a military fighting the shadowy battles of 'information warfare' might find itself engaging the country in foreign-policy tangles of a particularly messy kind."

90. As quoted by George Wilson. See George C. Wilson, "Like It or Not, Space Warfare Is Way of Future—and Past," *Air Force Times* 28 (June 1994), p. 70.

91. See Myron Hura and Gary McCleod, *Intelligence Support and Mission Planning for Autonomous Precision-Guided Weapons* (Rand Corporation, 1992).

92. See Jennifer Heroema, "A.F. Space Chief Calls War in Space Inevitable," *Space News*, 1–18 August 1996, p. 4.

93. See William Broad, "Military Hoping to Test-Fire Laser against Satellite," *New York Times*, 1 September 1997, p. 1.

94. W. Hays Parks, "Air War and the Law of War," 32 *A. F. L. Rev.* 1 (1990), p. 168.

95. William H. McNeill, *The Pursuit of Power* (1982), p. 369. This is also true with respect to much of the actual technology aboard the spacecraft. See Craig Covault, "NRO Radar Sigint Launches Readied," *Aviation Week & Space Technology*, 1 September 1997, p. 22: "The same technology employed by [the military satellites] will increasingly be applied to the commercial sector."

96. See, e.g., U.S. Space Command, *Guardians of the High Frontier* 16 (1996) (describing military satellite systems).

97. See notes 295 and 296 *supra* and accompanying text.

98. Jeffrey R. Barnett, *Future War: An Assessment of Aerospace Campaigns in 2010* (Alabama: Air University Press, 1996), p. xix.

99. Essentially, the concept of proportionality requires commanders to refrain from attacks when it "may be expected to cause incidental loss of civilian life, injury to civilians, damage to civilian objects or combination thereof, which would be excessive in relation to the direct and concrete military advantage anticipated." See AFP 110–131 *supra* note 266, at paragraph 5-3c(1)(b)(I)(c).

100. See *U.S. Space Command Vision for 2020* (1997), p. 6.

101. See, e.g., Article I, Treaty on Principles Governing the Activities of States in the Explorations and Use of Outer Space, Including the Moon and Other Celestial Bodies, 27 January 1967, 18 U.S.T. 2411, I.I.A.S. 6347; 610 U.N.T.S. 205 (the "Outer Space Treaty"). See Richard A. Morgan,

"Military Uses of Commercial Communications Satellites: A New Look at the Outer Space Treaty and 'Peaceful Purposes,'" *J. Air L. & Comm* 60 (fall 1994), p. 237.

102. Morgan, ibid.; see also Naval War College, Department of Oceans Law and Policy, *Annotated Supplement to the Commander's Handbook on the Law of Naval Operations* (1997), paragraph 2.9.2, note 114.

103. Among the problems with declaring space as an area of operations is the fact that there is no universally accepted definition of exactly where national sovereignty ends and "space" begins. See AFP 110–131, *supra* note 14, at paragraph 2-1h.

104. See Jonathan S. Landay, "The Next Arms Race? Drawing Battle Lines in Space?" *Christian Science Monitor*, 17 December 1997, p. 1.

105. See, e.g., *Hague Convention Respecting the Rights and Duties of Neutral Powers and Persons in the Case of War on Land* (1907): Communications facilities on neutral territory are inviolate from attack so long as they are made available to all belligerents.

106. See Michael R. Mantz, *The New Sword: A Theory of Space Combat Power* (Air University Press, May 1995), p. 12 (emphasis added).

107. National Science and Technology Council, *National Space Policy* (White House press release, September 19, 1996), p. 6.

108. See, e.g., Ben Bova, "Laser Foes Forget Crossbow's History," *USA Today* 7 January 1998, p. 15.

109. See Commander James N. Bond, USN, "Peacetime Data Manipulation as One Aspect of Offensive Information Warfare: Questions of Legality under the United Nations Charter Article 2(4)," Advanced Research Project, Naval War College, 14 June 1996 (unpublished manuscript).

110. See Charles J. Dunlap, Jr., "Cyberattack! Are We at War?" *J. of the Nat'l Computer Security Association* (NCSA News) (November 1996), p. 19.

111. Bond, *supra* note 352.

112. See, generally, Joseph W. Cook, III, Maura F. McGowan, and David P. Fiely, "Non-Lethal Weapons Technologies, Legalities, and Potential Policies," *USAFA J. of Legal Studies* 5 (1994/1995), pp. 23, 38.

113. Larry Lynn, Director, U.S. Department of Defense Advanced Research Projects Agency, says that "there is no such thing as nonlethal of course." See "One on One," *Defense News*, 19–25 February, 1996, p. 30.

114. See Cook et al., note 355, pp. 28–35.

115. See also Thomas E. Ricks, "Gingrich's Futuristic Vision for Re-Shaping the Armed Forces Worry Military Professionals," *Wall Street Journal*, 8 February 1995, p. 16 (contending that "many of the supporters of the military who lack firsthand experience . . . believe that gadgets can somehow substitute for the blood and sweat of ground combat").

116. See Anthony Zinni, "No Premium on Killing," *Proceedings*, December 1996, pp. 26–28 (arguing that nonlethal means should be used in tandem with lethal means).

117. A. J. Bacevich and Lawrence F. Kaplan, "The Clinton Doctrine," *Weekly Standard*, 30 September 1996, pp. 16, 20.

118. Parks, *supra* note 291, p. 142.

119. See Best, *supra* note, pp. 274–275.

120. H. R. McMaster discusses a similar theme in the context of the Vietnam War in his book *Dereliction of Duty* (New York: Harper Collins, 1997); ibid., p. 327 (emphasis added).

121. A. J. Bacevich and Lawrence F. Kaplan, *supra* note 360, pp. 20–21.

122. *JV 2010, supra* note 259, p. 18.

123. Compare George I. Seffers, "U.S. Army Puts Tactical Internet to Test," *Defense News*, 17–23 March, 1997, p. 3 (describing a battlefield information/communication system currently being tested).

124. See Captain Michael R. Lwin, U.S., and Captain Mark R. Lwin, USMC, "The Future of Land Power," *U.S. Naval Institute Proceedings* (September 1997), pp. 82, 83.

125. David S. Alberts, *The Unintended Consequences of Information Age Technologies* (National Defense University, 1996), p. 36.

126. *U.S. v. Calley*, 46 C.M.R. 1131 (C.M.A. 1973).

127. Stephen E. Ambrose, *Americans at War* (Jackson: University of Mississippi, 1997), p. 152.

128. See Lwin and Lwin, *supra* note 367.

129. Ibid.

130. Ibid.

131. David A. Fulgham, "Computer Combat Rules Frustrate the Pentagon," *Aviation Week & Space Technology*, 15 September 1997, p. 67.

132. Ibid.

133. See Pat Cooper and Frank Oliveri, "Air Force Carves Operational Edge in Info Warfare," *Defense News*, 21–27 August, 1995.

134. See, e.g., "Generals to Moms: At Ease!" *Omaha World-Herald*, 6 February 1996, p. 6 (discussing Israeli recruits arriving for training with personal cellular phones and using them to call their mothers to complain about various aspects of their military duties) and Lisa Hoffman, "E-Mail Will Link Troops to Families," *European Stars and Stripes*, 18 December 1995, p. 7.

135. As quoted in Nicholas Wade, "Bytes Make Might," *New York Times Magazine*, 12 March 1995, p. 28.

136. See, e.g., Brigid Schulte, "How a Fighter Pilot's Raw Account of Rescue Flashed around the Globe," *Philadelphia Inquirer*, 11 July 1995 (describing how a private e-mail allegedly containing "explicit descriptions of radio frequencies, pilot code names, exact times and weapons load for the mission" relating to the rescue of U.S. pilot Scott O'Grady in the Balkans became available to millions on the Internet).

137. See Wade, *supra* note 378; ibid.

138. John Leo, "Gadgetry's Power and Peril," *U.S. News & World Report*, 15 April 1991, p. 20.

139. See discussion on pages 18 and 19 *supra*.

140. Martin Van Creveld, "Technology and War II," in *The Oxford Illustrated History of Modern War*, ed. Charles Townsend (1997), p. 304 (emphasis in original).

141. Ronald Haycock and Keith Neilson, *Men, Machines, and War* (1988), p. xi.

142. Ibid., p. xii.

143. See Shukman, *supra* note, p. 8. See also Michael Loescher, "New Approaches to DoD Information-Systems Acquisition," in *Cyberwar: Security, Strategy, and Conflict in the Information Age*, ed. Alan D. Campen et al. (1996), p. 127 and Jeffery R. Barnett, *Future War* (1996), p. 17 (stressing the need to compress the procurement time for information technologies).

144. See, e.g., "The Software Revolution: The Information Advantage," *Economist*, 10 June 1995, p. 11.

145. See also Arsenio T. Gumahad II, "The Profession of Arms in the Information Age," *Joint Force Quarterly* (spring 1997), pp. 14, 15.

146. Stefan Possony and Jerry Pournelle, *The Strategy of Technology* (Cambridge, MA: University Press of Cambridge, 1970), p. xxxi is quoted in Chris Hables Gray, *Postmodern War* (1997), p. 172.

SLOUCHING TOWARD KOSOVO

MATCHING MORAL EXPECTATIONS
AND MILITARY CAPABILITIES IN MODERN WARFARE

CONRAD C. CRANE
United States Army War College

Recent military operations in the Balkans and the defense policy review by the Bush administration in Washington have inspired some defense commentators to herald a new Revolution in Military Affairs (RMA) where precision munitions delivered by stand-off platforms guided by new information systems promise swift and decisive results in war with little loss of life or collateral damage.[1] Contending views argue that such hopes are dangerous and unrealistic, and the impact of new technology is much more ambiguous.[2] New precision-guided munitions of great penetrating power have made warfare more lethal, though their promise has also inspired expectations that conflicts will now be less bloody. Space-based communications and computers have exponentially increased the amount of information available to commanders, but that has not necessarily increased the quality of intelligence, dispelled the fog of war, or made warfare more predictable.

Historical analysis can provide us with a tool to get a true perspective on whether these technologies have indeed brought fundamental changes to warfare. This chapter addresses the application of airpower, the element of military power most dependent on and responsive to technology. It compares conflicts in Korea and Kosovo to illustrate the relative continuity in the capabilities of military force to achieve a political settlement in such situations, and the resulting mismatch with current public expectations. This dichotomy, combined with a different set of ethical and legal dilemmas accompanying the new means of warfare, has created a new moral morass for military commanders and political leaders trying to combine force and diplomacy in international affairs today. Wars are usually decided by destroying an enemy's capability or will to fight. In World War II, American airmen espoused a doctrine of

The views expressed herein are those of the author and do not purport to reflect the positions of the United States Army War College, Department of the Army, or Department of Defense.

precision bombing of industrial targets that was perceived as more humane and efficient than the city-bombing conducted by Royal Air Force Bomber Command against German morale.[3] The fundamental tension between these approaches persists today, and was very evident in air operations in Kosovo.

ETHICAL DILEMMAS OF NEW TECHNOLOGY

The previous chapter has already provided us with an enlightening exposition of the moral and ethical problems produced by the new precision-guided munitions. As Charles Dunlap points out, even though the advent of new military technology that is such an important component of the American way of war often heightens expectations that warfare will become less bloody and more civilized, enemies usually react quickly to complicate things. Potential counters to PGMs include threatening a nuclear response, or using shields of noncombatants, both of which threaten to expand, not limit, levels of collateral damage. We will probably never again be so lucky to have an enemy who leaves military forces out in the open desert to be destroyed at our leisure. War-games project that future adversaries will hunker down in their cities and make friendly forces dig them out, all the while displaying civilian bodies on CNN. The accuracy of PGMs and interrelationship between the civilian and military sectors of the economy tempt decision makers to target many dual-use systems with the potential to cause considerable harm to noncombatants. Additionally the new military technologies require considerable civilian development and support, further blurring the line between combatant and noncombatant.

Recent events in Iraq have highlighted many of the limitations and counters for precision munitions according to Dunlap. After successful American air strikes against air defense positions in the no-flight zones, the Iraqis moved their antiaircraft guns into residential neighborhoods, and their command-and-control center into the historic ruins at Nineveh. Wary about the number of air attacks and claims of civilian casualties, the Turkish government limited the number of days jets can fly from Incirlik Air Base and forbade night operations. Faced with a situation where virtually no collateral damage is acceptable, the Air Force has resorted to filling two thousand-pound bombs with concrete instead of explosives. In a scene that is reminiscent of an episode from the *Flintstones*, multi-million dollar aircraft fly through enemy fire to deliver what are basically laser-guided rocks. A perfect hit is necessary to take out a target, and damage inflicted is much less, but there is little chance for the Iraqis to garner international sympathy by publicizing civilian casualties.[4]

The advent of "information warfare" has also complicated ethical decision making for leaders. With the development of seemingly benign advanced communication and data-processing technology has come the realization of the power it can provide to a military force that can use it properly while denying the same benefits to an enemy. This has produced a whole new set of legal and moral concerns for commanders. An electromagnetic pulse weapon or virus that disables a key computer or communication system can bring down an airliner or destroy an economy. Such assaults against us will probably be camouflaged. Hackers can route their attacks through many servers, and disguise their origin. The nature of the threat can also be very ambiguous. Department of Defense (DOD) computers are subject to about a quarter million intrusions each year, but the origin of many is unclear. They could be the result of terrorist attempts to secure information vital to national security, or just a prank by a teenager looking for a challenge. Effective retaliation or retorsion is impossible unless the perpetrators can be identified. Moreover, there will almost always be some uncertainty present that should limit the extent or intensity of response. There is also an ethical issue about levels of response to information attacks. Is it proper to react to a computer virus with a cruise missile? At what threshold does a nonlethal action with a potentially crippling impact on national infrastructure become an act of war?[5]

Information warfare also involves the extensive targeting and analysis of "dual-use" systems. Even if information attackers can be identified, objectives to be hit in defensive retaliation or offensive operations will be difficult to choose, since the nature of information systems makes delineation between military and civilian components particularly problematic. Parties of conflicts are required by the Geneva Conventions to direct operations only against military objectives, but international courts have recognized that some collateral impact on civilians is allowable as long as the intended target is primarily a military one. The relatively nonviolent and often temporary nature of information warfare attacks has the potential to permit operations against targets like dam controls or power systems that might normally be considered off-limits to conventional weapons. But the widespread and interrelated nature of information targets insures that any such mission will have some repercussions on civilians. A power grid that runs air defense system radios and computers might also pump fresh water to homes. Taking out military communications will also disable civilian traffic. Even the United States routes 95 percent of all DOD telecommunications over public networks. Determining a formula of proportionality between civilian and military aspects of such dual-use systems is open to much debate. Should the evaluation be based on lives or dollars saved or lost, or just on the amount of resulting permanent physical destruction?[6]

This ethical calculus also applies to precision munitions. Generally saving lives, on both sides, appears to have become the most important limiting consideration for modern warfare. Yet, just as with Harry Truman's justification for dropping the atomic bomb, concerns about friendly casualties predominate. Saddam Hussein was convinced that he could deter the United States with the threat of heavy losses. American actions after the loss of the eighteen Rangers in Somalia reinforce such perceptions. Joint Chiefs of Staff (JCS) planners today acknowledge that predicted friendly losses are a key factor in shaping any contingency operation. Yet RAND studies suggest that potential adversaries should be wary of assuming that killing a few soldiers will always result in American withdrawal. When casualties mount public opinion becomes less tolerant of the status quo, but aggressive and cohesive leadership can maintain support for current operations or even garner support for escalation.[7]

Lurking in the international consciousness is a suspicion that the United States is always willing to employ its military technology, especially airpower, rather indiscriminately to achieve its goals. The ethical question for American decision makers concerned about the impact of friendly casualties on public opinion remains: "What degree of risk to our service personnel is justifiable in order to save the lives of enemy civilians," a dilemma with many troubling implications under the Laws of War. Observers in the Third World and countries bombed by us in the past are quick to condemn any significant application of our airpower. After the Gulf War against Iraq that Martin Cook describes in the following chapter, Yasuo Kurata of the *Tokyo Shimbun* complained that Americans are insensitive to civilian casualties because they have never been bombed themselves, and tend to dismiss such "collateral damage" as an inevitable but acceptable "byproduct of aerial warfare." He implied that Asians and Europeans, sensitized by their own experiences of being bombed, were opposed to the air war against Iraqi cities but that Americans remained ignorant of the costs of such aerial bombardment and did not seem to care.[8]

Recent limited conflicts have highlighted continuing asymmetries about worldviews concerning the impact of new military technologies, as well as the aforementioned ethical dilemmas about their application. The American media and military have heightened expectations of the precision that can be achieved in applying force, and consequently obscured many of the realities of war and the American way of fighting it, even when we are not engaged in a total conflict like World War II.

KOREA AND KOSOVO

Almost a half century ago in Korea, the staff of the Far East Air Forces (FEAF) conducted the first systematic American study of the best way to apply airpower to produce a negotiated settlement in a limited war, our first of the nuclear era. They wrestled with a number of complex issues. Though the quantity of air assets was limited and much was of World War II vintage, Americans expected that their air force could overwhelm any enemy with atomic bombs and conventional firepower. The effects of the postwar draw down and high wages in private industry left the U.S. Air Force deficient in many technical specialties, and some such as photo interpreters would not be brought up to strength until well into the war. Airmen knew their limitations but were reluctant to reveal them to politicians or the press. By 1951 there was increasing disillusionment with airpower at command centers in Washington and UN forces headquarters in Tokyo, though the FEAF continued to operate on a shoestring. Disappointment was heightened by the marginal effectiveness of aerial interdiction in a relatively static war against an adaptable enemy. Planners looking for a new approach for the application of aerial weaponry in 1952 had great difficulty in selecting the proper alternate targets to influence enemy decision makers to accept desired terms. The FEAF staff did not know if the war was being run by leaders in Moscow, Beijing, or Pyongyang, how their minds worked, or what vulnerable items were important to them. Planners also had to deal with the inescapable fact that airpower is primarily a destructive force that is perceived very differently around the world. Its application could produce a political backlash in a Third World that still associated any American bombing with the devastation of Tokyo and Hiroshima, and even our United Nations allies were very reluctant to unleash its full fury.[9]

The FEAF first decided to attack a dual-use target that had been basically off-limits until mid-1952—North Korean hydroelectric dams and power complexes. While General Matthew Ridgeway had been in charge of the UN efforts he had forbidden any such operations, considering the power system as primarily a part of the civilian economy. However, his replacement, General Mark Clark, was more aggressive, and leaders in Washington were getting increasingly frustrated with seemingly interminable peace talks. They all approved the escalation in the air war, and the Americans bombed the power complexes in June 1952. The main impact was not in Moscow or Beijing but in London, where an enraged Parliament almost brought down Winston Churchill's government over charges the war was getting out of control. The raids also reinforced impressions in the Third World that Americans had no compunctions about bombing nonwhite peoples.[10]

FEAF next turned to an assault on supply and communication centers across North Korea, basically meaning that any town or village with standing buildings became a target. Aerial destruction of built-up areas reached phenomenal proportions during the war. Eighteen of the twenty-two largest North Korean cities were at least half obliterated. POWs observed that most towns were just "rubble or snowy open spaces." Civilian casualties far exceeded military losses. That still had not brought an armistice by 1953, so planners focused on what they considered to be the last viable target system, irrigation dams that sustained the North Korean rice crop. The FEAF commander, General Otto P. Weyland, would not allow attacks on such obviously civilian facilities, but his staff convinced him and Clark that holing some of the dams would wash out key rail lines. The UN commanders emphasized to Washington and subordinates that the objective of the operation would be interdiction of key transportation routes, but their planners really wanted to exploit the threat to enemy food supplies. The attacks were carried out in May and the railroads destroyed, though the flood from one of the dams also washed out twenty-seven miles of river valley and sent water into the streets of the North Korean capital. Communist countermeasures such as lowering water levels in reservoirs and building back-up barriers soon negated the impact of the dam attacks, shortly before the armistice was concluded in July 1953.[11]

The Air Force was quick to claim that the "Air Pressure" campaign against North Korean hydroelectric plants, supply centers, and irrigation dams was the decisive factor in persuading the Communists to accept an armistice. However, the actual impact of air operations at the time is unclear, though one important long-term legacy is the current North Korean missile development program inspired by memories of the destruction of most of their cities and towns by American bombing.[12]

Though aerial technology has continued to improve since the Korean War, so have public expectations and USAF promises about airpower's decisiveness and accuracy. As a result key decisions about the application of military force in most

American wars in the air age have been shaped by an overestimation of airpower's capabilities, and disappointing results have led to an escalation of bombing operations against civilians.

The recent air campaign over Yugoslavia repeated that pattern. Again there were high expectations for what airpower, along with the newest PGMs and information warfare, could accomplish, even if many were skeptical that primary objectives could be achieved without at least some threat of a ground war. It cannot be denied that airpower was the primary offensive arm that produced a settlement without risking ground casualties, though the results were not those envisioned when the campaign started.

When the bombing campaign commenced, President Clinton announced to the nation that the operation had three primary objectives: to stop the ethnic cleansing in Kosovo, to prevent an even bloodier Serb offensive against civilians there, and to "seriously damage" the Serb military capacity to do such harm. Bombing did not achieve any of those goals, and in fact helped exacerbate the second. The resulting massacre of thousands of Kosovars must be considered before anyone can triumphantly proclaim the relative "bloodlessness" of the air campaign. Serb ground forces in Kosovo responded to the high-tech air assault with a low-tech ravaging of the whole region. Peacekeepers on the ground are finding that initial estimates of the degradation of Serbian forces from air attacks were also exaggerated, primarily due to extensive use of decoys and deception. NATO has reduced its initial claims of tanks destroyed from 122 to 93, and admits that its investigators only uncovered 26 when they moved into Kosovo. Yugoslav vehicle commanders proved very adept at hiding in villages, using the surrounding community and inhabitants as the human shields foreseen by Dunlap. Whether or not the air campaign motivated Serbians to remove Milosevic from power or only strengthened his hand against a fragmented opposition is still debated. Achieving any of these objectives by airpower alone was made even more difficult by the gradual escalation in the pace of air attacks, which reinforced the lessons learned about the drawbacks of that approach in Vietnam. One of the harshest critics of that aspect of the air campaign against Yugoslavia was Colonel John Warden (retired), who developed the theories that inspired the aerial thunder and lightning of DESERT STORM that Martin Cook describes in the following chapter.[13]

The full impact of problems caused by consensus building for the air campaign within the nineteen-member NATO coalition have yet to be revealed, but it appears that targeting was micromanaged even more than in Vietnam. Exchanges highlighted the differences between American and European views of the application of military force. NATO commander General Wesley Clark and his air commanders wanted to hit power supplies, communications facilities, and command bunkers in Belgrade on the first night, but NATO political leaders wouldn't even approve strikes on occupied barracks, fearing too many dead conscripts.[14]

Eventually Clark got approval for a wider target array, but still had to get clearance to attack each objective from any nation with pilots or planes on the mission. New information systems facilitated an amazingly sophisticated target review and development system. A computer network linked NATO planners in Germany, Belgium, and the United States with data analysts in England and weapons experts in Italy. Military lawyers in Germany assessed each target in terms of the Geneva Convention, confirming its military nature and evaluating whether its value outweighed any risks of collateral damage. Clark held daily teleconferences with NATO and EUCOM leaders, and finished the process by passing target lists to the Joint Chiefs of Staff and the White House for a final blessing.[15]

The political and legal constraints resulting from this system produced rules of engagement for pilots as strict as seen in any war in history. Yet with all these controls and precision weaponry, young pilots searching for targets on four-inch square monitors made mistakes. Fears of Serb air defense kept aircraft at fifteen thousand feet or higher and further increased difficulties of target identification, contributing to the tragic attacks on tractor loads of refugees near Djakova on April 14. The video replay of the unfortunate destruction of a Yugoslav train passing over a bridge just as it was struck by a NATO missile was highlighted on newscasts around the world. And as Clark rapidly expanded his target lists, the quality of his intelligence declined markedly. Outdated CIA maps led to the accidental bombing of the Chinese embassy on May 7. Mid-level CIA analysts had actually tried to warn of the target misidentification, but could not get their input into the targeting process in time to halt the mission. Up to then no one at Clark's headquarters had thought to question the accuracy of the information in their target folders. *Newsweek* reports the mistake also resulted from a shortage of qualified photo interpreters, repeating a USAF deficiency from 1950. This time the technicians had been lured away by private satellite-imaging firms.[16]

These errors eroded support for the air war, and put considerable pressure on NATO political and military leaders to achieve results. Clark was close to running out of militarily useful and politically acceptable targets when he secured approval for probably the most important raid of the campaign on May 24. The destruction of the transformer yards of the Yugoslav power grid disabled everything from the air defense command-and-control network to the country's banking system. It demonstrated NATO's strength and dominance to the political leaders and the civilian population. Knocking out the power grid also took away electricity from hospitals and water-pumping stations, an example of the dilemmas highlighted in Martin Cook's chapter. Military lawyers made the moral implications clear to Clark. One recalled, "We'd have preferred not to have to take on these targets. But this was the Commander's call." All major Serb cities experienced extended power disruptions until a settlement was reached on June 10.[17]

Despite obvious differences in coalition members and munitions, there are many similarities between the airpower experience in Korea and Kosovo besides the last names of the theater commanders. Gauging the decision-making process, vulnerabilities, and will of targeted leaders again proved difficult. Problems with limited resources and allies' sensibilities affected the conduct of the air campaign in both conflicts, though there was an obvious escalation of the assault on dual-use targets as the conflicts continued. Attempts at aerial interdiction of Yugoslav forces appear to have exhibited many of the same shortcomings that appeared in Korea and Vietnam. No technology has yet been developed to control the weather, and unpredictable storms and clouds remain a particularly vexing problem for air operations. Even in Kosovo, airpower did get some important assistance from traditional land power and diplomacy. While a NATO ground offensive was not used, open discussions about its possibility and an apparent growing willingness to gather peacekeeping forces in the region probably had some influence on Yugoslav leaders. The KLA also was essential in drawing Serb forces out into the open where aircraft could attack them. As in Korea, the Russians, despite their vocal opposition to the NATO attacks, played a key role in persuading traditional allies to accept a settlement. They also assisted NATO by not upgrading Yugoslav 1970s-vintage air defense systems. Modernized antiaircraft technology would have downed more aircraft, and perhaps tested coalition solidarity if casualties had mounted.

It is clear, however, that whatever sort of "victory" this air campaign achieved was not by "plinking" tanks, or by causing the strategic or operational paralysis advocated by theorists like Warden. Despite European attempts to restrain attacks, a less than final settlement was achieved by the same sort of "imposed cost" strategy applied in Korea and Vietnam, resulting in massive destruction of the civilian infrastructure of Yugoslavia. Pentagon spokesman Ken Bacon speculated that the main factor in Milosevic's acceptance of terms "was the increasing inconveniences that the bombing campaign was causing in Belgrade and other cities." A broad definition of the term "dual-use" opened up a wide array of targets for NATO airmen, including bridges, heating plants, and television stations. Black humor in Belgrade determined that even bread shops were valid targets because "soldiers also eat bread." Serb propaganda videos of the damage and casualties wreaked by NATO airpower in attacks on cities, factories, and power plants gained some international sympathy, but the same images that fanned anti-NATO and anti-American sentiments may have also reinforced a sense of futility in the besieged civilian population, since their own air defenses seemed powerless to do anything to stop the mounting devastation. When the conflict ended, 45 percent of Yugoslavia's television broadcast capability was degraded and a third of military and civilian radio relay networks were damaged. Petroleum refining facilities were completely eliminated. Seventy percent of road and 50 percent of rail bridges across the Danube were down, affecting economies throughout the region. Destruction is what airpower does best, and it has contributed to an enormous Balkan repair bill that the president of the World Bank fears will use up any money available to deal with other humanitarian crises in Asia and Africa. Many Yugoslavs remain very bitter about the NATO bombing, and the Belgrade Center for Human Rights predicts "the biggest collateral damage will be the shattered possibilities for democracy in Serbia," because of the backlash against Western values.[18]

Though there was no hard evidence to support their claim, airmen in Korea were convinced that escalating their attacks to endanger the enemy rice crop forced a settlement. In Yugoslavia, it appears the growing intensity of attacks on dual-use targets in Belgrade and other cities served that purpose. Accordingly, there is a good probability that Yugoslav civilian casualties exceeded their military ones. This is particularly ironic considering the expectations for a bloodless war that were reinforced by NATO briefings on targeting accuracy. These high NATO expectations for extremely low casualties on both sides helped convince the more reluctant coalition members to support the air campaign, and increased the impact of each scene of civilian dead and wounded. Media images and accusations motivated UN war crimes prosecutors of the International Criminal Tribunal for the Former Yugoslavia to begin assessing evidence in December 1999 that NATO commanders had violated the laws of war with their air attacks. Michael Ignatieff has aptly pointed out that journalists' accounts of the maneuvering of cruise missiles in Iraq and fascination with precision munitions have reinforced a myth in Western publics that war can now be thought of as laser surgery. In the dogged pursuit of the ideal of "precision bombing," the USAF has improved its capabilities tremendously, but the term "surgical airstrike" remains an oxymoron. Some targeting errors and technical failures will always occur, and blast effects are often unpredictable. The attack on the Chinese embassy looks even more sinister when we claim perfection. And the two British Gurkhas who died trying to disarm some of the estimated 10,000 unexploded cluster munitions in the area are victims of the flaws that exist in even the most modern ordnance.[19]

The International Criminal Tribunal declined to pursue formal charges, though more war crimes accusations have come from Amnesty International, and the British Parliament's top foreign affairs panel criticized the bombing as being of "dubious legality." Estimates of civilian dead from air attacks range from 500 to 2,000. To judge these figures from a just war perspective, the timing of the deaths is more important than the numbers. If they were the result of air attacks aiming to prevent even more civilian casualties from ethnic cleansing in Kosovo, than they can be justified. If, however, the bombing was being conducted after most Serb actions against the Kosovars had already been completed, it can be classified as retaliation, and then killing civilians becomes much more questionable.[20]

Some ethicists are also troubled by NATO's decision not to risk ground troops and instead to conduct war from a distance. Yale legal philosopher Paul Kahn argues that "riskless warfare in pursuit of human rights" is a "moral contradiction." Michael Walzer criticizes Western leaders who would not send their own soldiers into battle but were willing to kill Serb soldiers by bombing and risk collateral damage to Serb and Kosovar civilians. He calls that an impossible moral position, and asserts, "You can't kill unless you are prepared to die." Just war theory cannot support the claim that Yugoslav lives are expendable, but American ones are not.[21]

One of the most significant similarities between Korea and Kosovo is that many key decisions in employing military force were based on inflated expectations of what technology could accomplish. Another is that the heaviest casualties in both conflicts were borne by civilians. We must be prepared to face the ethical implications of the success NATO airpower achieved because of the destruction wreaked on the civilian infrastructure and the resultant noncombatant casualties. That does not necessarily make this application of military force wrong, but it should dispel any mistaken impressions about the true nature of the destructive force of the new technology.

One nation has already begun to apply the lessons of Kosovo to its own international affairs. Though they opposed NATO air strikes on Yugoslavia, the Russians are now applying the same tactic against Chechnya, trying to force the withdrawal of Islamic militants from neighboring Dagestan without a bloody and unpopular ground war. Critics point out that Chechnya does not have an effective central government, nor does it control the invaders, but that has not halted the bombs. While Russian newspapers declare, "The Kremlin is using the scheme NATO applied in Kosovo," the Russian Air Force Commander conducts NATO-style briefings narrating combat footage of precision munitions striking targets in Grozny. His forces are also conscious of the need to justify the destruction of dual-use targets. Russian aircraft destroyed Chechnya's cellular telephone exchange to prevent the rebels from talking to each other, bombed oil refineries to deprive the rebels from black market revenues, and presumably attacked the television station to stop the transmission of misleading propaganda like NATO did. As the damage to the civilian infrastructure, and the civilian death toll, mounts, more than 100,000 Chechens have become refugees fleeing the violence.[22]

Instead of demonstrating how the RMA will allow righteous states to restrain transgressors with a minimum of bloodshed on both sides, the recent conflict over Kosovo has instead shown how aggressive belligerents with the right technology can inflict massive destruction at low cost to themselves. And modern technological change has brought a merging of the civilian and military sectors of society to an unprecedented degree, creating a broader target spectrum that can be justified for attack. Instead of restraining war or making it less likely, the new technology has done the opposite. It is now much easier to get domestic support to use force when all it requires is to launch a cruise missile or drop a precision bomb. The expectation is that results will be clean and decisive. When they are not, it is also much easier to escalate a conflict as impatience grows, especially when there is a considerable technological mismatch between belligerents. This reality will most likely accelerate the search for ways to counter the new technologies as Dunlap described in his chapter, and further mute the effects of whatever revolution in military affairs may have occurred. Instead of heading for the sort of future envisioned by airpower theorists like John Warden, when paralyzing attacks on military structures will end wars quickly and with relatively little impact on the civilian sphere, we may be headed for that predicted by Giulio Douhet, when new weapons will decide wars by inflicting the maximum amount of distress on the civilian population. As Douhet predicted, civilian will appears to be more vulnerable to the destructive power of modern technology than military capability. After concluding that the attacks on Yugoslav civilians were the key to ending the conflict, one journalist wrote, "That may produce an uncomfortable lesson for the politicians who call the shots during the next war: The most merciful way to conduct a war may be to end it swiftly and violently."[23]

During World War II, the Army Air Forces staff created a model reply to answer any letters they received questioning the humanitarian application of their new technology. One section read:

> We see air warfare as being different only in the range of its potential destruction. The air gives uncurbed bestial instincts a wider field of expression, leaving only

humanity and common sense to dictate limitations. Law cannot limit what physics makes possible. We can depend for moderation only upon reason and humane instincts when we exercise such a power.[24]

The new military and information technology has also given warfare a "wider field of expression." Expectations that it has changed the fundamental nature of warfare and somehow made it less violent or bloody could be dangerously misplaced.

And what rough beast, its hour come round at last, Slouches toward Bethlehem to be born?[25]

NOTES

1. For some recent examples of versions of this point of view, see Christian Lowe, "Air Force QDR; America's New 911 Force?" *Defense Week*, 8 January 2001, p. 1; John Keegan, "West Claimed Moral High Ground With Air Power," *London Daily Telegraph*, 16 January 2001.
2. For an eloquent exposition of the ways new technology could make wars more common and destructive, see Michael Ignatieff, *Virtual War: Kosovo and Beyond* (New York: Henry Holt, 2000).
3. For more on the different airpower approaches in World War II, see Conrad C. Crane, *Bombs, Cities, and Civilians: American Airpower Strategy in World War II* (Lawrence: University Press of Kansas, 1993).
4. Steven Lee Myers, "U.S. Wields Defter Weapon against Iraq: Concrete Bomb," *New York Times*, 7 October 1999, p. 3-A.
5. Mark Russell Shulman, *Legal Constraints on Information Warfare* (Maxwell AFB, AL: Air University, March 1999).
6. Ibid.
7. Benjamin C. Schwarz, *Casualties, Public Opinion, and U.S. Military Intervention: Implications for U.S. Regional Deterrence Strategies* (Santa Monica, CA: RAND, 1994); Eric V. Larson, *Casualties and Consensus: The Historical Role of Casualties in Domestic Support for U.S. Military Operations* (Santa Monica, CA: RAND, 1996).
8. Yasuo, Kurata, "Americans Are Insensitive to Casualties Because Their Country Hasn't Been Bombed," *Kansas City Star*, 5 May, 1991, p. 2-K, reprinted from the *Tokyo Shimbun*.
9. On the Korean air war, see Conrad C. Crane, *American Airpower Strategy in Korea, 1950–1953* (Lawrence, KS: University Press of Kansas, 1999).
10. Ibid., pp. 118–122.
11. Ibid., pp. 123–125, 168–169.
12. For the USAF assessment of its performance in Korea, see Robert F. Futrell, *The United States Air Force in Korea, 1950–1953*, rev. ed. (Washington, D.C.: USGPO, 1983) and James T. Stewart, ed., *Airpower: The Decisive Force in Korea* (Princeton: Van Nostrand, 1957). For a different perspective, see Crane, *American Airpower Strategy in Korea*, pp. 164–165. On the inspiration for North Korean missile programs, see Selig Harrison, "The Missiles of North Korea: How Real a Threat?" *World Policy Journal* 17 (fall 2000), pp. 13–24.
13. For the stated objectives of the bombing campaign, see R. W. Apple "A Fresh Set of U.S. Goals," p. A-1 and the text of President Clinton's speech, p. A-15, in the March 25, 1999, *New York Times*. On the Serb use of decoys and estimates of damage, see Steven Lee Myers, "Damage to Serb Military Less Than Expected," *New York Times*, 28 June 1999, p. 1. On how NATO damage estimates matched their findings after occupying Kosovo, see Richard J. Newman, "The Bombs that Failed in Kosovo," *U.S. News and World Report* 127 (September 20, 1999), pp. 28–30. Warden's ideas are expressed in his book, *The Air Campaign: Planning for Combat* (New York and London, Pergamon-Brassey's, 1989). The best critique of his theories is LTC David S. Fadok, "John Boyd and John Warden: Airpower's Quest for Strategic Paralysis" in *The Paths of Heaven: The Evolution of Airpower Theory*, ed. Col. Phillip S. Meilinger (Maxwell AFB, AL: Air University Press, 1997).
14. Michael Ignatieff, "The Virtual Commander: How NATO Invented a New Kind of War," *New Yorker*, 2 August 1999, p. 32.
15. Ibid., pp. 32–34.

16. Ibid., p. 34; "The Buzz," Newsweek, CXXIV, 13, 27 September 1999, p. 8.
17. Ignatieff, "Virtual Commander," p. 35; Martin L. Cook, "Applied Just War Theory: Moral Implications of New Weapons for Air War," The Annual of the Society of Christian Ethics (1998), pp. 199–219; Rebecca Grant, The Kosovo Campaign: Aerospace Power Made It Work (Arlington: The Air Force Association, 1999), p. 22.
18. Michael Dobbs, "Post-Mortem on NATO's Bombing Campaign," Washington Post National Weekly Edition, 19–26 July 1999, p. 23; Grant, p. 22; Bert Roughton, Jr., "Yugoslavs Still Bitter toward U.S.," Atlanta Journal and Constitution, 25 March 2001, p. 12.
19. Dobbs; Ignatieff, "Virtual Commander," p. 32. For insight on the impact of NATO air attacks on civilians, see Dobbs. He estimates that the Serbs suffered 1,600 civilian and 1,000 military casualties. In contrast, he accepts a figure of as many as 10,000 massacred Kosovars.
20. Jamie Dettmer and Jennifer G. Hickey, "British MPs Question Legality of Kosovo Intervention," Insight on the News, 3–10 July 2000, p. 6. The low figure of 500 comes from the group Human Rights Watch. They were still very critical of NATO targeting practices and concluded that half the casualties could have been avoided. Elizabeth Becker, "Rights Group Says NATO Killed 500 Civilians in Kosovo War," New York Times, 7 February 2000, p. A-10.
21. Ignatieff, Virtual War, p. 162; Michael Walzer, "Kosovo," Dissent 46 (summer 1999), pp. 5–7.
22. Michael R. Gordon, "Imitating NATO: A Script Is Adapted for Chechnya," New York Times, 28 September 1999, p. A-3.
23. Newman, p. 30. For a fine analysis of Douhet's theories see Col. Phillip S. Meilinger, "Giulio Douhet and the Origins of Airpower Theory," in The Paths of Heaven.
24. "Suggested Reply to Letters Questioning Humanitarian Aspects of Air Force," in Humanitarian Aspects of Airpower Binder (papers of Frederick L. Anderson, Hoover Institution on War, Revolution and Peace, Stanford University, Stanford, CA).
25. W. B. Yeats, "The Second Coming."

STRATEGIC THEORY, MILITARY PRACTICE, AND THE LAWS OF WAR

THE CASE OF STRATEGIC BOMBING

MARTIN COOK

United States Air Force Academy

From its origins, air war has been subject to a peculiarly bifurcated way of thinking. In its ability to leap across borders and attack virtually anywhere, airpower has threatened to undo the last shreds of just war's effort to keep fighting among soldiers and its insistence on the immunity of noncombatants from direct and deliberate attack.

The combatant/noncombatant distinction had been under pressure from the industrialization of war for some time before airpower's advent, of course, but the prospect of air war's deliberate attack on urban centers seemed likely to render it permanently moot. Especially in the immediate aftermath of World War I, airpower offered a much-desired possibility of breaking out of stagnant wars of attrition and defensive lines. Direct attack on enemy vital centers promised a new era of quick, humane war that would target the industrial and logistical support of the war effort directly, and only secondarily human beings, whether in or out of uniform.

This prospect, early enthusiasts of airpower suggested, would enormously reduce the length and carnage of war by focusing violence on the economic and industrial bases necessary to sustain conflict. As it evolved in practice through World War II and beyond, it began to appear that the prophecy of the obliteration of the combatant/noncombatant distinction would be fulfilled while precision targeting of vital centers was far more a rhetorical than a real possibility. Amid all the variations of targeting strategy for nuclear weapons in the Cold War, it seemed increasingly clear that the moral restraints on war that lay at the core of the just war tradition were archaic, at least in regard to air war conducted by well-equipped air forces. It did not require a subtle mind to determine that a full-scale conventional war between NATO and the Warsaw Pact would, in any credible scenario, inevitably evolve into at least a theater-wide total war with nuclear weapons. Almost equally certainly, it would cascade to global total war. In either case, noncombatant immunity would, to put it mildly, certainly not be respected.

Some shreds of just war thinking might remain in the law books, and occasionally in practice in small-scale wars. For direct conflict between the United States and the Soviet Union, however, the probability that war would be conducted within meaningful restraints of the just war was essentially nil. This was true most especially, perhaps, in regard to air war. Strategic bombing would inevitably lead to bombing of targets in major population centers. Such bombing would, either by design or in fact (due to the limitations of the targeting mechanisms and weaponry available) be tantamount to World War II–style area bombing. Whatever the claims, bombing would inevitably involve huge numbers of direct civilian deaths due to inaccurate weapons and navigation.

The uses of airpower in the Persian Gulf War and in the Kosovo bombing campaign, however, challenge this apparently inevitable historical progression. In those conflicts, vast applications of airpower produced very little destruction of civilian life and property (leaving aside for the moment targets bombed with precision, but in error), even in the bombing of targets in highly urbanized environments. For the first time in the history of airpower, it looked as though the promise of precision strategic bombing might, at last, be fulfilled.

Of course there were many characteristics unique to the Gulf War that give us pause in drawing too sweeping conclusions about the future of air war generally. The new technologies of the F-117, cruise missile, and various kinds of precision munitions made a dramatic debut in the Gulf War,[1] and they both presage whole new classes of precision weapons in future air war.

On the other hand, the desert environment in which frontline troops met allowed the use of inherently indiscriminant weapons such as "dumb bombs" (the vast majority of the weapons discharged in the war) without endangering civilian lives. Further, the total air supremacy of Coalition forces in the theater was an element that may not be assumed in future conflicts.

The Kosovo campaign marks yet a further evolution, both in technology and in strategy. On the one hand, the weapons systems employed were another generation ahead of those in the Gulf War. For example, the difficulties with laser-designators as guidance systems, easily confused by dust and smoke, were largely solved by the use of the global positioning system of satellite signals to direct weapons to their targets. The B-2 bomber made its combat debut, making possible far larger precision strikes by stealth platforms than the F-117 was capable of delivering.

On the other hand, clearly the new air weapons tempt political leaders to "air only" campaigns of dubious strategic value.[2] The "down side" of the Gulf War's precision, especially on the *jus ad bellum* dimension of just war theory, was made abundantly clear by the decisions regarding how to use precision airpower in the Kosovo campaign. It now seems clear that the very precision of airpower, coupled with the impunity given by stealth and stand-off weapons capability, serve dramatically to lower the threshold to the use of military force.

Still, the emergence of precision weapons and new tactics for their use marks a distinctive turn in the attempt to assimilate air war to the laws and moral principles of just war. It is a turn that marks very good news indeed in the prospect of at last bringing air war under the umbrella of the central moral principles of just war. But it also points to novel areas for moral reflection on the use of such new weapons.[3]

HISTORICAL CONSIDERATIONS

From its very beginning, airpower has been the subject of fantasy as much as of careful rational thought about its military potential. As Michael Sherry observed in *The Rise of American Air Power,* "Never viewed solely as a weapon, the airplane was the instrument of flight, of a whole new dimension in human activity. Therefore it was uniquely capable of stimulating fantasies of peacetime possibilities for lifting worldly burdens, transforming man's sense of time and space, transcending geography, knitting together nations and peoples, releasing humankind from its biological limits."[4]

From the first moments after its invention, the laws of war rushed to accommodate and attempt to regulate the new possibilities for the conduct of war the airplane made possible. In the Hague Conference of 1907, prohibition was made of "bombardment, by whatever means" of "undefended" cities.[5] Such efforts seem quaint given the subsequent history of the use of airpower. But it is important to note that as early as this there was the recognition that the indiscriminate attacks on cities made possible by aerial bombardment would be legally and morally unacceptable. Further, the Hague Conference recognized that such attacks, if they ever were to be accepted as means of legitimate warfare, would obliterate the prohibition on the deliberate attack on civilians that lay at the heart of just war restrictions.

Speculation about the practical military uses of airpower consistently traded on the ambiguity of two quite different targeting ideas. On the one hand, early theorists such as Billy Mitchell imagined strategic uses of airpower to attack the "vital centers" of an enemy, thereby avoiding the need to confront line armies in the field.[6] In this use, ideal targets would be those essential facilities of production of war matériel, and of command, control, and communication, which made it possible to sustain a fighting force in the field. On the other hand, airpower made it possible to entertain the possibility of direct strikes at enemy civilian populations in hope of sapping the *will to fight.*

This possibility was explicitly laid out and advocated by the Italian theorist Douhet in his highly influential 1921 book, *The Command of the Air.* Douhet's idea was not that airpower should destroy targets of direct and demonstrable relation to the capabilities of fielded military forces. Instead, direct wholesale bombing of urban populations would serve to end war quickly due less to the physical destruction of the enemy's weapons and communications systems and more to the collapse of the civil society that sustained and fielded those forces. As Douhet wrote, "How could a country go on living and working under this constant threat, oppressed by the nightmare of imminent destruction and death? How indeed!"[7] The efficacy of such attacks was, apparently, deemed to be so obvious that further argument was unnecessary.

When Douhet-inspired thinkers such as Britain's Trenchard wrote to address the moral justification of such a plan of attack, they were, of course, aware that intentionally bombing civilian populations would obliterate the noncombatant immunity principle. Thus, with tortured logic, Trenchard insisted that bombing of whole urban areas was not "for the sole purpose of terrorising [sic] the civilian population" but rather that it had its legitimate military purpose in bombing "to terrorise [sic] munitions workers (men and women) into absenting themselves from work"[8] The very illogic of such a "distinction" bears tribute to the strongly felt need to find a moral defense of the suggestion.

The point is the ambiguity in strategic thinking, and the consequent confusion about the most efficacious (never mind, morally preferable) use of strategic bombing. On one interpretation, the purpose of strategic bombing is to destroy specific identifiable targets. These targets are selected because intelligence indicates that they are the sources of production or distribution of specific items essential to the conduct of military operations or are the crucial points of command, control, intelligence coordination, or other important military functions. On the other hand, however, so-called strategic bombing is really a euphemism for deliberate attacks on populated areas with the intended purpose of demoralizing the population. The rationale for this mode of attack is the belief that the consequent demoralization and disorientation of the civilian population will force enemy political and military leadership to capitulate. Of course the limited accuracy of the technology of bombardment through the Second World War made the distinction largely moot in practice. Still, it remained an important conceptual distinction, and one that would have practical consequence as the technology of air war evolved.

Although it is too complex to rehearse in detail here, in many ways the history of the use of airpower in World War II can be mapped as a complex interplay between these two distinct, yet often blurred-together fundamental ideas. The differing opinions of the British and American air arms regarding the preferred method of bombing Germany early in the war play out this doctrinal dispute. American doctrine argued for "precision daylight" bombing. Partly as a consequence of the repugnance at wholesale terror bombing, partly because it believed it would be more militarily effective, American theorists argued for careful targeting of key nodes in the enemy's economic and military system. Sherry writes, "[Precision bombing] promised victory independent of the other branches of the armed forces, with minimal demands on and risks for Americans, employing the bomber as an instrument of surgical precision rather than indiscriminate horror, laying its high explosives (not gas or incendiaries) on its targets with pinpoint accuracy, incapacitating the enemy without slaughter."[9] In contrast the British advocated forthrightly bombing of built-up areas for the purpose of terrorization, believing this would cause German society to collapse and quickly end the war.

Despite these theoretical differences, in practice American technology was only slightly more able than British to deliver on the promise of precision bombing for the whole of the war. This became even more the case as German air defense improved and forced the bombers to higher altitudes for their bomb runs. American and British decision makers perceived the need to show some means of bringing home the war, first to the German and then to the Japanese public, which pushed in the direction of terror bombing. Altogether, these factors combined made area bombing the actual practice of the Allied air forces throughout the war.[10]

Indeed, by the end of the war American bombing was directed *away* from certain strategic operations such as mine laying in the sea lanes (which might well have had a direct impact on the enemy's ability to wage war) *in favor of* a policy of incendiary bombing of Japanese cities,[11]

But for bombing in urban areas, to repeat the point, the debate regarding pinpoint versus area bombing was pretty much a distinction without a difference. Even in 1941, close analysis of the effect of a hundred air raids into Germany revealed that "not one bomb in three had hit within five miles of its designated target, and there were extreme errors of up to a hundred miles."[12] Given these realities, clearly area bombing was the reality, regardless of the intent.

Again, the historical record of World War II is well known and well documented, and for our purposes here does not require rehearsing in detail. What is clear is that it was not technically feasible to engage in pinpoint strategic bombing given the technology available at the time. But *neither was it generally deemed desirable* to refrain from area bombing or to attempt to restrict civilian deaths to the category of reasonable collateral damage within the framework of such a careful bombing campaign.

It is only with the wisdom of hindsight after World War II that American Air Force doctrine on this point emerged into relative clarity. Until quite recently, Air Force doctrine identified "two basic target sets" for strategic bombing: "those that would affect enemy capability to conduct military operations and those that would affect enemy will to continue fighting."[13] Even this formulation, of course, begs the question of which targets might affect "enemy will"—targets that demoralize combatants, or direct attacks on civilian populations? But clearly the possibility of targeting civilians is under consideration, since it notes that it rarely works: "Strategic attack has rarely affected enemy morale to the degree anticipated by early airpower enthusiasts."[14] Further, in a footnote:

> Early airpower theorists assumed that civilian populations would be more vulnerable and susceptible to the psychological impact of massed airpower than would military personnel in combat. Ironically, history appears to demonstrate that civilian resistance tends to stiffen under persistent strategic air attacks, while the morale of soldiers on the battlefield has often been totally shattered by relatively small strikes.[15]

Increasingly after World War II it was apparent that the use of area bombing campaigns with the intent to terrorize civilian populations and demoralize enemy citizens was a dubious use of military resources. Compared to the efficacy of attack on targets that directly affect the enemy's capability to conduct military operations, it was almost always ineffective.

Although recognized in theory, this realization had little opportunity for large-scale testing in Korea and Vietnam, where much of the use of airpower was the air support mission to ground troops rather than engaging strategic targets. When strategic bombing was attempted, the inaccuracy of weapons made such pinpoint targets notoriously difficult to destroy until laser-guided munitions became available toward the end of the Vietnam War. Further, when strategic bombing was conducted in Vietnam in the Linebacker II operation, even though exclusively military targets were selected, collateral damage was extensive. This damage was due partly to the inaccuracy of unguided munitions dropped from B-52s, and partly to Vietnamese air defense weapons that, having missed their targets, returned to earth and exploded.

In this period, thinking about truly strategic air war was relegated to the planning of the use of nuclear weapons. Even in nuclear planning, however, the counterforce vs. countervalue targeting debate and issues of the prudence of thinking about "winnable" nuclear war failed to truly help the discussion. And needless to say, the enormous destructive force of the weapons themselves made it difficult to distinguish pinpoint from area bombing in practice, regardless of the targeting theory.

Only in the Persian Gulf War and in the Kosovo war did technology, political circumstance, and the nature of the enemy social organization combine to provide a new "experiment" in the efficacy of pinpoint strategic bombing. In its aftermath it is apparent that air war has entered a genuinely new phase in its history. The experience of the Gulf War suggested that the prophecies of early air war visionaries might finally be possible to a large degree.[16] Still the very success of the air campaign points to new issues for exploration in the ongoing dialogue on international law and the law of nations regarding just conduct in war.

INTERNATIONAL LEGAL AND ETHICAL ISSUES

In 1922–1923, legal experts convened at The Hague to draft rules for air war that would, at a minimum, prohibit avoidable killing of civilians. Although these rules were never ratified by any state, many air forces did incorporate the gist of these rules into operational manuals[17] and leaders still spoke of using airpower within the restraints of the just war. For example, in 1938, in an address to the House of Commons, the British Prime Minister said,

> In the first place, it is against international law to make deliberate attacks upon civilian populations. In the second place, targets that are aimed at from the air must be legitimate military objects and must be capable of identification. In the third place, reasonable care must be taken in attacking those military objects so that by carelessness a civilian population in the neighbourhood is not bombed.[18]

Despite this appearance of agreement prior to World War II, the course of the war evolved a style of air war where all pretense of maintaining this moral line was erased. Deliberate "area" or "carpet" bombing of cities became the standard of practice, especially for the Allies. Partly, this was a result of technological and operational constraints on the aircraft, targeting, and navigation systems available at the time. Partly it was a result of an explicit attempt to make civilian morale a direct object of attack. And partly it was an emotionally driven response to the German use of grossly indiscriminate weapons such as the V-1 and V-2.

This common practice did not in any way alter the legal understanding that direct attacks on civilian populations were prohibited. At the close of the war, the Nuremberg Tribunals were chartered to consider "wanton destruction of cities, towns, and villages, or devastation not justified by military necessity."[19] Nuremberg declined to prosecute cases involving air war on the part of Axis powers, at least partially in recognition that Allied practice would be subject to precisely the same strictures.

The major shift in international law on point is marked by the passage of Additional Protocol I to the Geneva Convention in 1977. Although unratified by the United States and most other major powers, it nonetheless establishes a binding understanding of the customary law of war in the minds of U.S. military officials.[20] Additional Protocol I, Article 48, clearly codifies what (arguably) had been unclearly stated previously:

> The basic rule requires that a distinction must be made at all times between the civilian population and combatants and between civilian objects and military objectives, and that operations must accordingly be directed only against military objectives.[21]

Further, the Protocol states that attackers must take "every precaution" to minimize incidental civilian losses and to insure that such losses and/or damage not be excessive in relation to the concrete and direct military advantage sought.[22]

In his comprehensive review of international law as it bears on air war, W. Hayes Parks writes:

> Article 48 states the fundamental principle of discrimination, a principle on which there should be no disagreement. Indeed, military efficiency calls for discrimination to the extent that it is reasonably possible, and the United States historically has used its technological superiority to endeavor to gain increased accuracy in order to be as discriminate as possible in placing munitions on the target.[23]

However one judges the morality and legality of the kind of air war the Allies conducted in World War II,[24] a similar pattern of targeting and target selection would clearly be illegal in the contemporary context. This is codified as official Air Force interpretation of international law. After reviewing the conduct of air operations in World War II, official U.S. Air Force interpretation of the laws of war states:

> The civilian population as such, as well as individual civilians shall not be made the object of attack. Acts or threats of violence which have the primary object of spreading terror among the civilian population are prohibited.[25]

This understanding of the legal situation dovetails nicely with both an improved understanding of the militarily efficacious uses of airpower. Further, the technological developments reviewed earlier now permit the application of airpower in ways largely congruent with such principles.[26]

CONTEMPORARY DOCTRINE OF THE U.S. AIR FORCE

Understandings of international law regarding armed conflict have practical force only insofar as they are incorporated in the doctrinal statements, the operational planning and training, and even the weapons acquisition pattern of armed forces of nations. Only insofar as military forces incorporate those legal principles into the routines of "how we do business" do they have real action-guiding force. It is appropriate, therefore, to survey the official articulations of doctrine and theory regarding the application of airpower in contemporary U.S. Air Force thinking.

The most influential thinker regarding strategic bombing in the contemporary Air Force is John A. Warden III. His book, *The Air Campaign: Planning for Combat*, has been incorporated into the teaching at the U.S. Air Force Academy and at the various levels of professional military education—the various professional schools officers attend as they advance through the ranks. To a great extent, the air campaign executed in the Persian Gulf War was the product of Warden's theories, and was actually planned by his close associates. Rick Atkinson wrote in *Crusade*, his history of the Gulf War, "In war no less than in peace, success has a thousand fathers, and paternity claims in the Persian Gulf War would mount in direct proportion to allied achievements. Yet no claim is stronger than Warden's."[27]

Warden's book begins with the assertion that planning for effective air war has been hampered by the lack of coherent thinking about the *operational* level of war planning. By "operational" Warden means the middle level, lying between the grand *strategic* plan for the overall conduct of the war and the *tactical* level, which concerns achieving of reasonably discrete and identifiable objectives in battle. The operational level "is primarily concerned with how to achieve the strategic ends of the war with the forces allotted," and is generally the concern of the theater commander (rather than, say, of the Joint Chiefs of Staff).[28] In short, Warden's theory purports to guide the theater planner in finding the right "fit" between the overall goals of the war, on the one hand, and the panoply of resources available in theater for accomplishing those goals.

Warden argues strenuously that the Air Force has historically been crippled by an excessively narrow, "tactical," kind of thinking about the proper application of airpower. Modern weapons make possible (at last) the fulfillment of much of the over-promised capability of air power from its inception: the direct attack on enemy "centers of gravity."[29] This requires more careful thought about the operational level of planning, above the tactical level.

Warden schematizes his theory in terms of five concentric circles of increasing radius, representing the five "centers of gravity" in an enemy state. The central and smallest circle represents enemy leadership. The second represents infrastructure and supplies essential to military operations such as petroleum and electrical power. The third includes other elements of infrastructure such as transportation. Fourth is the enemy population, and fifth the fielded military forces of the enemy. In a dramatic statement of his theory, Warden writes, "Strategic warfare is only indirectly concerned with what is happening on some distant battlefield"; instead, it should aim at vital centers usually far behind the lines.[30]

Warden's theoretical ideas, articulated in *The Air Campaign*, received their baptism of fire in the planning for the air campaign in Desert Storm. Although Warden's strategic campaign plan was initially dismissed by senior officers as the raving of an "airpower airhead," the essential framework of Warden's staff at the Pentagon (known as "Checkmate") survived in the plan for the opening phase of the Desert Storm air campaign.[31]

Warden's views are thoroughly reflected in official U.S. Air Force doctrinal statements.[32] Regarding strategic targeting, for example, official Air Force guidance states:

In large measure, successful strategic attack operations depend on proper identification of the enemy's major vulnerabilities—centers of gravity. Against a modern industrialized opponent . . . a center of gravity may be discerned by a careful analysis of the enemy's industrial infrastructure, logistics system, population centers, and command and control apparatus."[33]

Further, it notes, "The capability to put any asset an enemy possesses at extreme risk, at any time, largely fulfills the theory of strategic airpower expressed by aviation's pioneers and visionaries."[34]

Unfortunately, neither Warden's own work nor Air Force manuals are as clear on the issue of deliberate targeting of civilians as one would wish, or as international law would require. Warden, for example, writes:

The theater commander should consider all kinds of operations that might have an influence on the campaign. *If the will of the enemy people is vulnerable, the theater commander may want to concentrate efforts against that target.*[35]

Similarly, *Air Force Manual 1-1, volume II* (superceded only in 1998) writes:

A basic premise of early airpower theorists was that political and industrial targets deep behind enemy lines presented the most vulnerable and lucrative areas for attack and provided the greatest leverage for a favorable outcome to a war. The advent of airpower made possible direct strikes against such targets, thus presenting the prospect of ending a conflict quickly by destroying an enemy's ability to wage war or by convincing him to desist without first having to fight and defeat his military forces. In the development of these theories, two basic target sets emerged: those that would affect enemy capability to conduct military operations and those that would affect enemy will to continue fighting.[36]

On the issue of deliberate attack on enemy civilian morale, however, the manual comments only weakly and with understatement ". . . [S]trategic attack has rarely affected enemy morale to the degree anticipated by early airpower enthusiasts."[37] Only buried in a footnote do we find the more precise statement:

> Early airpower theorists assumed that civilian populations would be more vulnerable and susceptible to the psychological impact of massed airpower than would military personnel in combat. Ironically, history appears to demonstrate that civilian resistance tends to stiffen under persistent strategic air attacks. . . ."[38]

Contemporary doctrine of the U.S. Air Force has advanced the discussion to a degree. Current *Air Force Doctrine Document 2-1.2*, "Strategic Attack" (20 May 1998), writes:

> The historic focus of classic U.S. strategic attack theory since its development in the 1930s has been on the war-making capacity and will of the enemy. . . . Today, while these traditional goals and sequential attack techniques may still have relevance during prolonged major conflicts, *the advent of precision munitions, stealth technology, advanced information warfare (IW) techniques, and near-real-time capable command, control and intelligence systems has fostered different possibilities.*
>
> For example, *one approach involves the parallel, rather than sequential, attack of a series of targets.* The goal is to cripple the enemy's national political and military leadership's ability to act and bring elements of the national infrastructure and, resources permitting, operational and tactical targets under attack. Through overwhelming parallel attack of critical centers, the enemy's strategy is defeated by reducing or removing its capability to conduct military operations. *No longer must air forces serially destroy each target class before moving on to the next.*[39]

The emphasis in contemporary Air Force thinking is on "centers of gravity" (defined as "those characteristics, capabilities, or localities from which a military force, nation, or alliance derives its freedom of action, physical strength, or will to fight"[40]). It is not the total destruction of a set of targets that matters, so contemporary Air Force doctrine opines, but the "synergistic effect" of a swift attack on the "system of systems" upon which the enemy depends for situational awareness and coordinated defense and attack. Strategic planning informed by this view aims not at destruction of targets necessarily, but is "effects based," attempting to achieve clear disruption of enemy capability rather than large-scale physical destruction of property.

At the level of official doctrine, therefore, contemporary Air Force writing and thinking is still somewhat ambiguous. On the one hand, the legal guidance is quite clear regarding deliberate attacks on civilians and civilian objects. On the other, both Warden's writing and Air Force policy statements allow for the possibility that, in some particular set of military circumstances, World War II–style direct attacks on civilians with the hope of undermining enemy morale *might* be a center of gravity. In such a case, they suggest civilians would be the correct target set for a particular theater commander. Rather than noting the legal *prohibition* of such attacks, both content themselves with the pragmatic observation that attacks on civilians are rarely effective.

THE GULF WAR: LESSONS LEARNED

Despite the somewhat ambiguous statements of doctrine, in practice planners of the air campaigns in the Gulf War were extremely careful in target selection to minimize civilian casualties. Very self-consciously they avoided any hint of deliberate targeting of civilians. Further, they were extremely cautious to minimize even foreseeable collateral damage to civilians and civilian objects that might result from targeting of clearly military targets.

Both at the level of political leadership, and as implemented at the level of the targeting staff, the language and constraints of JWT were extensively employed in planning of those air campaigns. Legal advisors were assigned to the targeting staff to insure that the bombing campaign conformed to the requirements of international law.[41] Obviously the motives for this were mixed. Among the mix of reasons were a real growth in understanding of the legal and moral constraints required in air war, the availability of weapons of sufficient precision to make constrained conflict possible, and, of course, a political concern with public opinion and a desire to avoid adverse press coverage.

However multivariate the causes, the air campaign in the Persian Gulf War marks a "revolution in warfare."[42] Although an extremely large number of weapons were delivered, many in built up urban areas, for the first time in the history of air war, noncombatant injuries and death as a result of direct discharge of weapons were remarkably few. Apart from clear (although serious) mistakes civilian casualties seem largely to be proportionate collateral damage, secondary to attacks on legitimate military targets. Furthermore, airpower's long-promised and never delivered abilities to destroy pinpoint targets and thereby to disable enemy air defense, command, control communications, intelligence, and logistic operations were fulfilled to a truly remarkable degree.

The study of civilian casualties in Iraq conducted by Middle East Watch, although dramatically titled *Needless Deaths in the Gulf War: Civilian Casualties During the Air Campaign and Violations of the Laws of War*, is remarkably thin in actual cases. Disposed to be highly critical, even this study admits, "[I]n many if not most respects the allies' conduct was consistent with their stated intent to take all feasible precautions to avoid civilian casualties." Indeed the "violations of the laws of war" they cite rest almost entirely on dubious interpretations of the provisions of Additional Protocol I to the Geneva conventions. For example, they suggest that bombing legitimate military targets in civilian areas should have been conducted exclusively at night, rather than during the day when civilians were more likely to be near them—a nice idea when technically possible, but hardly a requirement of the laws of war! Further, the study cites very likely self-serving Iraqi official accounts of large numbers of civilian casualties and then notes that their own interviews with Iraqi physicians yielded a far lower set of casualty figures. It arrives at the conclusion that, apart from the single significant loss of life in the bombing of Ameriyya shelter, civilian casualties as a direct result of Coalition bombing were very low indeed.[43]

Clearly, for the first time in the history of the use of military aviation, there were few or no deaths of civilians due to *direct and deliberate* targeting of them or of civilian structures. Inherently inaccurate weapons (so-called "dumb bombs") were not used in tactical situations where large numbers of civilian deaths were foreseeable and direct civilian deaths were reduced to very low numbers indeed.

It is too strong, of course, to claim that the air war in the Gulf achieved perfection in bringing air war into conformity with the principles of noncombatant immunity. But it certainly *is not* an exaggeration to say that the combination of new weapons and platforms, combined with improvements in Air Force doctrine, hold out the promise of future air war that would go far toward abiding by those rules and limitations.

To say they hold out promise is, of course, not to claim that those promises have been fulfilled. As the Government Accounting Office evaluation of the air war noted, despite its obvious success, the air war was hampered in its desired effectiveness by a number of factors.[44] Deficiencies of timely Bomb Damage Assessment (BDA) were marked, and such deficiencies necessitated restriking targets. Obviously, restrikes put both civilians and pilots at additional and, in principle, unnecessary risks. Further, an understandable emphasis on pilot and aircraft survivability resulted in delivery of weapons from much higher altitudes than were used in training.[45] Such tactics degraded considerably the accuracy of some weapons, increasing the risk of civilian death due to missing of targets that would have been reduced had lower altitude releases been possible. Bad weather, smoke, and the deliberate firing of oil wells by Iraqi forces further degraded weapon accuracy in weapons that depended on optical sensors or on pilot laser designation of targets. Clearly, these difficulties indicated the need for enhanced sensor capability in the next generation of such weapons to work around these difficulties—precisely the kinds of improvements that were demonstrated in the Kosovo campaign's improved weapons systems.[46] Still, the experience of the Gulf War points to an area where further careful thought needs to be given in order to further enhance the salutary direction in which air war is evolving in bringing its conduct more squarely within the scope of JWT.

The most pressing and difficult is the moral status of dual-use targets—targets whose destruction is reasonably believed to afford a real military advantage but the destruction of which has clearly foreseeable and significant impact on civilian health, well-being, and (perhaps) even survival. This problem is by no means unprecedented in earlier air war. But it achieves a much sharper focus in light of the development of weapons, weapons platforms, and tactics after Desert Storm. In the pursuit of the asymptotic goal of "one bomb, one target"[47] it is foreseeable that in future war there can be less and less direct destruction of civilian life and property as a result of deliberate targeting.[48] This goal is asymptotic, rather than realistic, of course, due to inevitable equipment failures, intelligence failures in target identification, and simple human error. But there can be no question that, from a legal and moral perspective, further development in these directions is to be applauded and pursued.[49]

Even in an imagined "one bomb, one target" environment, with the benefit of perfect intelligence as to the nature of the targets selected, the moral concern to protect civilian life and property to the greatest extent possible points to an area where

considerable further thought is indicated. In any reasonably modern society, the complex web of technical infrastructure necessary to maintain life and health of the population is enormously interdependent. Modern urban life for civilians depends on
available clean water, electrical power, sanitation, and garbage removal. Further, in
the wartime context, treatment of casualties as well as the routine aspects of civilian
health care depend on electrical power for refrigeration of medicines and foodstuffs
and for use of technical equipment for health care provision. Even an imagined "perfect" air war might avoid all *direct* civilian casualties and still, in its destruction of
dual-use targets, create huge numbers of civilian deaths and injuries—all, of course,
of the "bomb now, die later" variety, rather than direct casualties of bombing.

Ramsey Clark's provocative book, *The Fire this Time: U.S. War Crimes in the
Gulf,* documents in detail the effects of sanctions on the civilian population of Iraq.
Clearly, the deliberate targeting of aspects of the civilian infrastructure, while it does
not involve immediate and direct destruction of civilian life, exacerbated to a large degree the suffering and death of the civilian population.[50] Further, *it was intended to
do so* in the hope that Iraq would perceive the need to seek external help to restore infrastructural elements such as electrical power, and be motivated to shorten the war.[51]

To some degree these issues are addressed (at least in principle) under the classical rubric of proportionality. One assesses the "distinct military advantage offered
at the time" (Additional Protocol I, Geneva Convention) of targets in relation to
these foreseen effects on civilians. But the concept of proportionality here is highly
elastic and imprecise, especially in determination of the relevant span of time within which proportionality is to be assessed.

Morally and legally conscientious targeteers are not oblivious to this issue. In
the Gulf War, for example, there was a serious, if largely ineffective, effort to take such
matters into consideration. *The Gulf War Air Power Survey, Summary Report* writes
that in response to written directives of Buster C. Glosson,

> Planners wished to minimize long-term damage to Iraq's economic infrastructure,
> even as they provided for attacks against both electricity and oil targets. This constraint
> led air planners and targeting specialists to try to restrict attacks on Iraqi electric
> power to strikes on transformer/switching yards and control buildings rather than on
> generator halls, boilers, and turbines in order to minimize recuperation time after
> the conflict ended. Similarly, attacks on oil production were supposed to concentrate
> on refined-product storage; distillation and other refining areas were to be aimpoints
> only if they produced military fuels.[52]

For a variety of technical reasons (primarily the inability of pilots to distinguish
among the buildings at the plant due to smoke, haze, and the stress of combat) these
attempts to restrict targets were ineffective. Attacks on electrical power had the following effects:

> [T]he attacks rapidly shut down the generation and distribution of commercial elec-
> tric power throughout most of Iraq, forcing the Iraqi leadership and military on to
> back-up power. Ultimately, almost eighty-eight percent of Iraq's installed generation

capacity was sufficiently damaged or destroyed by direct attack, or else isolated from the national grid through strikes on associated transformers and switching facilities, to render it unavailable. The remaining twelve percent, mainly resident in numerous smaller plants that were not attacked, was probably only available locally because of damage inflicted on transformers and switching yards.[53]

Similar points could be made regarding the destruction of petroleum products, transportation systems and other dual-use targets. As a result of the bombing of electrical power, for example, "the Harvard Study Team reported sharply increased levels of gastroenteritis, cholera, typhoid, and malnutrition in Iraqi children due to the delayed effects of the Gulf War."[54] William M. Arkin, of Greenpeace, estimates 111,000 civilian deaths as a result of the indirect detrimental health effects of the war.[55] These effects occurred despite the fact that the "Iraqis restored commercial power considerably faster then anticipated."[56] Another study claimed "bombing of electrical power 'contributed to' 70,000–90,000 *postwar* civilian deaths above normal mortality rates over the period April–December 1991, principally because of the lack of electricity in Iraq for water purification and sewage treatment following the cease-fire."[57]

KOSOVO CAMPAIGN: LESSONS LEARNED

The Kosovo bombing campaign, while it bore many signs of continuity with the Gulf War, was also in many respects quite different. First, the technology had evolved considerably. The difficulties with laser and optical guidance systems the Gulf War had revealed were largely overcome by the development of global positioning system guidance systems for the precision munitions. The first combat use of the B-2's fargreater ordinance capacity within a stealthy platform greatly enhanced the delivery of PGMs in large quantities.

On the other hand, the political context of the Kosovo campaign did not allow air planners to execute anything like a doctrinally correct air campaign. The fragility of the NATO coalition and highly debatable legal and moral justification of the campaign itself forced political considerations to radically constrain all aspects of the air campaign, from micromanaging target selection and, most importantly, severing entirely the air campaign from its doctrinally mandated connection to the follow-on ground campaign.[58]

The initial phase of the air campaign was highly successful in taking down Serbian air defenses. But the commitment to an "air only" war forced planners farther and farther down the target list, resulting in colossal errors such as the Chinese embassy bombing. That commitment further, since political leadership was committed to achieving victory using the air-only strategy, forced ever-widening attacks on Serbian infrastructure—in effect, making the will of the civilian population and its political support of the regime once again the target. Fortunately, the campaign ended when it did. Had it continued much longer in a commitment to victory via an air campaign only, the "bomb now, die later" consequences to the civilian population would have mounted quickly.

Further, the mismatch between the dispersed Serbian ground forces conducting the ethnic cleansing in Kosovo and the high-altitude fast-fighters committed to the mission made airpower seem impotent (as it largely was against that kind of force). There is, and will remain, a dispute over whether it was mere risk aversion that prevented use of the Apache helicopters and other air assets against those ground forces, or whether the ability of any airpower to deal with such a dispersed ground force points to another inherent limit to airpower.

What Kosovo reveals most graphically is that precision delivery of munitions has very real limits in achieving promised effects. Timothy J. Sakulich has captured the problem perfectly in the phrase, ". . . the causal relationship between aerial attacks and political outcomes remains murky."[59] Sakulich further distinguishes "exactness" (precision of the weapon) from "correctness" (matching the attack to the foreseen effect), and points out that the connection between the two is a purely hypothesized black box.

Of course, some Air Force thinkers claim the problem is entirely that they were hamstrung and unable to execute the Kosovo air campaign as they would have seen fit left to their own devices. Surely there is some truth in that claim. But Sakulich correctly argues the problem lies deeper than that in the still murky understanding of the connection between destruction of any given target set and the desired political outcomes of the campaign. In Air Force jargon, the ability effectively to understand an adversary correctly enough to determine genuine "centers of gravity" remains a challenge.

CONCLUSIONS

Airpower is emerging into a new historical phase in terms of its capabilities and limitations. The first word, from the perspective of ethics, must be a positive one. At least for some conflicts and in some applications, airpower can at last be used as a discriminate force and once again fit into the moral universe of just war constraints.

New capabilities raise new questions, of course. Regarding the use of newfound capabilities of airpower, questions arise on both the *jus in bello* and the *jus ad bellum* dimensions of just war thinking.

1. Competent militaries will certainly have anticipated disruption of basic infrastructure such as power grids and prepared work-around solutions to them. Given that reality, how do we make a reasonable assessment of the military "value at the time" of such dual-use targets as electrical power in planning future air campaigns? The mere fact that it is reasonable to think that attack on such targets will achieve *some* military effect is not sufficient to relieve the burden of proof that the civilian consequences are acceptable, legally and morally. The fact that coping with disruptions to normal services and infrastructure certainly will require diversion of personnel and resources from other military activities to some indeterminate degree is not, by itself, sufficient justification either.

A calculation of proportionality requires at least a rough degree of quantification of these matters. We know pretty clearly the significant costs on the civilian side of the equation. It is important to ask for some equal attention to quantifying the military side of the ledger. For example, it is true that Iraqi air defenses were effectively neutralized early in the conflict. But it is also true that the absence of grid electrical power made a minor contribution at best to that neutralization. Far more important was the direct suppression of enemy air defenses by direct missile attack on targeting radars whenever they were engaged.

2. W. Hayes Parks is certainly correct when he suggests that Additional Protocol I to the Geneva Conventions errs on the side of assigning too much—indeed nearly absolute—moral and legal responsibility for the welfare of civilians to the *attacker*. Clearly, there is a correlative responsibility *of the defender* to take reasonable precautions to separate civilian populations as much as possible from obvious military targets.[60] Certainly when an adversary such as Iraq routinely attempts to use civilian population, civilian structures, and hostage foreign nationals and prisoners of war to shield military equipment and activity, such efforts cannot be given the permission of international law.[61]

But destruction of basic civilian *infrastructural elements* is indeed primarily the responsibility of the attacker. A defender sincerely concerned with the welfare of its civilian populations might take care to segregate infrastructural elements into military and civilian categories. It might declare (and in good faith, *insure*, perhaps even inviting in neutral observers to verify) that some essential infrastructural elements are solely for civilian use in an effort to spare its population. Still, it is unreasonable to ask that defenders segregate, say, civilian power grids from military ones. Indeed, in the absence of mutually trusted observers to verify such segregation, a defender's claim that it is doing so would hardly be credible.

But it is reasonable to require *a good-faith effort on the part of the attacker* to determine the genuine military necessity of attacks on targets with significant civilian value and use. Such a good-faith effort is necessary if one is to make a proportionality judgement of the "military value at the time" of attacks on such targets that err on the side of protecting civilian infrastructure.

3. How, insofar as we wish to take the moral basis of noncombatant immunity seriously, might we instrumentalize these considerations sufficiently to provide practical action guidance to targeting staffs in future air war? At a minimum, might it not be worthwhile to collect and analyze a series of real cases of difficult targeting decisions for use in the training of targeteers? Targeting staff officers should train routinely in making moral and legal as well as technical military judgments in war-gaming air campaigns.

4. The Gulf War and Kosovo disclosed even more sharply than ever before the interdependence of airpower effectiveness and intelligence, both in target identification and in Battle Damage Assessment (BDA).

Only insofar as theater commanders possess reliable target identification information can they successfully conduct air operations against truly essential military targets and diminish unnecessary disruption to civilian life and infrastructure. The promise of swift and simultaneous attack on centers of gravity that will rapidly remove an adversary's capacity to resist and wage war requires a level of understanding of both the military systems of the adversary and of the political context. This level of understanding remains elusive. At the level of strategic value, the "mistakes" in bombing the Chinese embassy in Belgrade and the Al Firdos structure containing civilians in Baghdad clearly illustrate that even precision attack based on bad intelligence can threaten to unravel the strategic value of airpower.

Further, only insofar as BDA is accurate and timely can unnecessary restricting of targets be avoided, further diminishing the risks to aircrews and the destruction of civilian life and property that is part of the friction of war.

5. The last and most perverse unintended consequence of the advance in airpower is on the *jus ad bellum* side of just war thinking, however. Kosovo seems to illustrate that the existence of the new technologies of air war (stealth, stand-off munitions, and precision guidance combined) may serve to lower the threshold to the recourse to the use of the military instrument. Rather than serving the just war requirement of last resort, the possession of capability to employ military means with impunity demonstrably tempts political leaders to use airpower rather than the State Department to "send a message."

The moral foundation of the last resort requirement is the recognition that, because lives are placed at risk by military action, one should have recourse to it reluctantly and sparingly. Admittedly, the weight of human life is more palpable to political leaders when the lives in question are those of their own soldiers and citizens. But from the perspective of ethics, unequal weighing of the value of human life is impermissible, and the fact of virtual immunity of one's own military personnel engaged in military action does not in the least justify neglect of the lives of the adversary hazarded in the recourse to military force.

NOTES

1. Of course, each of these weapons systems had been employed to some degree in earlier conflicts—precision guided munitions in Vietnam and beyond, and F-117s saw some action in Panama. Still, "debut" seems an appropriate use here in that, for the first time, these systems were employed in large quantity and in pursuit of an integrated vision of strategy.
2. For a detailed discussion of the evolution of the technology and strategic thinking regarding airpower, see Benjamin S. Lambeth, *The Transformation of American Air Power* (New York: Cornell University Press, 2000). See also Robert A. Pape, *Bombing to Win: Air Power and Coercion in War* (New York: Cornell University Press, 1996) for a detailed analysis of the uses of air power historically and their efficacy.
3. See *GWAPS*, vol. II, 348–370 for a detailed discussion of whether the Gulf War is a "revolution in military affairs."
4. Michael Sherry, *The Rise of American Air Power: The Creation of Armageddon* (New Haven: Yale University Press, 1987), p. 2.
5. Sherry, p. 5.
6. Sherry, p. 19.
7. Quoted in Sherry, p. 25.
8. Quoted in Sherry, p. 25.
9. Sherry, p. 53.

10. See Sherry, pp. 99–100.

11. Sherry, pp. 256–300. Sherry uses this point as support of the thesis that the WWII Air Corp was in the total thrall of the ideal of terror bombing. Thomas Keaney helpfully points out that the B-29s were, in fact, designed for strategic bombing. The strategic theory of the time made it seem to the planners that diverting their efforts toward sea lanes would be a misuse of the weapons system and would prevent their efficient fulfillment of the goal of crippling Japan and ending the war without the need for an invasion. Whether such models were correct seems, in hindsight, unlikely.

12. James L. Stokesbury, *A Short History of Air Power* (New York: William Morrow and Co., 1986), p. 190.

13. *Air Force Manual 1-1*, vol. 2, p. 148.

14. *Air Force Manual 1-1*, vol. 2, p. 148.

15. *Air Force Manual 1-1*, vol. 2, no. 3, p. 158.

16. For a much grimmer assessment of the future value of such weapons, see Charles J. Dunlap's provocative piece, "How We Lost the High-Tech War of 2007," *Weekly Standard*, 29 January 1996, pp. 22–28. Essentially, Dunlap argues that enemies will quickly find ways to exploit the very precision of such weapons to make it still more difficult for high-tech forces to fight effectively. For example, one would anticipate that the use of "human shields" of civilians or POWs would become routine.

17. Geoffrey Best, *War and Law Since 1945* (Oxford: Oxford University Press, 1994), p. 200.

18. Quoted in Best, p. 200.

19. Best, p. 204.

20. Private communication. Lt. Col. William G. Schmidt, USAF, U.S. Air Force Academy, Department of Law.

21. International Committee of the Red Cross, *Summary of the Geneva Conventions of August 12, 1949 and Their Additional Protocols* (Geneva: International Committee of the Red Cross, 1988), p. 17.

22. ICRC, *Summary*, p. 17.

23. W. Hays Parks, "Air War and the Law of War" *Air Force Law Review* 32 (1), (1989), p. 113. Parks very extensively and helpfully analyzes the difficulties with the language of Protocol I in five areas: (1) the definition of "attack," (2) the definitions of "civilian" and "combatant," (3) the definition of military object, (4) the apparent equation in value of civilian life and civilian property, and (5) the weight of responsibility for civilian welfare assigned to attacker and to defender. For our purposes, however, this level of detail is not important. What is important is the clear and agreed upon prohibition of indiscriminate bombing.

24. Michael Walzer, in *Just and Unjust Wars*, makes a complex and interesting argument in favor of area bombing in the very early phases of the war. For this discussion, see *Just and Unjust Wars: A Historical Argument with Historical Illustrations*, 2nd ed. (New York: Basic Books, 1992), pp. 255–263. He argues that military necessity made such attacks acceptable for a small window of time when it was the only practical means to attack Germany. Whatever one thinks of this argument, however, he agrees as well that the justification for area bombing ceased fairly quickly when other means became available.

25. Ibid. 5-3 a.l.a.

26. However, for a much grimmer assessment of the future value of such weapons, see Dunlap.

27. Rich Atkinson, *Crusade: The Untold Story of the Persian Gulf War* (Boston: Houghton Mifflin Co., 1993), p. 56.

28. John A. Warden, *The Air Campaign: Planning for Combat* (Washington, D.C.: National Defense University Press, 1988), p. 4.

29. Atkinson, p. 58.

30. Quoted in Atkinson, p. 59.

31. Atkinson, p. 63.

32. E.g., *Air Force Manual 1-1, Volume II: Basic Aerospace Doctrine of the United States Air Force* (March, 1992).

33. Ibid., p. 151.

34. Ibid., p. 152.

35. Warden, p. 8.

36. *AFM 1-1*, vol. 2, p. 148.

37. Ibid.

38. Ibid., p. 158.

39. Ibid. p. 13, all emphasis original.

40. Ibid., p. 15.
41. Personal communication, Lt. Col. William G. Schmidt, Dept. of Law, USAF Academy. Lt. Col. Schmidt was the chief of the International Law Division in Riyadh, Saudi Arabia, during the Gulf War.
42. See Thomas Keanyey and Eliot A. Cohen, *Gulf War Air Power Survey: Summary Report* (Washington, D.C.: U.S. Government Printing Office, 1993), Chapter 10 for a nuanced discussion of this claim.
43. Middle East Watch, *Needless Deaths in the Gulf War: Civilian Casualties During the Air Campaign and Violations of the Laws of War* (New York: Human Rights Watch, 1991), pp. 17–20.
44. U.S. General Accounting Office, *Operation Desert Storm: Evaluation of the Air War (PEMD-96-10)* (Washington, D.C.: General Accounting Office, July 1996).
45. It is important to note that there is always tension between the desire to protect one's own troops and the development of weaponry. For example, laser-guided munitions, which clearly make possible highly accurate bombing, also require pilots to fly straight and level in order to hold the laser designator on the target. This requires pilots to forego evasive maneuvers they would commence immediately after release of more traditional bombs.
46. See U.S. General Accounting Office, *Weapons Acquisition: Precision Guided Munitions in Inventory, Production, and Development (NSIAD-97-134)* (Washington, D.C.: Government Accounting Office, June 1995), pp. 40–41, for specific GAO analysis of these shortcomings. See also Benjamin S. Lambeth, *The Transformation of American Air Power* (New York: Cornell University Press, 2000) for a detailed technical discussion of the nature and scope of those improvements.
47. GAO, *PEMD-96-10*, p. 4.
48. It is important to note that "[c]ontrary to the general public's impression about the use of guided munitions in Desert Storm, . . . approximately 95 percent of the total bombs delivered against strategic targets were *unguided*; 5 percent were guided. Unguided bombs accounted for over 90 percent of both total bombs and bomb tonnage. Approximately 92 percent of the total tonnage was unguided, compared to 8 percent guided" (GAO/NSIAD-97-134, 69). Given these numbers, the lack of significant civilian collateral damage is extraordinary—perhaps an artifact of the location of many strategic targets in Iraq away from population centers? The accuracy of weapons delivery from the F-117 Stealth was also overplayed considerably in the popular media. See the detailed analysis of the accuracy of F-117 bombing at GAO/NSIAD-97-134, 127–143. In general, this study shows that there were considerable numbers of bomb misses—counting as "misses" anything from 3.2 meters to 178.1 meters from aimpoints. This moderates considerably the expectation of certain destruction of targets through the use of guided munitions in future conflicts. On the other hand, this is an improvement of orders of magnitude in the distance of misses from World War II or even Vietnam—a fact that is important when one focuses on civilian collateral damage. That is, even if targets were not destroyed by such weapons, at least they seem largely to have fallen in the immediate target area rather than far afield where the probability of damage to civilian life and property would be raised considerably.
49. See GAO/NSIAD-97-134, 123 for a detailed analysis of the degree to which this "one bomb, one target" goal was not attained. The main conclusion was that "the average number of LGBS [laser guided bombs] dropped per target was four."
50. Wesley Clark, *Waging Modern War* (Cambridge, MA: Perseus Books Group, 2001), pp. 59–84. I am entirely sympathetic to Clark's concern and insistence that a great deal of care needs to be taken in future conflicts to make good faith judgments of the relative military value of such targets in comparison to the costs to civilian populations. I do not agree, however, that international law is, as yet, very clear on this point—and certainly not that we can with any confidence refer to the infrastructure destruction in the Gulf War as "war crimes."
51. Clark, pp. 62–63.
52. GWAPS, *Summary Report*, p. 71.
53. GWAPS, *Summary Report*, p. 73.
54. *Harvard Study Team Report: Public Health in Iraq after the Gulf War* (May 1991), pp. 12–13; quoted in GWAPS, *Summary Report*, p. 75.
55. Beth Osborne Daponte, "Iraqi Casualties from the Persian Gulf War and Its Aftermath"; quoted in GWAPS, *Summary Report*, p. 75.
56. GWAPS, *Summary Report*, p. 74.
57. GWAPS, *Summary Report*, p. 75. See also p. 75, footnotes 44–45 for additional citations on point.
58. See Wesley K. Clark, *Waging Modern War* (Cambridge, MA: Perseus Book Group, 2001), pp. 192–220 for a full and painful description of the inner working of the air campaign.

59. Timothy J. Sakulis. "Precision Engagement at the Strategic Level of War: Guiding Promise or Wishful Thinking?" (unpublished manuscript, submitted to the faculty in partial fulfillment of the graduation requirements, Air Force Fellows Program, Air University, Maxwell Air Force Base, Alabama, 2001).
60. Parks, p. 156.
61. This lack of balanced assessment in the responsibilities of both attackers and defenders is one of the major flaws in the critique offered by Ramsey Clark and other extreme critics. While they are right to document the destruction of the war, they are often lacking in even-handed assessment of the moral and legal responsibilities of the parties.

INDEX